CIVIL SERVICE SYSTEMS IN EAST AND SOUTHEAST ASIA

This book compares contemporary civil service systems across East and Southeast Asia, a dynamic region of greater diversity in local administrative tradition, imported models of modern administration, and the character of prevailing political institutions.

Featuring chapters on Japan, South Korea, Taiwan, Singapore, Hong Kong, Vietnam, Indonesia, Thailand, Malaysia, and the Philippines, this book provides a detailed analysis of key aspects of the civil service system, including centralization, recruitment, classification, openness of positions, performance assessment, promotion, training, and senior civil service. It distinguishes four modes of public employment, namely, bureaucratization, professionalization, politicization, and marketization, to develop a conceptual framework for comparing the civil service system at the operational level. The region's contemporary civil service systems appear to be hybrid systems that combine, at varying degree, these modes of public employment, responding to administrative reform pressures. The patterns of public employment across East and Southeast Asia reflect local administrative traditions, imported Western models of administration, and the relative timing of democratization and bureaucratization.

With contributions from leading local experts across the region, this book will be invaluable to students, scholars, and practitioners interested in Asian public administration, especially civil service systems.

Chong-Min Park is Professor Emeritus of Public Administration and former dean of the College of Political Science and Economics at Korea University, Seoul, South Korea.

Yousueng Han is Assistant Professor in the Department of Global Public Administration at Yonsei University, Wonju, South Korea.

Yongjin Chang is Associate Professor in the Faculty of Global Management at Chuo University, Tokyo, Japan.

"This book about the diverse civil service systems of East and Southeast Asia continues an important line of research that covers more than five decades. . . . Scholars and practitioners with serious interests in civil service systems will want this book."

James L. Perry, *Distinguished Professor Emeritus, Chancellor's Professor of Public and Environmental Affairs Emeritus, Paul H. O'Neill School of Public and Environmental Affairs, Indiana University*

"This insightful book uses the cultural aspects of the Confucian tradition and non-Confucian traditions to explore and compare the variations in the modes of public employment among ten countries in East and Southeast Asia."

Soonhee Kim, *Professor, KDI School of Public Policy and Management, South Korea*

"It is very rare and convenient to find in a single volume such clear and concise analyses by a dozen experts who carefully considered the changing contexts and conditions of the civil service."

David Chan, *Professor of Psychology & Director, Behavioural Sciences Initiative, Singapore Management University*

CIVIL SERVICE SYSTEMS IN EAST AND SOUTHEAST ASIA

Edited by
Chong-Min Park, Yousueng Han
and Yongjin Chang

LONDON AND NEW YORK

First published 2023
by Routledge
4 Park Square, Milton Park, Abingdon, Oxon OX14 4RN

and by Routledge
605 Third Avenue, New York, NY 10158

Routledge is an imprint of the Taylor & Francis Group, an informa business

© 2023 selection and editorial matter, Chong-Min Park, Yousueng Han and Yongjin Chang; individual chapters, the contributors

The right of Chong-Min Park, Yousueng Han and Yongjin Chang to be identified as the authors of the editorial material, and of the authors for their individual chapters, has been asserted in accordance with sections 77 and 78 of the Copyright, Designs and Patents Act 1988.

All rights reserved. No part of this book may be reprinted or reproduced or utilised in any form or by any electronic, mechanical, or other means, now known or hereafter invented, including photocopying and recording, or in any information storage or retrieval system, without permission in writing from the publishers.

Trademark notice: Product or corporate names may be trademarks or registered trademarks, and are used only for identification and explanation without intent to infringe.

British Library Cataloguing-in-Publication Data
A catalogue record for this book is available from the British Library

Library of Congress Cataloging-in-Publication Data
Names: Park, Chong-Min, editor. | Han, Yousueng, editor. |
   Chang, Yongjin, editor.
Title: Civil service systems in East and Southeast Asia / edited by
   Chong-Min Park, Yousueng Han and Yongjin Chang.
Description: Abingdon, Oxon ; New York, NY : Routledge, 2023. |
   Includes bibliographical references and index.
Identifiers: LCCN 2022030092 (print) | LCCN 2022030093 (ebook) |
   ISBN 9781032353579 (hardback) | ISBN 9781032351216 (paperback) |
   ISBN 9781003326496 (ebook)
Subjects: LCSH: Civil service—East Asia. | Civil service—Southeast Asia. |
   Public administration—East Asia. | Public administration—Southeast
   Asia.
Classification: LCC JQ1499.A67 C58 2023 (print) | LCC JQ1499.A67
   (ebook) | DDC 352.6/3—dc23/eng/20220923
LC record available at https://lccn.loc.gov/2022030092
LC ebook record available at https://lccn.loc.gov/2022030093

ISBN: 978-1-032-35357-9 (hbk)
ISBN: 978-1-032-35121-6 (pbk)
ISBN: 978-1-003-32649-6 (ebk)

DOI: 10.4324/9781003326496

Typeset in Bembo
by Apex CoVantage, LLC

CONTENTS

List of figures	*ix*
List of tables	*x*
List of contributors	*xii*
Acknowledgments	*xv*

Comparing Civil Service Systems: Bureaucratization, Professionalization, Politicization, and Marketization 1
Chong-Min Park, Yousueng Han, and Yongjin Chang

PART I
Civil Service Systems With the Confucian Tradition **25**

1 Japan 27
Motomichi Otani

2 South Korea 45
Juhyun Nam

3 Taiwan 58
Bennis Wai Yip So

4 Singapore 71
James Low

viii Contents

5 Hong Kong 80
Wilson Wong and Raymond Hau-yin Yuen

6 Vietnam 98
Ngo Thanh Can

PART II
Civil Service Systems With Non-Confucian Traditions 117

7 Indonesia 119
Eko Prasojo, Defny Holidin, and Fajar Wardani Wijayanti

8 Thailand 151
Amporn Tamronglak

9 Malaysia 171
Khadijah Md Khalid and Nur Hairani Abd Rahman

10 The Philippines 203
Maria Fe Villamejor-Mendoza and Minerva Sanvictores Baylon

Conclusion 235
Chong-Min Park, Yongjin Chang, and Yousueng Han

Index *242*

FIGURES

1.1	National Personnel Authority	29
1.2	Current situation of basic labor rights	33
1.3	Process of remuneration recommendation	34
1.4	Basic framework of the personnel evaluation system	37
1.5	Utilization of evaluation results	38
1.6	Double piece model	40
1.7	Training programs provided by the National Personnel Authority	42
2.1	Composition of civil service	49
2.2	Civil service rank system of central administration	49
2.3	Training program of civil service	53
3.1	Structure of central government in Taiwan	59
6.1	The structure of the Ministry of Home Affairs	102
6.2	The local administrative organizational levels	106
6.3	The training institute system	113
7.1	The civil servant recruitment process	124
7.2	ASN composition	131
7.3	Communication between BKN and the public on social media (Twitter)	132
7.4	Promotion, rotation, and career of civil servants in Indonesia	137
7.5	Improvement of performance management	138
8.1	Performance management process in Thai public sector	160
9.1	Malaysian government structure (Mokhtar 2011)	174
9.2	Organizational chart	178
9.3	Secondment, temporary transfer, and permanent exchange	187
10.1	The organizational chart of the civil service commission	206

TABLES

0.1	Modes of public employment: East and Southeast Asia, 2015	13
3.1	Juxtaposition of government's and Examination Yuan's office terms	61
3.2	Training institutes of central government agencies in Taiwan	68
5.1	Number of officers leaving the service	89
5.2	Officers leaving the service during 2019–2020 – By wastage types and terms of appointment	89
5.3	Principal officials who were former civil servants (1997–2021)	90
6.1	Structure of the national government	101
6.2	Numbers of civil servants and public servants	101
7.1	Civil servant positions	142
7.2	Hierarchical level and typology of positions of JPT	142
8.1	Members of the Civil Service Commission	153
8.2	Duties and responsibilities of CSC in brief	155
8.3	Levels of measurement	162
8.4	Competency-based assessment using hybrid scale	164
8.5	Deduction points criteria	164
9.1	Breakdown of the number of public servants (as of 2018)	176
9.2	List of service classification	182
9.3	Appointment grade	183
9.4	Service structure	183
9.5	Numeric grading according to entry qualification	183
9.6	Common (open) and closed service	188
9.7	Lists of training institutes/providers	195
10.1	Number of CSC personnel by office, 2018	208
10.2	Number of government personnel, by year and major subdivision, 1964–2017	211

Tables **xi**

10.3	Number of government personnel, by classification of position, 2004–2017	212
10.4	Levels of career appointments	212
10.5	QS for division chiefs and executive/managerial positions in the second level	214
10.6	PRIME HRM maturity level rating, percentage of agencies	217
10.7	Rating scale of the SPMS	220
10.8	Category and number of CSC-recognized learning and development institutions	224
10.9	Career executive service officer rank, salary grade, and equivalent CES positions	225

CONTRIBUTORS

Minerva Sanvictores Baylon is a retired professor of Public Administration and Public Policy of the National College of Public Administration and Governance (NCPAG), University of the Philippines. Her areas of expertise are on the Philippine administrative system, political economy of electricity regulation, public sector/enterprise reform and governance, and combating corruption.

Ngo Thanh Can is an associate professor in the Viet Nam National Academy of Public Administration and dean of Public Administration science and Personnel Organization. Some areas of his research interest are public administration organization, human resource management, public administration reform, and organization culture. He had worked for the Government Committee on Organization and Personnel and then the Ministry of Home Affairs. From 2008 up to now, he has been in the National Academy of Public Administration as a vice-dean and senior lecturer.

Yongjin Chang is an associate professor in the Faculty of Global Management at Chuo University, Tokyo, Japan. He teaches Public Management, Public Human Resource Management, and Public Policy. He earned his Ph.D. from the School of Public Affairs at American University, Washington DC, USA. His research interests include public human resource management, administrative ethics, corruption, whistleblower protection, quality of bureaucracy, and comparative public administration.

Yousueng Han is an assistant professor in the Department of Global Public Administration at Yonsei University, Wonju, South Korea. He received a Ph.D. in Public Affairs from the Paul H. O'Neill School of Public and Environmental Affairs at Indiana University-Bloomington. His research and teaching interests include public personnel administration, public accountability, bureaucracy, and governance.

Contributors **xiii**

Defny Holidin is an assistant professor of Public Administration and Policy at Universitas Indonesia and serves as a national bureaucracy reform policy consultant with the Government of Indonesia. He works on comparative government reform trajectories, democratic governance, decentralization and local autonomy, public policy transfer, and innovation.

Khadijah Md Khalid is professor of Political Science at Universiti Malaya, Malaysia. She received her Ph.D. in Political Studies from the School of Oriental and African Studies (SOAS), University of London, the United Kingdom. Khadijah is an expert in Malaysian Politics and Foreign Affairs, Political Economy, International Politics, and Comparative Politics.

James Low is a principal researcher with the Institute of Governance and Policy, Civil Service College, Singapore. His research areas include public sector governance, particularly whole-of-government coordination, crisis management, and international relations. James also teaches case study methodology.

Juhyun Nam is an HR expert who worked in Korean government (Civil Service Commission and Ministry of Personnel Management), and OECD Korea Policy Centre, and now serves as Vice President of HR Innovation Department at LG Energy Solutions. She obtained Ph.D. at LSE, and compensation and global HR are her main interests.

Motomichi Otani is professor of the Faculty of Law at Dokkyo University, Japan. His research interest is public administration, mainly public service personnel affairs.

Chong-Min Park is professor emeritus of Public Administration and director of the Varieties of Governance (VoG) Center of Korea University in South Korea. He serves as the principal investigator of a Social Science Korea project "Quality of Government and Varieties of Governance," funded by the National Research Foundation of Korea. He directs the Asian Barometer Survey in Korea.

Eko Prasojo is a professor and former dean of the Faculty of Administrative Science, Universitas Indonesia, and president of Asian Group for Public Administration. He was vice minister of Administrative Reform in Indonesia. He received Braibant Lecture Award 2019, Habibie Award 2019, and MIPI Award 2018.

Nur Hairani Abd Rahman is a senior lecturer in Social Policy at Universiti Malaya, Malaysia. She obtained her Ph.D. in Public Policy from the Universiti Sains Malaysia. Her research interest includes social policy (social care, care system and governance, social inclusion/exclusion), public administration, and policy.

Bennis Wai Yip So is professor in the Department of Public Administration, National Chengchi University, Taiwan. His recent research interests are in civil

xiv Contributors

service systems in East Asia, performance management of the public sector, and application of design thinking to public service.

Amporn Tamronglak is a public administration professor at Thammasat University's Faculty of Political Science in Bangkok, Thailand, and holds a doctorate in public administration from Virginia Tech University, Virginia, USA. Currently, she serves as president of the Public Administration Association of Thailand (PAAT) and the Asia Pacific Society for Public Affairs (APSPA), as well as an advisor to the Senate Commission on Political Party Development and People Participation, the Election Commission, and other organizations. Her research interests include governance, transparency, integrity, accountability, TQM, HRM, HRD, administrative tools, project management and evaluation, and other public administration topics.

Maria Fe Villamejor-Mendoza is professor of Public Administration and Public Policy and former dean of the National College of Public Administration and Governance (NCPAG), University of the Philippines. Her areas of expertise are on regulatory governance, competition, and regulation; public sector/enterprise reform; collaborative governance, bureaucracy, and quality of government services; and climate change adaptation and mitigation.

Fajar Wardani Wijayanti is a junior researcher and lecturer assistant at the Faculty of Administrative Science, Universitas Indonesia. Currently, she is pursuing a master's degree at the University of Bristol. She is actively involved in various research areas: administrative reform, strategic management, and digital governance.

Wilson Wong is the director and associate professor of Data Science and Policy Studies (DSPS) Programme, Faculty of Social Science, the Chinese University of Hong Kong. His core research areas include digital governance, public management, public budgeting and finance, and comparative public policy and administration.

Raymond Hau-yin Yuen is a political specialist focusing on political development, policy trends, and cross-cutting issues in relation to Hong Kong and its role in China and global political economy. He had taught in major universities in Hong Kong on global studies, political science, and public management.

ACKNOWLEDGMENTS

This long-awaited book arose as part of a multiyear Social Science Korea (SSK) project on "Quality of Government and Varieties of Governance" supported by the Ministry of Education of the Republic of Korea and the National Research Foundation of Korea (NRF-2018S1A3A2075609). Over the years of the project, we have been aware that public bureaucracy matters to effective governance and that the civil service system as an institution of public employment plays a crucial role in establishing a competent and professional bureaucracy for effective governance. Against this backdrop, we brought together a group of Asian scholars and practitioners to examine the state of public bureaucracy in East and Southeast Asia, a dynamic region facing various administrative reform challenges associated with modernization, democratization, and globalization at the societal level. The conference, of which this book had its genesis, was held in Seoul on July 6–7, 2018. After securing research fund in 2019, we planned to publish a volume on civil service systems in East and Southeast Asia and asked conference participants to provide more information on core aspects of the civil service system, including centralization, recruitment, classification, openness of positions, performance assessment, promotion, training, and senior civil service. Yet, the outbreak of the COVID-19 pandemic in 2020 halted our work to transform the contributions into an edited volume. In mid-2021, we resumed the work with all the updates from the contributors and finally came to fruition after two years of effort. We greatly appreciate the patience and understanding of our contributors.

We are grateful to everyone who participated in the Seoul conference as presenters, discussants, or chairs, including Seoyong Kim, Chang-Gil Lee, Tan Sri Dr. Sulaiman Mahbob, Enkhmandakh Tsagaach, Gyunsoo Yoon, and Mingzheng Xiao. We are particularly grateful to our former colleague, Nara Park, who helped in initiating the book project. We also thank our publishers for their support and assistance, particularly Commissioning Editor, Yongling Lam, and Editorial Assistant, Kendrick Loo. We cannot conclude without once again thanking the contributors without whom this volume would not have been possible.

COMPARING CIVIL SERVICE SYSTEMS

Bureaucratization, Professionalization, Politicization, and Marketization

Chong-Min Park, Yousueng Han, and Yongjin Chang

The primary objective of this edited volume is to describe and compare national civil service systems across East and Southeast Asia, a region of greater diversity in culture and tradition. Over the past decades, there have been various administrative reform pressures across much of the region. The priorities and strategies each country emphasized in responding these pressures varied widely, reflecting local administrative traditions, imported models of modern administration, and types of political regime or the character of prevailing political institutions (Painter and Peters 2010; Burns and Bowornwathana 2001; Wong and Chan 1999; Pollitt and Bouckaert 2011). Some prioritized bureaucratic rationalization or professionalization of public employment. Others emphasized strengthening democratic or political control of public employment. Still others promoted market-based control of public employment. As a result, the region exhibits greater variation in national civil service systems than any region of the world.

In this introductory chapter we propose a conceptual framework for describing various civil service systems across the region. The framework is primarily drawn from the historical evolution of the modern civil service system. Notably, it distinguishes four modes of public employment, largely based on different patterns of control over entry and promotion. It is not assumed that national civil service systems necessarily converge because of similar administrative reform pressures. The evolutionary trajectory of the civil service system may differ from one country to another. Depending on local administrative traditions, imported models of administration, and types of political regime, national civil service systems may differ in prioritizing mechanisms of control over entry and promotion. We consider the proposed modes of public employment to be useful in characterizing civil service systems across the region. As discussed in detail later, we call these modes of public employment bureaucratization, professionalization, politicization, and marketization, respectively. They reflect institutional responses to administrative

DOI: 10.4324/9781003326496-1

2 Chong-Min Park, Yousueng Han, and Yongjin Chang

reform pressures coming from modernization, democratization, and globalization at the societal level.

Civil Service System as an Institution of Public Employment

Our research emphasizes the civil service system as an institution of public employment. The field of comparative public administration once focused on formulating a grand general theory of administrative systems (Brans 2012). To this end, it attempted to develop concepts and categories that would classify administrative systems all over the world. Yet, its endeavor to produce such a theory largely failed. Since then, scholarly efforts have shifted from formulating a grand general theory to developing a mid-range theory (Pierre 1995). So, comparative research on public administration has centered around sub-themes.

Over the last two decades, the civil service system became one of such themes in comparative public administration. Initiating comparative research on the civil service system, Bekke et al. (1996) define the civil service system as "mediating institutions that mobilize human resources in the service of the affairs of the state." This definition suggests that the civil service system links the state to administration. It also emphasizes that the dominant concern of the civil service system lies in human resources, not financial or physical resources. Following this line of inquiry, in this volume we deal with the civil service system as an institution of public employment, especially those operational aspects associated with entry and promotion.

By exploring the historical evolution of public employment of the modern state, we seek to develop a conceptual framework for comparing contemporary civil service systems. Raadschelders and Rutgers (1996) examine the evolution of the modern civil service system in Western countries in which it originated. They emphasize two key distinctions in analyzing the developmental trajectory of state employment. One pertains to the distinction between the public and private and the other, that between politics and administration. There was little public-private distinction prior to the emergence of the modern state. In the patrimonial state lacking the public-private distinction, private or personal control of entry and promotion was a dominant pattern. Therefore, making the public-private distinction was a crucial step toward rationalizing state employment. To ensure the public nature of state employment, impersonal merit-based control of entry and promotion had to be established. In other words, it was necessary to replace entry and promotion based on patronage or nepotism with those based on technical competence. This distinction between the public and the private led to the bureaucratic rationalization of state employment. Indeed merit-based recruitment became equated with the modern civil service system.

The other distinction pertains to the separation between politics and administration. While it was once common for senior officials to perform both political and administrative tasks at the same time, the modern civil service system was not yet consolidated until politics and administration became distinguished from each other, particularly in management of entry and promotion. The distinction between politics and administration has replaced partisan control of public employment with merit-based neutral control.

The most recent neoliberal managerial reform seems to add a further layer of complication to these sweeping distinctions. By emphasizing the use of private sector management tools for public employment, this reform renders the distinction of the public and private blurred. However, removing the public–private distinction driven by the managerial reform was not meant to reverse the rationalization of public employment, that is, a return to a patrimonial and patronage system. Rather, it emphasizes the substitution of rules-based control of public employment with market-based control (Pierre and Peters 2017).

In view of the historical evolution of civil service systems, we may identify four modes of public employment at the operational level: bureaucratization, professionalization, politicization, and marketization. They reflect distinct patterns of control over entry and promotion. Specifically, both bureaucratization and professionalization emphasize meritocratic neutral control over entry and promotion. While they share much in common, they differ in that bureaucratization prioritizes entry based on formal examination, whereas professionalization, entry based on professional qualification. Politicization emphasizes partisan and political control over entry and promotion. Marketization highlights performance-oriented and contract-based pragmatic control over entry and promotion.

Distinguishing these modes of public employment appears to be useful in analyzing state responses to administrative reform pressures. Heredia and Schneider (2003) develop three historical models of state administrative reform, namely, civil service model, democratizing (accountability) model, and managerial model. The main objective of the civil service model, the first historical model, is to eliminate patrimonialism, amateurism, and spoils. The reform measures include recruitment through formal examination or professional qualification, merit-based promotion, tenure protection, reasonable remuneration, and rules-based management. The reform aims to reduce patronage and clientelism by abolishing personalistic or partisan control of public employment. Second, the democratizing model seeks to expand democratic control and political accountability in response to a lack of administrative responsiveness and coherence. Countering a loss of political control over executive agencies resulting from the civil service model, the democratizing model promotes the expansion of popular control through political appointments and dismissals. The reform measures include expanding the scope of partisan or party control over public employment. Finally, the most recent managerial model is a response to administrative inefficiency and ineffectiveness. Not only the civil service model but also the democratizing model produces rules and constraints which result in administrative formalism and managerial rigidity. The reform measures include the use of tools borrowed from the private sector, such as decentralized and individualized personnel management, results-based management such as management contracts and performance-related pay, and elimination of red-tapes and overregulation.

However, these historical models of civil service reform fail to distinguish between bureaucratization and professionalization as modes of public employment, as emphasized in this study. In fact, Heredia and Schneider conflate both modes in their civil service model. Silberman (1993) considers such a distinction important in fully understanding the rise of the rational modern state. He distinguishes between an organizational model and a professional model as alternative methods of rationalizing the administrative apparatus of the modern state. He maintains that it would be quite limited in analyzing authority relations to simply differentiate the traditional model from the legal-rational model. According to him, there are two, not one, models of rationalizing the state at the opposite side of the traditional model: one is the organizational model based on a closed system of recruitment and the other, the professional model based on an open system. Both models are distinguishable in patterns of control over entry and promotion. In the organizational model, there are standardized rules of appointment for senior positions. These rules emphasize early entry into the civil service. There are restrictions on eligibility for senior positions. Initial entry is open to those who complete university courses or are trained in apprenticeship. It is necessary to start early civil service education and training. The predictability of career advancement induces early initial entry. To this end, appointment for senior positions is limited only to those who have made early commitment to the civil service. It takes a form of predictable promotion, which is based on years of service and minimizes lateral entry. This incentive structure limits eligibility to senior positions. Unless one makes early initial entry, she or he will not be advanced to senior positions. It promotes post-entry specialization by ministry or agency. Moving from one ministry to another is discouraged because skills acquired from one ministry may not be readily transferred to another ministry. Internal promotion as well as seniority-based advancement tends to prevail. The organizational model has features such as limited entry into high-ranking positions, higher organizational boundaries, specialization by ministry, and predictable career ladders. This bureaucratic model is closely associated with career-focused closed civil service systems.

By contrast, in the professional model profession-related education and training are the primary criterion for getting public jobs including senior positions. Professional qualifications required for positions are acquired by individuals before initial entry into the civil service. Social and economic incentives are used to motivate individuals to pursue professional education and training. There is no need to induce early commitment to the civil service. Incentives are offered to professionals through remuneration, lateral entry, flexible placement, and greater discretion and autonomy. Seniority does not matter much in promotion and there exist fast tracks. The emphasis on professional training and competences facilitates the movement not only between the public and private sectors but also between ministries or agencies, which lowers organizational boundaries. This professional model is closely linked to position-focused open civil service systems.

Although both the organizational and professional models equally seek to rationalize state administration, they are contrasting in the principles and norms underlying control over entry and promotion. The organizational model emphasizes organization-centered meritocratic control while the professional model, profession-centered meritocratic control. Recognizing these differences, in this study we distinguish between bureaucratization and professionalization, as distinct modes of control over public employment, although both are commonly associated with efforts to rationalize state administration.

Modes of Public Employment

In the previous section, we identify four modes of public employment, that is, bureaucratization, professionalization, politicization, and marketization, drawn from the historical evolution of the modern civil service system. We argue that contemporary civil service systems are cumulative outcomes of country-specific responses to administrative reform pressures and embody varying levels of these modes. In this section we examine key features of each mode of public employment in detail.

Bureaucratization

The bureaucratization of public employment indicates the extent to which the pattern of control over entry and promotion reflects key features of Weberian bureaucracy. Weber's ideal type of bureaucracy primarily represents a body of officials who have following characteristics (Weber 1946, 1947). First, officials obey higher authority only in relation to official duties. Second, they are organized as hierarchies of duties. Third, each job is clearly defined in a legal sense. Fourth, the official in charge of the job is filled by a free contractual relationship. Fifth, officials are selected by technical competence, which can be verified by examination or education or a combination of both. They are not elected but appointed. Sixth, they are compensated by fixed monetary payments and usually have pension rights. Seventh, for them jobs are considered the only or at least primary occupation. Eighth, their duties constitute careers. In other words, there is a system of advancement primarily based on years of service (seniority) or merit or a combination of both. Ninth, their works are completely separated from the ownership of means of administration. Finally, they are subject to strict and systematic discipline and control in the conduct of their duties.

Being aware of the multidimensional nature of Weberian bureaucracy, Hall (1968) empirically distinguishes between several aspects of bureaucratization. They include hierarchy of authority, division of labor, rules, impersonality, and technical competence. He finds that a higher level of bureaucratization at one dimension is not necessarily associated with a higher level at another dimension. One of the notable findings is that the dimension of technical competence was negatively related to other dimensions, suggesting that technical competence should be distinguished from other aspects of bureaucratization.

The bureaucratization of public employment indicates that the pattern of control over initial entry and promotion shifts from patronage-based to merit-based, especially exam-based. The technical competence of Weberian bureaucracy emphasizes the impartial use of objective standards in entry and promotion. Selection is determined by testing and education while promotion, largely by seniority.[1] The conditions of advancement tend to be fixed and objective. Prior to the bureaucratization of public employment, entry and promotion were based on kinship relations or personal connections. Yet, bureaucratization ushered in meritocratic impersonal control of public employment to ensure the rationality and objectivity of state administration.

Yet, it should be noted that the technical competence envisioned by Weberian bureaucracy may be seen as reflecting some degree of professionalism. However, it is worth emphasizing here a subtle difference between specialization and professionalization. Weber's emphasis on technical competence refers to the impartial use of objective standards by an administrative organization, which ensures the rationality of state administration. In this regard, recruitment through objective testing constitutes a key component of the bureaucratization of public employment, which led to the replacement of a patrimonial or patronage bureaucracy with a rational modern bureaucracy.

The bureaucratization of public employment emphasizes post-entry learning of skills or expertise while the professionalization, pre-entry possession of job-related skills or expertise. Both bureaucratization and professionalization seek to rationalize state administration but differ in the way in which they secure job-related skills or expertise. The kind of expertise promoted by bureaucratization is acquired through post-entry specialization. Public employees are not expected to acquire job-related skills before their entry to the civil service. After being selected and assigned to a specific ministry or agency, they begin to acquire skills or expertise through conducting various job assignments. Here, skills or expertise develops or increases through job experience. Having longer years of service means more job experience and thus more skills or expertise. Therefore, seniority serves as a good basis of promotion. Early entry to the civil service constitutes a main path to senior positions. Hence, lateral entry to the civil service is limited and internal promotion is a common practice. Skills or expertise acquired from one ministry or agency cannot be readily transferred to another. This is a traditional form of post-entry specialization distinguishable from pre-entry professionalization. Open objective testing required for initial entry is intended to ensure the impersonality of public employment rather than selecting the best or right candidate for a specific position or job.[2] Similarly, education requirements, which attest to general knowledge rather than specialized knowledge, are meant to ensure at least the impersonality and impartiality of public employment.[3]

In sum, the bureaucratization of public employment refers to the extent to which meritocratic control over entry and promotion is based on general competence testing defined by an administrative organization. Hence, the degree of bureaucratization of public employment indicates the number of public officials who are selected through general competence testing, promoted largely based on seniority, and guaranteed lifelong employment.[4]

Professionalization

Half a century ago, Mosher (1968) anticipated the emergence of the professional state distinct from the administrative state by pointing to a growth of professionals in government employment. As the number of professionals employed by the government rapidly increased, he claimed that the administrative apparatus of the state became professionalized. As emphasized earlier, the type of skills or expertise associated with professionalization is distinguishable from those associated with bureaucratization. Post-entry specialization by ministry or agency occurs as job experience is accumulated largely through learning by doing. The main agent of specialization is one's ministry or agency. In contrast, the kind of skills or expertise associated with professionalization is obtained mainly through professional education and training. The main agent of professionalization is one's profession. While a specialist may be trained by her or his affiliated administrative organization, a professional is to be trained by an institution of her or his profession.

Mosher (1978) regards a profession as an occupation that provides a lifetime career while requiring professional education and training. As scientific knowledge and technology expands, professions multiply and become diverse. It is not always clear whether a particular occupation is a profession or not. He distinguishes between two types of professions in relation to government employment. One is general professions whose members can be employed in both the public and private sectors. The government competes with the private sector to recruit and retain these professionals. The other is public service professions whose members are wholly or mainly employed by government agencies. The status of professionals is recognized by licenses, credentials, and educational certificates. The extent of recruiting license holders, credential holders, and master or doctoral degree holders may indicate the extent of professionalization of public employment.

As discussed earlier, one of the important characteristics of Weberian bureaucracy is the kind of skills or expertise that is accumulated within an organization with vertical and horizontal specialization of labor. This type of meritocratic recruitment is not based on testing of such skills or expertise, which is assumed to be acquired later through learning by doing after entry to the civil service. On the other hand, professionalization emphasizes recruitment through screening of technical competence required for specific jobs. Professional qualifications such as licenses, credentials, and educational certificates are prerequisites for employment. In this regard, meritocratic recruitment based on professional skills or expertise constitutes a major indicator of professionalization of public employment.

Although professionalization is often regarded as an antithesis of bureaucratization, both may be considered alternative ways of rationalizing state administration. Ritzer (1975) points out that Weber viewed professionalization as an aspect of the rationalization of society as in the case of bureaucratization and refutes the view emphasizing the potential conflict between them. He claims that profession, along with market and bureaucracy, is a structure that promotes rationality in the West.

8 Chong-Min Park, Yousueng Han, and Yongjin Chang

However, the distinction between professionalization and bureaucratization may not always be clear. For instance, Weber's Prussian bureaucracy was staffed by recruiting graduates who completed legal education at universities. Suppose that one completes legal education at a university, has practical training, and then is finally recruited as a civil servant. In this case, we may say that the civil service system is, to some extent, professionalized, although it is far less so than a civil service system which directly recruits lawyers. The key is whether officials acquire skills or expertise through learning by doing after their entry to the civil service or pre-entry professional education and training. Nonetheless, considering the legal-rational basis of Weberian bureaucracy, Prussia, where legal education was emphasized, was distinguishable from the United Kingdom, where liberal education was emphasized (Fischer and Lundgreen 1975). As Mosher notes, the professionalization of public employment started in the middle of the twentieth century. Traditional subjects such as law and humanities are replaced by science and technology as government activities become more complicated and diverse (Page and Wright 1999). The growth of science and technology and the proliferation of institutions of higher education in the wake of the expansion of government in size and complexity lead to greater recruitment of various professionals, which results in the full-scale professionalization of civil service systems.

Professions tend to set their own standards of qualifications and competences. Even personnel management specialists have a hard time evaluating the qualifications and performance of professionals. Thus, a central personnel organization or an independent civil service commission tends to delegate personnel matters (particularly qualification assessment) to a profession. Professionals acquire skills or expertise not within administrative organizations but through professional institutions. The socialization of professionals is primarily done by professions, not by administrative organizations. Professional education and training rarely distinguish between the public and private sectors, so professionals can be recruited by both sectors and there is little barrier to their movement between them. Bureaucratization develops loyalty to an administrative organization, while professionalization, loyalty to a profession. Professionalization emphasizes the operational autonomy of professionals from hierarchical organizational control (Wilson 1989).

In brief, the professionalization of public employment refers to the extent to which meritocratic control over entry and promotion is based on education and training defined by a profession. Hence, the degree of professionalization indicates the number of public officials who are employed and promoted through qualifications accredited by their professions and seek profession-oriented career opportunity.

Politicization

According to Rouban (2012, 2015), the politicization of civil service system indicates at least three distinct phenomena. The first indicates that civil servants participate in political decisions (Aberbach et al. 1981). The second emphasizes that the appointment and promotion of civil servants are politically controlled. The third refers to political activism of civil servants. In this study we focus on the second aspect of politicization.

The second meaning of the politicization of civil service system refers to political control over public employment, beyond meritocracy and professionalism (Dahlström et al. 2012). In other words, general or professional competencies are replaced by party affiliation and political connections for entry and promotion (Peters and Pierre 2004). The main targets of politicization are often high-ranking officials, but since political patronage extends to lower levels of administration, lower officials also constitute the targets of politicization, especially in developing countries. Party-based or policy-oriented political appointments are often distinguished from patronage appointments based on personal connections. Grindle (2012) sees recruitment in exchange of personal loyalty to elected politicians as a form of politicization. Hence, the politicization of public employment may be extended to include not only formal party-based politicization but also informal patronage-based one.

Peters and Pierre (2004) discuss some misunderstandings about politicization of public employment that should not be overlooked. One is that politicization of public employment can be legal and legitimate. The reason for politicization is that an elected government ought to respond to what the electorate wants. The spoils system is justified by and developed from this logic. In other words, political appointment is promoted as a means of democratic responsiveness and accountability of state administration. The other is that politicization of public employment does not necessarily indicate a lack of professional competence. For instance, in France and Germany, senior officials are specialists or professionals even though they remain partisan loyalists. Having said that, politicization may be accompanied by incompetence or corruption, especially when political appointments are based on cronyism or clientelism.

Furthermore, Peters and Pierre (2004) present six issues to consider when dealing with the politicization of public employment. The first is whether political intervention in personnel decisions is out of legal bounds. The second is the nature of political criteria used in appointing public officials. Partisan affiliation or allegiance to a political party is often a main criterion, but sometimes policy vision can be more important. Sometimes it may reflect personal loyalty to a political boss or a patron-client relationship. The third is whether the use of political criteria is related to the performance of an administrative system. Merit criteria are used in initial entry while political criteria may be used in promotion. Depending on what purpose political criteria are used for, and whether political criteria used include policy goals or political connections, the effects of politicization may differ. The fourth is that politicization may mean that officials take on tasks that are considered political. The fifth is that politicization may imply de-politicization of administration when partisan control substitutes for the close connection of interest groups with administrative agencies. That is, the influence of interest groups is weakened while the influence of political parties is strengthened. The last one is that political criteria may be more important in promoting democratic values. Replacing lifelong employment with political appointment can improve the linkage between election outcomes and government policy. Among these, the second and third issues are directly relevant for the politicization of public employment in this study.

The political control of public employment in the modern state is an attempt to make the government more responsive and accountable to what the electorate wants. The policy direction will be maintained if loyal party members, instead of neutral civil servants, hold key high-ranking positions. For the same reason, career civil servants who agree with the policy of an incumbent government and share its policy vision may be appointed to key positions. Patronage is another form of politicization of public employment. It is used to compensate electoral supporters or to encourage them to display personal allegiance to individual politicians. In contrast to party-based political appointment, patronage-based political appointment may cause inefficiency and corruption. In this study, not only institutionalized party-based appointment but also particularistic patronage-based appointment is regarded as indicating the politicization of public employment.

In sum, the politicization of public employment refers to the extent to which control over public employment is exercised by political parties or individual politicians. The number of high-ranking officials who are appointed or dismissed by the top political leadership is an important indicator of the degree of politicization of public employment, but the number of low-ranking officials who are employed or promoted through political connections may be more relevant for assessing the level of politicization, especially in developing countries.

Marketization

The marketization of public employment means market-based control over entry and promotion. It emphasizes human resources management practices in the private sector as means of improving efficiency and effectiveness in the public sector. It is linked to the neoliberal New Public Management (NPM) reform movement. Hood (1991) identifies key elements of the NPM reform: agencification of public sector business units; the delivery of public services based on competition and contracts; the introduction of management principles of the private sector; the economic use of public resources, transparent, practical, and professional management; the introduction of measurable performance standards; and an emphasis on performance evaluation. The type of public employment driven by the NPM reform emphasizes the application of market mechanisms to entry and promotion in the public sector.

Open competition and incentives, which represent key market mechanisms, weaken the modern foundation of control over public employment based on the private-public distinction underlying bureaucratization and politicization. Both bureaucratization and politicization are distinguishable from marketization in their emphasis on the private-public distinction. To the extent that professionalization does not distinguish between the public and private sectors, it is more compatible with marketization which blurs the distinction. Both bureaucratization and professionalization protect the status of officials from personal capriciousness or political intervention by emphasizing either organization- or profession-oriented careers. On the other hand, marketization emphasizes the flexibility of employment and contract-based employment instead of lifelong employment and performance-based monetary compensation instead of fixed compensation (Christensen and Laegreid 2001).

The marketization of public employment encourages the delegation of control over entry and promotion from a central personnel agency to line managers of an administrative organization. It promotes internal competition between administrative organizations as well as external competition between the public and private sectors. The legalistic approach which emphasizes the protection of public officials based on rights is viewed as constraining flexible management of hiring and promotion. Hence, marketization seeks to deregulate rules-based control over public employment toward business-like pragmatic control (Battaglio and Ledvinka 2009).

The marketization of public employment increases flexibility, competitiveness, and openness in the control over entry and promotion. It includes fixed employment contracts, private sector-style recruitment, and reduced legal employment protection (Bezes and Lodge 2015; Bach and Kessler 2007). It emphasizes open and competitive recruitment, which means the selection of candidates who are most qualified for specific positions and the mobility between the inside and outside of the civil service.

The marketization of public employment emphasizes individualized performance-based control over entry and promotion. An emphasis on performance leads to the introduction of incentives that link contract and performance to compensation, which makes the promotion of high performers or the demotion or dismissal of poor performers easier (Christensen and Laegreid 2001). The reason for the introduction of performance-related pay is that a traditional pay system based on standardized pay rate is not suitable for individualized performance management, so that the motivation of individual employees is strengthened through making compensation dependent on performance. Second, it lowers the level of compensation rise and controls total personnel expenses. Third, it promotes accountability of public employees for their work and shows that wages increase only in relation to performance (OECD 2005; Bach and Kessler 2007).

The neoliberal NPM reform emphasizes managerial flexibility and autonomy based on results. It replaces rules-based control with results-based control. To the extent that result-based control emphasizes greater managerial autonomy, the marketization of public employment is likely to weaken the bureaucratic or political control over public officials. As noted earlier, marketization seems more compatible with professionalization than either bureaucratization or politicization. Yet, there could be a trade-off even between them because the main agent of marketization is the managerial class of an organization while that of professionalization, a profession outside the organization.

Public Employment in East and Southeast Asia

In this study we emphasize the civil service system as an institution of public employment for state administration and identify four modes of public employment associated with societal changes in the environment of state administration. As the historical evolution of civil service systems indicates, modernization leads to the bureaucratization of public employment to ensure the impartiality and rationality of state administration. With the proliferation of science and technology, modernization also facilitates the professionalization of public employment to improve skills or expertise of state administration. Democratization encourages the politicization of public employment to strengthen political responsiveness and accountability of state administration. Globalization promotes the marketization of public employment to enhance the efficiency and effectiveness of state administration. Contemporary civil service systems represent varying mixtures or combinations of the four modes of public employment, responding to administrative reform pressures associated with modernization, democratization, and globalization at the societal level.

In this section, by applying these four modes of public employment, we describe and compare contemporary civil service systems across East and Southeast Asia. To this end, we utilize country-level data from the Expert Survey conducted by the Quality of Government Institute (QoG).[5] Of three waves of the QoG Expert Survey we choose the second one conducted in the mid-2010s because it provides some items roughly capturing the four modes of public employment (Dahlström et al. 2015). Analysis is confined to the cases where data are available. The cases include Hong Kong, Indonesia, Japan, Malaysia, the Philippines, Singapore, South Korea, Taiwan, Thailand, and Vietnam. At the risk of simplification, we present the patterns of public employment prevalent in our cases and characterize their civil service systems at the operational level.

We first turn to the level of bureaucratization of public employment. As discussed earlier, the bureaucratization of public employment refers to the extent to which control over entry and promotion reflects key features of Weberian bureaucracy. Specifically, they include early initial entry, promotion based on seniority, and lifelong employment. That is, the degree of bureaucratization indicates the number of public employees who are selected through an entrance examination, promoted on the basis of the length of service, and guaranteed lifelong tenure. We select two survey items to assess these aspects of bureaucratization of public employment: one pertains to initial entry based on an examination and the other, lifelong employment. Table 0.1 shows the extent of bureaucratization of public employment across the region.

TABLE 0.1 Modes of public employment: East and Southeast Asia, 2015

	HKG	IDN	JPN	MYS	PHL	SGP	KOR	TWN	THA	VNM
Bureaucratization										
Exam-based recruitment	4.60	6.24	6.75	–	5.92	4.33	6.70	6.67	5.20	5.67
Lifelong tenure	5.60	5.71	6.13	5.00	4.08	3.67	5.90	5.67	5.40	5.67
Average	*5.1*	*6.0*	*6.4*	*–*	*5.0*	*4.0*	*6.3*	*6.2*	*5.3*	*5.7*
Professionalization										
Skill/merit-based recruitment	6.20	4.29	5.88	4.33	5.33	6.67	6.05	5.00	3.60	2.5
Open/wide search for candidates	7.00	4.94	3.88	5.67	5.50	6.00	5.50	5.00	4.75	3.00
Average	*6.6*	*4.6*	*4.9*	*4.1*	*5.4*	*6.3*	*5.8*	*5.0*	*4.2*	*2.8*
Politicization										
Recruitment based on political connections	1.60	4.18	1.88	4.67	3.92	2.00	2.40	2.67	4.20	6.17
Political appointment of senior officials	2.40	4.65	2.88	6.33	5.25	4.33	4.95	3.67	3.60	5.33
Average	*2.0*	*4.4*	*2.4*	*5.5*	*4.6*	*3.2*	*3.7*	*3.2*	*3.9*	*5.8*
Marketization										
Performance-related pay	3.75	2.94	4.13	4.67	4.18	6.00	4.26	4.33	4.40	1.33
Pay competitiveness	4.75	3.00	4.63	3.00	3.09	6.67	3.47	3.00	3.60	2.00
Average	*4.3*	*3.0*	*4.4*	*3.8*	*3.6*	*6.3*	*3.9*	*3.7*	*4.0*	*1.7*

1=hardly ever occurs and 7=almost always occurs.
Source: QoG Expert Survey II.

First, most cases examined appear to select public employees through a civil service examination. On a 7-point scale from 1 (hardly ever occurs) to 7 (almost always occurs), Japan, South Korea, Taiwan, Indonesia, the Philippines, and Vietnam scored above the mid-point of 4, suggesting that they more often select public employees through an entry examination. Although Singapore and Hong Kong still scored about the mid-point, they seem less dependent on a formal examination than their neighbors. Notable is that Japan, South Korea, and Taiwan are most committed to exam-based neutral testing.

As regards another feature of bureaucratized public employment, most cases except Singapore and the Philippines tend to guarantee lifelong employment, with scores higher than the mid-point. As is well known, Japan proves to be most committed to lifelong employment. It was followed by South Korea.

By averaging scores of both aspects, we ascertain the level of bureaucratization of public employment. Japan displayed the highest score. It was closely followed by South Korea and Taiwan. Their civil service systems appear to be most bureaucratized in the region, indicating that their civil servants are most likely employed through an examination and guaranteed lifelong employment. By contrast, the civil service system in Singapore appears to be least bureaucratized, with an average score of 4, indicating that its civil servants are less likely employed through an examination and guaranteed lifelong employment than any in the region.

We now turn to the level of professionalization of public employment, which refers to the degree to which control of entry and promotion is based on professional education and training. Professionalization emphasizes entry and promotion through screening of job-related skills or expertise. Since merit-based recruitment includes entry based on all forms of testing, free from partisan influence, it does not necessarily indicate professionalization of public employment. While recognizing the ambiguity of merit-based entry and promotion, we select two survey items to assess the degree of professionalization of public employment: one pertains to skills-based hiring and the other, open search for the best candidates. As presented in Table 0.1, most cases except Vietnam and Thailand scored above the mid-point of 4, indicating some degree of skills-based employment. Of them Singapore seems most committed to skills-based employment. It was followed by Hong Kong, South Korea, and Japan. By contrast, the civil service system in Vietnam is least skills-based. It is followed by Thailand. Both countries remain weak in skills-based recruitment. Notable is that even though Singapore displays the lowest score on entry based on an examination, it shows the highest score on skills-based recruitment. It suggests that entry based on an examination does not necessarily indicate skills-based employment. The level of professionalization, as captured by this item, indicates that the civil service systems in Singapore, Hong Kong, and South Korea tend to be more professionalized than any in the region.

Another feature of professionalization emphasizes selection of the best-suited candidate for each position, either by external recruitment or internal promotion, which requires open search for highly qualified candidates. Hong Kong registers the maximum score, indicating that it almost always hunts for the best candidates for specific positions. It is followed by Singapore. By contrast, Vietnam displays the lowest score, suggesting that it is least active in open search for best-suited candidates.

By averaging scores on both items, we ascertain the level of professionalization of public employment. Hong Kong displays the highest score. It is followed by Singapore and South Korea, all with scores higher than the mid-point. By contrast, Vietnam displays the lowest score, lower than the mid-point. The civil service systems in Singapore and Hong Kong appear to be more professionalized than any in the region. By contrast, the civil service system in Vietnam is least professionalized.

Next, we examine the level of politicization of public employment, which refers to the extent to which control of entry and promotion is party-based or patronage-based. Appointment and promotion are controlled to meet political needs by political parties or individual politicians. For a highly politicized civil service system, top political leadership readily appoints and dismisses senior officials. Accordingly, the scope of high-ranking officials who are politically appointed is an important indicator for assessing the level of politicization. To assess the level of politicization of public employment, we choose two survey items: one pertains to recruitment based on political connections, and the other, the appointment and dismissal of senior officials by top political leadership.

First, on the recruitment based on political connections Vietnam, the only one-party system among the cases examined, displays the highest score, suggesting that its civil service system is more politicized than any in the region in this respect. In fact, this is the only country that receives a score higher than the mid-point. Hong Kong, Japan, Singapore, South Korea, and Taiwan all receive scores lower than the mid-point, suggesting that their civil service systems are least politicized. Notable is that at least in the mid-2010s Hong Kong was judged as least politicized in this respect.

Second, as regards another feature of politicization, Malaysia, which has long promoted a policy of affirmative action for bumiputras, displays the highest score on the appointment and dismissal of senior officials by top political leadership. It was followed by Vietnam. In these countries political leaders from the top command the appointment and dismissal of senior officials. By contrast, Hong Kong displayed the lowest score. It was followed by Japan, Taiwan, and South Korea. They all register scores lower than the mid-point. The civil service systems in Malaysia and Vietnam are most politicized in this respect while those in Hong Kong, Japan, Taiwan, and South Korea, least politicized.

The level of politicization, as captured by averaging these aspects of politicization is that Vietnam, a political regime with one party-rule, shows the highest level of politicization. It was followed by Malaysia, Indonesia, and the Philippines, the latter two of which are competitive electoral regimes. Especially, in Vietnam political command extends to selection of public officials in general. In Malaysia, a non-competitive electoral regime with uneven playing field, political control is stronger in managing senior public officials. Overall, Japan, South Korea, and Taiwan as well as Hong Kong and Singapore remain distinguishable from most Southeast Asian neighbors in the extent of politicization of public employment.

We finally turn to the level of marketization of public employment, which is linked to the neoliberal New Public Management (NPM) reform whose aim is to make the civil service employment more like the private sector employment. It refers to the degree to which control of entry and promotion is based on market mechanisms used in the private sector, which emphasizes performance, open competition, and incentives. Individualized performance-related pay is one of the characteristics of marketized public employment. It is contrasted with compensation based on seniority and grades. Open competition for entry and promotion constitutes another feature of marketized public employment. It entails pay comparability between the public and private sectors. To ascertain the level of marketization of public employment, we choose two survey items: one pertains to performance-related pay and the other, pay schemes benchmarked to private sector competitors.

First, on assessment of performance-related pay Singapore scored far higher than the mid-point, suggesting its more marketized public employment in this respect. By contrast, Vietnam scored far lower than the mid-point. It is followed by Indonesia and Hong Kong. Both scored lower than the mid-point, indicating a weakness in linking pay to performance. The remaining cases displayed scores around the mid-point, suggesting that if they adopt a performance evaluation system, it may be linked to promotion and advancement, not necessarily pay.

Second, pay schemes benchmarked to private sector competitors indicate linking pay to the wider market and more open recruitment. Singapore again displayed the highest score, indicating its more marketized public employment. It is followed by Hong Kong and Japan, both of which scored the mid-point. Among the cases, Singapore is the only country that most actively introduces market-type reform measures. Not surprisingly, socialist Vietnam displayed the lowest score, indicating least marketized public employment.

By averaging scores on both aspects of public employment, we assess the level of marketization of public employment. Singapore proves to be the only case that receives a score higher than the mid-point. Vietnam is the only case whose score is far lower than the mid-point. The remaining cases displayed scores about the mid-point. Overall, the marketization of public employment develops a body of senior officials to lead their organization toward more efficiency and effectiveness. Whether they start from professionalized position-oriented systems or bureaucratized career-oriented systems, most of the cases examined seem to move slowly in that direction. Singapore turns out to be a leader among them.

In summary, based on some measures of each mode of public employment, it is found that most civil service systems across East and Southeast Asia emphasize initial entry based on neutral testing of either general or professional competencies. Yet, the civil service systems in Japan, South Korea, and Taiwan emphasize testing of general competencies while those in Singapore and Hong Kong, screening of professional competencies. The civil service systems in Vietnam and Malaysia turn out to be least free from political intervention across the region. The civil service system in Singapore is more open to the marketization of public employment than any in the region.

As we will bring up in the concluding chapter, the civil service systems examined here appear to be hybrid systems, combining, to a varying degree, different modes of public employment. For instance, Japan displays high levels of bureaucratization, moderate levels of professionalization and marketization, and low levels of politicization; South Korea and Taiwan, high levels of bureaucratization, fairly high levels of professionalization, and fairly low levels of marketization and politicization; Singapore, high levels of professionalization and marketization, moderate levels of bureaucratization, and fairly low levels of politicization; Hong Kong, high levels of professionalization, fairly high levels of bureaucratization, moderate levels of marketization, and low levels of politicization; Indonesia, high levels of bureaucratization, moderate levels of professionalization and politicization, and fairly low levels of marketization; Malaysia, fairly high levels of bureaucratization and politicization, moderate levels of professionalization, and fairly low levels of marketization; the Philippines, fairly high levels of bureaucratization and professionalization, moderate levels of politicization, and fairly low levels of marketization; Thailand, fairly high levels of bureaucratization, moderate levels of professionalization and marketization and fairly low levels of politicization; and Vietnam, fairly high levels of politicization and bureaucratization and low levels of professionalization and marketization. A notable finding is that in most cases examined, bureaucratization is more prevalent than any other mode of public employment, suggesting the predominance of career-oriented closed civil service systems across much of the region.

The cases analyzed here differ in local administrative traditions, imported Western models of modern administration, and types of political regime (Painter and Peters 2010; Berman 2011). Japan, South Korea, and Taiwan inherited the Confucian tradition[6] and imported the Continental European model of modern administration (under Japanese colonial rule in the cases of South Korea and Taiwan). They maintain competitive electoral regimes and develop civil service systems with high levels of bureaucratization and low levels of politicization. Singapore and Hong Kong inherited the Confucian tradition and imported the Anglo-American model of modern administration under British direct colonial rule. They maintain noncompetitive electoral regimes and develop civil service systems with high levels of professionalization or marketization and low levels of politicization. Vietnam inherited the Confucian tradition and imported the Continental European model of modern administration under French colonial rule. It establishes a one-party political regime with Soviet model of administration after the communist revolution and develops a civil service system with substantial levels of politicization and bureaucratization.

The remaining cases with no Confucian traditions appear to be distinguishable from the cases with the Confucian tradition. Indonesia imported the Continental European model of modern administration under Dutch colonial rule. It recently establishes a competitive electoral regime and develops a civil service system with high levels of bureaucratization and moderate levels of politicization. Malaysia imported the Anglo-American model of modern administration under British indirect colonial rule and maintains a noncompetitive electoral regime. It develops a civil service system with substantial levels of bureaucratization and politicization. The Philippines imported the Anglo-American model of modern administration under American colonial rule and recently establishes a competitive electoral regime. It develops a civil service system with substantial levels of bureaucratization and professionalization and moderate levels of politicization. Thailand imported the Continental European model of modern administration. It maintains a noncompetitive electoral regime controlled by a coalition of military-civilian bureaucratic elites and develops a civil service system with substantial levels of bureaucratization and lower levels of politicization.

Outline of the Book

In this introduction, we develop a conceptual framework for analyzing national civil service systems based on different modes of public employment and apply

18 Chong-Min Park, Yousueng Han, and Yongjin Chang

them to describe and compare contemporary civil service systems in East and Southeast Asia.

As presented in the preceding section, there exist notable differences in patterns of public employment across the region. The differences seem to reflect national variation in local administrative traditions, imported models of modern administration, and types of political regime. Bureaucratization or professionalization appears to be the most prevailing mode of public employment across much of the region. The movement of civil service systems toward politicization or marketization appears to differ, depending on local administrative traditions, imported models of modern administration, and types of political regime. The region's contemporary civil service systems seem to develop varying combinations of these modes of public employment partly due to these differences, despite similar administrative reform pressures.

We bring together local scholars and experts across the region to examine their contemporary civil service systems. Considering the underlying influence of local administrative traditions, we organize their contributions into two parts. Part I includes the cases with the Confucian tradition (Japan, South Korea, Taiwan, Singapore, Hong Kong, and Vietnam), and Part II, the cases with non-Confucian traditions (Indonesia, Malaysia, the Philippines, and Thailand). Each chapter presents key aspects of the civil service system, including centralization, recruitment, classification, openness of positions, performance assessment, promotion, training, and senior civil service. We briefly summarize notable features of contemporary civil service systems reported in the following chapters.

We have six cases with the Confucian tradition. Of them, three (Japan, South Korea, and Taiwan) transplanted the Continental European model of modern administration, two (Singapore and Hong Kong), the Anglo-American model, and the one (Vietnam), the Soviet model on top of the Continental European model. We begin with three cases with Confucian tradition which imported the Continental European model of modern administration. The major features of Japan's national civil service system are its "closed career system" and centralized "ministerial personnel management." Once hired at the bottom, employees continue to work for the same ministry until retirement without any lateral transfers. Hiring takes place through open competitive entrance examination. It is rare that higher positions are filled directly from the outside the bureaucracy. Political neutrality of public bureaucracy is emphasized, and lifetime employment is guaranteed. The evaluation of ability and performance of civil servants is to some extent reflected in salary and promotion. Their salaries are somewhat compatible with the private sector employee in charge of similar responsibilities. Overall, the civil service system in Japan remains strongly bureaucratized and adopts some measures of professionalization or marketization.

The main path to the civil service in South Korea remains an open competitive examination. There are two types of entrance examination: first, a majority of newly recruits are selected through testing of general competence, and second, a minority, through screening of skills or expertise for specific positions. Lifelong employment is guaranteed for most civil servants, which renders public employment highly attractive in comparison to employment in the private sector. Since the introduction of a performance-based pay system in the late 1990s, a range of public officials whose annual salaries are determined by their performance has gradually expanded, indicating some degree of marketization in public employment. Overall, the Korean civil service system remains strongly bureaucratized, although it introduced some measures of professionalization or marketization.

The civil service system in Taiwan is separately administered under the examination branch that is independent of the executive branch of government. Civil servants are recruited mainly through civil service entrance examination that is open and competitive. There exists little chance of mid-career entry into the civil service. Career civil servants are legally protected as permanent officials, pursing a lifelong career. Different levels of education are required for different levels of positions. On the other hand, fixed-term contract employees are directly hired by government agencies, and they cannot become permanent staff unless they pass a civil service entrance examination. Any abuse of power and favoritism in the selection procedures is inhibited, although some positions are politically appointed. Overall, the civil service system in Taiwan remains strongly bureaucratized and slowly embraces some measures of professionalization or marketization.

We now turn to two Confucian cases which imported the Anglo-American model of modern administration. Singapore has made significant progress in professionalization and marketization of public employment. Some reform measures were undertaken to render state administration highly efficient and least corrupt. Most human resource management (HRM) functions are delegated to ministries, which have operational autonomy in recruitment, appointment, promotion, performance appraisal, and training. Public employment is not subject to political interference. Work experience, skills, professional qualifications and credentials, academic performance, internships, and other co-curricular activities are required for hiring. The principle of pay-for-performance is applied to employees with frequent performance evaluation and feedback. Lifelong employment is not guaranteed. Civil servants can be appointed to senior officers, depending on merits including experiences and performance. Overall, the civil service system in Singapore remains highly professionalized and marketized, indicating a significant departure from the traditional bureaucratic model.

In Hong Kong, applicants need to pass Common Recruitment Examination as a prerequisite for applying most of the civil service positions in entry ranks. Candidates passing the examination apply for departments they want to work for and need to pass interview. Before the major civil service reform in the late 1990s, generally, permanent employment offers a very stable career for civil servants. However, since the early 2000s some measures associated with the New Public Management reform have been introduced to enhance the flexibility of civil service. A security of tenure for new appointees in basic rank has been replaced by agreement (contract) terms and longer probationary period is required before being appointed to the permanent terms. External recruitment is usually available from ad hoc positions requiring strong professional training and skills. The authority to create posts is delegated to the policy branches and departments. Most "directorate" officers, a majority of whom are senior civil servants, are appointed at the entry level and incrementally promoted through seniority and performance appraisal in general, although a political appointment system was introduced in the early 2000s. The pay increments are still more associated with seniority, not performance. Overall, the civil service system in Hong Kong remains highly professionalized and bureaucratized. Yet, it should be noted that the level of politicization has increased since it was transferred to China in the late 1990s.

We now turn to Vietnam, a Confucian case which imported the Soviet model on top of the Continental European model of modern administration. In this one-party regime, the Communist Party functions as leadership of governmental branches. In each organization, there is a party unit that supervises an administrative unit. Civil servants as permanent state employees work for the ruling party organizations. In the 2000s and the 2010s civil service reform programs were undertaken to make state administration more professional, flexible, and effective. Four kinds of objective tests are introduced, and good performance is rewarded by increased salary. However, civil servants are evaluated annually, based on comments from a party cell about observance of the guidelines and policies of the Party, political qualities, ethics, and lifestyle. Despite recent administrative reform measures, the civil service system in Vietnam remains highly politicized while moving toward bureaucratization.

We now turn to four cases with non-Confucian traditions. Of them two (Indonesia and Thailand) imported the Continental European model of modern administration while the other two (Malaysia and the Philippines), the Anglo-American model. The civil service reform in Indonesia has placed a strong emphasis on meritocracy, open career system, and professionalism accompanying performance-based management since the mid-2010s. The government has introduced a Computer Assisted Test (CAT) in the recruitment process. CAT consists of basic and technical competence tests. The announcement of various job positions can be accessed via an agency's official website. The civil servants consist of permanent employees and contract-based employees, and the recruitment system has been based on a merit system. Performance evaluation remains largely subjective, and a pay-for-performance system has not yet developed systematically. Overall, the civil service system in Indonesia remains substantially bureaucratized and slowly moves toward professionalization.

In Thailand, the centralization of human resource management has reduced individual agencies' operational autonomy in handling their own personnel matters. To be a civil servant, applicants need to take a general competitive examination designed and operated by a central agency. Application for civil service positions is fully open to all citizens. However, a minimum level of education, certificate or diploma is required to become a civil servant at the entry level. The tenure of civil servants is secured. Political appointees are just allowed for a very limited number of personal aide positions. There is little change in the number of professional positions. The reform of "pay for performance principle" was introduced in the

Comparing Civil Service Systems **21**

late 2000s, suggesting its slow adoption of marketization of public employment. Overall, the civil service system in Thailand remains substantially bureaucratized and slowly moves toward professionalization.

Since the 2000s, Malaysia has promoted civil service reforms for making state administration more efficient and less corrupt. One of the most attractive benefits from working in the civil service was lifetime employment protected by law. However, facing rising public sector debt, since the mid-2010s, "Exit Policy" has been introduced to deal with underperforming employees, and an increasing number of staff have been hired on a contractual basis to lessen the public sector debt. The recruitment or appointment of officers holding certain positions is made on the basis of political considerations. Political appointees do not come from the conventional pool of the civil servants, but outside the civil service. Overall, the civil service system in Malaysia remains substantially politicized and bureaucratized.

In the Philippine Civil Service Commission is a central human resource management unit, independent from the three branches of government. Career service is characterized by competitive entrance examination and security of tenure. Non-career service is contract-based employees, meeting education, training, and experience requirements of specific positions. The number of such positions is increasing. Each government agency is allowed to develop its own screening process including examination and interview. Lateral entry is not limited. Performance management for senior officials is formally based on merit, but many senior positions have been still filled by political appointees. Overall, the civil service system in the Philippines remains substantially bureaucratized as well as professionalized while moderately politicized.

Overall, at the risk of simplification, it can be said that the cases with the Confucian tradition except for Vietnam tend to display low levels of politicization. Of them those with the Continental European model of modern administration tend to display high levels of bureaucratization while those with the Anglo-American model, high levels of professionalization or marketization. By contrast, the cases with non-Confucian traditions tend to display substantial levels of politicization. Of them those with the Continental European model of modern administration tend to display higher levels of bureaucratization than those with the Anglo-American model. The patterns of public employment found across the region seem to reflect local administrative traditions, imported Western models of modern administration, and types of political regime.

Notes

1 In a strict sense, promotion by seniority appears to contradict a value pattern of achievement, but it may be considered as its variant in a broad sense.
2 Dahlström et al. (2012) distinguish between closed bureaucracy primarily characterized by exam-based appointment and professional bureaucracy characterized by meritocratic recruitment.
3 Evans and Rauch (1999) measure meritocratic recruitment by using appointment through examination and the number of civil servants with bachelor's degree or more (Rauch and Evans 2000).

4 While examination and seniority are considered fixed and objective criteria, evaluation of merit by superiors is considered a subjective criterion (Halaby 1978).
5 The QoG Expert Survey is a research project established by the Quality of Government Institute at the University of Gothenburg in Sweden. The aim of the survey is to empirically capture the organizational design of public bureaucracies and bureaucratic behavior in countries around the world (Dahlström et al. 2015).
6 The mode of recruitment based on examination is known to be one of key features of Confucian state bureaucracy (Woodside 2006).

References

Aberbach, J. D., Putnam, R. D. and Rockman B. A. (1981) *Bureaucrats and Politicians in Western Democracies*, Cambridge: Harvard University Press.

Bach, S. and Kessler, I. (2007) 'HRM and the new public management', in P. Boxall, J. Purcell and P. Wright (eds) *The Oxford Handbook of Human Resource Management* (pp. 469–88), Oxford: Oxford University Press.

Battaglio, R. P., Jr. and Ledvinka, C. B. (2009) 'Privatizing human resources in the public sector: Legal challenges to outsourcing the human resource function', *Review of Public Personnel Administration*, 29(3): 293–307.

Bekke, H. A. G. M., Perry, J. L. and Toonen, T. A. J. (1996) 'Introduction: Conceptualizing civil service systems', in H. A. G. M. Bekke, J. L. Perry and T. A. J. Toonen (eds) *Civil Service Systems in Comparative Perspective* (pp. 1–10), Bloomington: Indiana University Press.

Berman, E. M. (2011) 'Public administration in Southeast Asia: An overview', in E. M. Berman (ed) *Public Administration in Southeast Asia: Thailand, Philippines, Malaysia, Hong Kong, and Macao* (pp. 1–26), Boca Raton, FL: CRC Press.

Bezes, P. and Lodge, M. (2015) 'Civil service reforms, public service bargains and dynamics of institutional change', in F. M. van der Meer, J. C. N. Raadschelders and T. A. J. Toonen (eds) *Comparative Civil Service Systems in the 21st Century*, 2nd edn (pp. 136–61), Basingstoke: Palgrave Macmillan.

Brans, M. (2012) 'Comparative public administration: From general theory to general frameworks', in B. G. Peters and J. Pierre (eds) *The SAGE Handbook of Public Administration*, Concise 2nd edn (pp. 445–65), London: Sage.

Burns, J. P. and Bowornwathana, B. (2001) *Civil Service Systems in Asia*, Cheltenham: Edward Elgar.

Christensen, T. and Laegreid, P. (2001) 'New public management: The effects of contractualism and devolution on political control', *Public Management Review*, 3(1): 73–94.

Dahlström, C., Lapuente, V. and Teorell, J. (2012) 'The merit of meritocratization: Politics, bureaucracy, and the institutional deterrents of corruption', *Political Research Quarterly*, 65(3): 656–68.

Dahlström, C., Teorell, J., Dahlberg, S., Hartmann, F., Lindberg, A. and Nistotskaya, M. (2015) *The QoG Expert Survey Dataset II*, University of Gothenburg: The Quality of Government Institute.

Evans, P. and Rauch, J. E. (1999) 'Bureaucracy and growth: A cross-national analysis of the effects of "Weberian" state structures on economic growth', *American Sociological Review*, 64(5): 748–65.

Fischer, W. and Lundgreen, P. (1975) 'The recruitment and training of administrative and technical personnel', in C. Tilly (ed) *The Formation of National States in Western Europe* (pp. 456–562), Princeton: Princeton University Press.

Grindle, M. S. (2012) *Jobs for the Boys: Patronage and the State in Comparative Perspective*, Cambridge: Harvard University Press.

Halaby, C. N. (1978) 'Bureaucratic promotion criteria', *Administrative Science Quarterly*, 23(3): 466–84.

Hall, R. H. (1968) 'Professionalization and bureaucratization', *American Sociological Review*, 33(1): 92–104.

Heredia, B. and Schneider, B. R. (2003) 'The political economy of administrative reform in developing countries', in B. Schneider and H. Heredia (eds) *Reinventing Leviathan: The Politics of Administrative Reform in Developing Countries* (pp. 1–29), Miami: North-South Center Press at University of Miami.

Hood, C. (1991) 'A public management for all seasons?' *Public Administration*, 69(1): 3–19.

Mosher, F. C. (1968) *Democracy and the Public Service*, New York: Oxford University Press.

Mosher, F. C. (1978) 'Professions in public service', *Public Administration Review*, 38(2): 144–50.

OECD (2005) *Paying for Performance; Policies for Government Employees*, Paris: OECD, available at: www.sigmaweb.org/publicationsdocuments/38708031.pdf.

Page, E. C. and Wright, V. (1999) *Bureaucratic Elites in Western European States: A Comparative Analysis of Top Officials*, Oxford: Oxford University Press.

Painter, M. and Peters, B. G. (2010) *Tradition and Public Administration*, London: Palgrave Macmillan.

Peters, B. G. and Pierre, J. (2004) 'Politicization of the civil service: Concepts, causes and consequences', in B. G. Peters and J. Pierre (eds) *Politicization of the Civil Service in Comparative Perspective: The Quest for Control* (pp. 1–13), London: Routledge.

Pierre, J. (1995) 'Conclusion: A framework of comparative public administration', in J. Pierre (ed) *Bureaucracy in the Modern State: An Introduction to Comparative Public Administration* (pp. 205–18), Aldershot: Edward Elgar.

Pierre, J. and Peters, B. G. (2017) 'The shirking bureaucrat: A theory in search of evidence?' *Policy & Politics*, 45(2): 157–72.

Pollitt, C. and Bouckaert, G. (2011) *Public Management Reform: A Comparative Analysis*, 3rd edn, Oxford: Oxford University Press.

Raadschelders, J. C. N. and Rutgers, M. R. (1996) 'The functions of civil service systems', in H. A. G. M. Bekke, J. L. Perry and T. A. J. Toonen (eds) *Civil Service Systems in Comparative Perspective* (pp. 67–99), Bloomington: Indiana University Press.

Rauch, J. E. and Evans, P. B. (2000) 'Bureaucratic structure and bureaucratic performance in less developed countries', *Journal of Public Economics*, 75(1): 49–71.

Ritzer, G. (1975) 'Professionalization, bureaucratization, and rationalization: The views of Max Weber', *Social Forces*, 53(4): 627–34.

Rouban, L. (2012) 'Politicization of the civil service', in B. G. Peters and J. Pierre (eds) *The SAGE Handbook of Public Administration*, Concise 2nd edn (pp. 340–51), London: Sage.

Rouban, L. (2015) 'Political-administrative relations: Evolving models of politicization', in F. M. van der Meer, J. C. N. Raadschelders and T. A. J. Toonen (eds) *Comparative Civil Service Systems in the 21st Century*, 2nd edn (pp. 317–33), Basingstoke: Palgrave Macmillan.

Silberman, B. S. (1993) *Cages of Reason: The Rise of the Rational State in France, Japan, the United States, and Great Britain*, Chicago: Chicago University Press.

Weber, M. (1946) *From Max Weber: Essays in Sociology*, New York: Free Press.

Weber, M. (1947) *The Theory of Social and Economic Organizations*, New York: Free Press.

Wilson, J. Q. (1989) *Bureaucracy: What Government Agencies Do and Why They Do It*, New York: Basic Books.

Wong, H. and Chan, H. S. (eds) (1999) *Handbook of Comparative Public Administration in the Asia-Pacific Basin*, New York: Marcel Dekker.

Woodside, A. (2006) *Lost Modernities: China, Vietnam, Korea, and the Hazards of World History*, Cambridge: Harvard University Press.

PART I

Civil Service Systems With the Confucian Tradition

1

JAPAN

Motomichi Otani

History

Pre-war Japanese officials are "emperor's officials" who were appointed on the basis of the emperor's authority to oversee the governing power. They were obliged to serve the emperor faithfully and with absoluteness, and remuneration were paid in an amount appropriate for maintaining the position and appearance as a government official. Moreover, there was also a pension system. For a while, after the establishment of the new Meiji government in 1868, officials were appointed on the basis of personal motives of powers in feudal clans. However, with the establishment of the Cabinet system, at the end of the nineteenth century, it was decided that the appointment of government officials should be based on the merit system.

Since pre-war officials were opposed to the public as the emperor's officials, and – along with the military – formed a large force in the country's governing mechanism, the official system was radically reviewed with the post-war democratization of Japan. As the Constitution of Japan was established in 1946, public employees were considered to be servants for the entire nation – not some people – and their selection and dismissal were considered to be the unique rights of the public, the sovereign of the nation. The National Public Service Act was enacted in 1947, but there were some inadequacies. In the following year, major revisions were made, including restrictions on the basic labor rights of national public employees – thereby strengthening the independence of the National Personnel Authority, which is the central agency for personnel administration – and the addition of recommended provisions. In this way, the framework of the current national public service system was established (Morizono et al. 2015, pp. 5–13).

The national public service system established aims at guaranteeing the democratic and efficient operation of public affairs. To secure this purpose, the National Public Service Act stipulates the following principles: the performance-based

DOI: 10.4324/9781003326496-3

28 Motomichi Otani

principles that required recruitment through competitive exams; principles guaranteeing status and stating that layoffs will not occur unless the conditions stipulated by law are satisfied; and the basic principle of job-based pay, stating that duties are analyzed and salaries are paid accordingly. In addition, there were restrictions on political acts, strict service regulations, such as prohibition of strikes, and the Establishment of the National Personnel Authority with authority over affairs concerning recruitment examinations, remuneration recommendations, and equity processes.

In the mid-1990s, scandals, such as corruptions by public employees and policy failures, occurred in quick succession, which initiated the reform of the national public service system. The National Public Service Act was amended in 2007 to ensure thorough personnel management, based on ability and performance. This rests on the idea that it is essential to improve upon the efficiency of public affairs by allocating personnel in the right places and realizing varied salary treatment, based on the capabilities and achievements of each staff member, rather than uniform personnel management, such as conventional appointment and salary treatment that focuses on the type and year of recruitment examinations to make the best use of national public employees as human resources. In addition, the National Public Service Act was revised in 2014 to tackle the sectionalism in each ministry. The personnel affairs of executives, which had been carried out by each ministry, were to be centrally managed under the Cabinet, and the Cabinet Bureau of Personnel Affairs was established in the Cabinet Office (Otani 2021, pp. 186–7).

Overview: Current System

Japan's national administrative organization is made up of the Cabinet Office, 11 ministries, and two agencies, all of which are placed under the Cabinet. There are about 589,000 national public employees in Japan (as of April 1, 2022) (National Personnel Authority 2022, p. 3).

National public employees can be categorized as either "special service" or "regular service" employees. The former category consists of those who are responsible for political affairs, such as ministers and deputy ministers; those who belong to the legislative and judicial branches of the government, such as parliamentary staff and judges; and others who must be treated separately owing to the nature of their duties, such as officials with the Ministry of Defense (SDF officials). The majority of these are, in fact, staff at the Ministry of Defense.

Those who do not fall into the special service category are regarded as regular service. These employees are subject to numerous provisions set out in the National Public Service Act, including regulations concerning the elimination of favoritism in appointments, guarantee of status, and rigorous service discipline. Within the regular service, staff working for each ministry or for their branch offices at the local level are subject to the Remuneration Act (Otani 2021, pp. 174–5). This chapter discusses regular-service employees.

Central Personnel Administrative Agency

The National Personnel Authority is a neutral third-party specialist agency that conducts personnel management for national public employees positioned under the Cabinet Office jurisdiction. The Authority is a consultative organization made up of three personnel commissioners, one of whom serves as the President. As the country's central agency for personnel administration, the Authority sets out criteria for personnel management as implemented by appointed officials and performs the overall coordination of personnel management.

Specifically, the National Personnel Authority (1) sets criteria and implements training for recruitment tests, appointments, and dismissals in order to ensure fairness in the personnel management of public employees; (2) makes recommendations to the Diet and the Cabinet regarding reforms to labor conditions such as salaries to compensate for restrictions on basic labor rights; and (3) conducts surveys and studies on human resources systems in Japan and overseas and develops

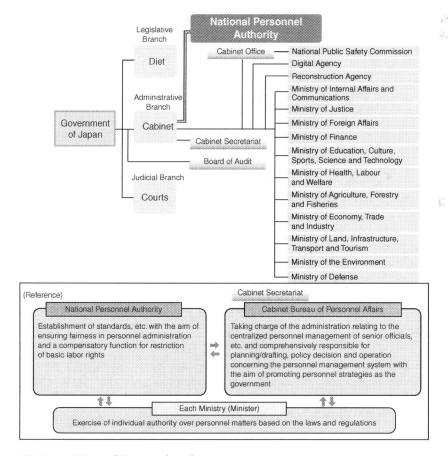

FIGURE 1.1 National Personnel Authority

Source: Modified from National Personnel Authority (2020, p. 1).

30 Motomichi Otani

personnel policies that meet contemporary demands as a specialized agency for personnel administration (National Personnel Authority 2020, pp. 1–2).

Recruitment

Two major features of Japan's national public service personnel system are (1) its "closed career system": national public employees are hired as new graduates and are transferred and promoted internally until they reach the age of retirement, and (2) "ministerial personnel management" in which recruitment takes place at the government ministry level. Once hired, employees continue to work for the same ministry until retirement without any lateral transfers.

Thus, employees are generally hired directly out of university or high school and then work their way up from the bottom. It is extremely rare for individuals with certain capabilities or experience to actively be sought out for any particular position, except for those with term limits.

Recruitment is based on performance. In principle, hiring takes place through competitive exams that are open and fair to ensure that opportunities are available to all citizens and that candidates are evaluated impartially. Only in exceptional cases can a candidate be chosen through a method of evaluation other than an exam.

There are two types of recruitment exams. The Career Track (*sōgō-shoku*) Examination is for those who have a graduate degree or equivalent, or a bachelor's degree or equivalent, while the General Track (*ippan-shoku*) Examination has a category for those who have a bachelor's degree or equivalent and a category for those who have a high school diploma or equivalent. In addition, there are two versions of the specialist exam for roles such as national tax specialists or prison officers: one version is given to those with a bachelor's degree or equivalent and another for those with a high school diploma or equivalent.

In the case of the Career Track Examination (targeting those with a bachelor's degree or equivalent), intended for hiring employees who could potentially become high-ranking officials, qualified candidates are those between the ages of 22 and 30 at the time of recruitment who have either graduated or are expected to graduate from university, or those who are deemed by the National Personnel Authority to have credentials equivalent to a university degree. The preliminary exam consists of a "fundamental skills" test involving general subjects as well as a test for specialized subjects. The latter involves law and economics, among other subjects, for administrative candidates, and engineering, agricultural science, and the like for technical candidates. These are multiple-choice exams. The second stage of the exam involves a written test concerning specialized subjects, an essay on policy issues, and interviews. Those who have passed these exams are invited to visit the respective ministries for an interview. Only about one-third of applicants receive job offers.

Another feature of Japan's national public service personnel system is its use of recruitment test tracks known as "career" and "non-career" tracks for entrance selection. "Career" track employees are those who have been recruited via the Career Track (*sōgō-shoku*) Examination for the Recruitment of National Public Employees. In this ministry, these employees are recruited as candidates for executive posts and account for no more than a small percentage of all employees.

"Non-career" track employees are employees outside the "career" track who have been recruited via the General Track (*ippan-shoku*) Examination for the Recruitment of National Public Employees. These employees are mainly recruited by local-level branch offices and play an active role as officials who provide practical support for those on the career track.

Personnel management of "career" candidates for senior positions and other "non-career" positions is carried out separately. Another feature of this system is a seniority-based model of personnel management that places an emphasis on the year in which a given employee entered public service. This makes it nearly impossible for a career- or non-career track employee to be promoted ahead of a colleague on the same track who joined the public service at an earlier date (Otani 2021, pp. 174–8; National Personnel Authority 2020, p. 4).

In addition to the division between the career and non-career tracks, another categorical distinction among Japan's national public employees is that between administrative officials (*jimukan*) and technical officials (*gikan*). Even for the same career-track and general-track recruitment examinations, multiple examination categories exist depending on the applicant's fields of expertise. Here, "administrative officials" are those recruited through clerical recruitment examinations, while those recruited via technical recruitment examinations are known as "technical officials."

At the Ministry of Land, Infrastructure, Transport and Tourism and the Ministry of Agriculture, Forestry and Fisheries, technical officials are recruited in numbers that match or even surpass administrative officials. Technical officials are transferred within a narrower range than administrative officials and are trained in a manner that cultivates a high level of technical expertise. Administrative officials trained as generalists are often given preferential treatment in terms of promotions.

Moreover, the world of technical officials is highly exclusive, as evidenced in part by the fact that personnel plans for technical officials are drafted by senior officials with backgrounds as technical officials, such that it is sometimes known as an "independent kingdom."

Because technical officials have a high degree of technical expertise, they form tightly knit policy networks (i.e., connections with policy experts) that include contacts with related industries and legislators, and exert a strong influence over national policy formation processes (Mabuchi 2020, pp. 312–18).

Civil Service Classification and Status

National public employees are appointed by authorized appointers such as ministers. As stated earlier, national public employees in Japan are hired as recent graduates and are then transferred and promoted internally until they retire. Lifetime employment is guaranteed by the National Public Service Act. While layoffs related to restructuring or budget cuts are legally possible, they rarely occur in practice. Although there is a system for hiring fixed-term employees who have expertise and experience in areas that are lacking within the organization, the number of people who are actually hired under this system is extremely low.

Working conditions for national public employees are determined by law. Salaries consist of basic wages, which are determined according to the complexity and difficulty of the work performed by employees, the responsibilities they undertake, and various allowances. There is a salary schedule for each type of work, such as administration, taxation, public safety, education, and research. Salaries are paid in accordance with the pay schedule.

The salary schedule sets out basic monthly wage amounts that are determined according to position and years of experience. This system follows the basic principle of duty-based pay; once standard government positions and the ability to perform standard duties necessary for those positions have been established, salaries are paid according to employees' duties. For example, the Administrative Service (1) Salary Schedule has 10 grades based on work categories, and each grade has as many as 125 different payment levels (steps). Once hired, employees begin with grade 1, the bottom level, and work their way up toward higher grades.

The basic labor rights of national public employees are subject to some restrictions. For national public employees in the so-called regular service, the "right to organize" and form labor unions, for example, is respected. However, while "collective bargaining rights" involving negotiations over labor conditions with personnel management offices are permitted, the "right to conclude collective agreements" that arise as a result of the former is not permitted. Moreover, the "right to strike" is also not respected. In other words, it is not possible to determine labor conditions through negotiations between labor and management. As compensation for this, the National Personnel Authority has prepared a recommendation system.

Regarding the determination of remuneration levels, the National Personnel Authority conducts a survey of remuneration levels in the private sector every August and delivers recommendations to the Diet and Cabinet regarding differences compared with national public employee remuneration. In most cases, remuneration revisions are carried out in line with these recommendations, and remuneration for national public employees are comparable with those of workers in private firms. This is known as "private sector compliance."

It is worth noting that the 2019 survey of private sector remuneration levels, after taking into consideration industry type and enterprise scale, randomly extracted data from places of business with at least 50 employees, collecting and analyzing remuneration data from approximately 550,000 employees in about 12,500 places of employment. On the basis of this data, we compare the remuneration of people with the same conditions (region, position, educational background, age group),

Category		Right to organize	Right of Collective Bargaining		Right to Strike
				Right to Conclude Collective Agreements	
National public employees	Employees under the Remuneration Act	○	△ (×2)	×	×
	Police officials Coast Guard officials Penal institution employees	×	×	×	×
	Employees of agencies engaged in administrative execution	○	○	○	×

(×1) ○ indicates a right recognized; △ indicates a right partially denied; and × indicates a right denied.

(×2) Labor-management negotiations can be carried out.

FIGURE 1.2 Current situation of basic labor rights

Source: National Personnel Authority (2020, p. 18).

from the public and private sectors, and draw appropriate remuneration levels. As of April 2021, the average age of national public employees is 43.0, and the average monthly remuneration is about 407,000 yen along with basic wages and various allowances (excluding commuting allowance and overtime allowance) (Otani 2021, pp. 178–9; National Personnel Authority 2020, pp. 14–18; Ministry of Internal Affairs and Communications 2021, p. 6).

Openness of Posts/Positions

As stated earlier, Japanese national public employees are hired as recent graduates under a closed career system and are transferred and promoted internally until retirement. Unlike an open career system under which candidates are actively sought from both inside and outside the organization whenever job vacancies arise, available positions under this system are filled by candidates within the organization through staff reassignment. In other words, candidates are not actively sought for particular positions.

As an exceptional way to recruit human resources from outside, recently, a system for mid-career recruitment, fixed-term recruitment, and personnel exchange system with the private sector have been established. This aims at addressing the need to flexibly recruit the necessary human resources from outside the organization to provide high-quality administrative services, as administrative issues become diversified and complicated. However, the proportion of such recruitments are extremely small in the total number of recruited people (Otani 2021, pp. 184–6; National Personnel Authority 2006).

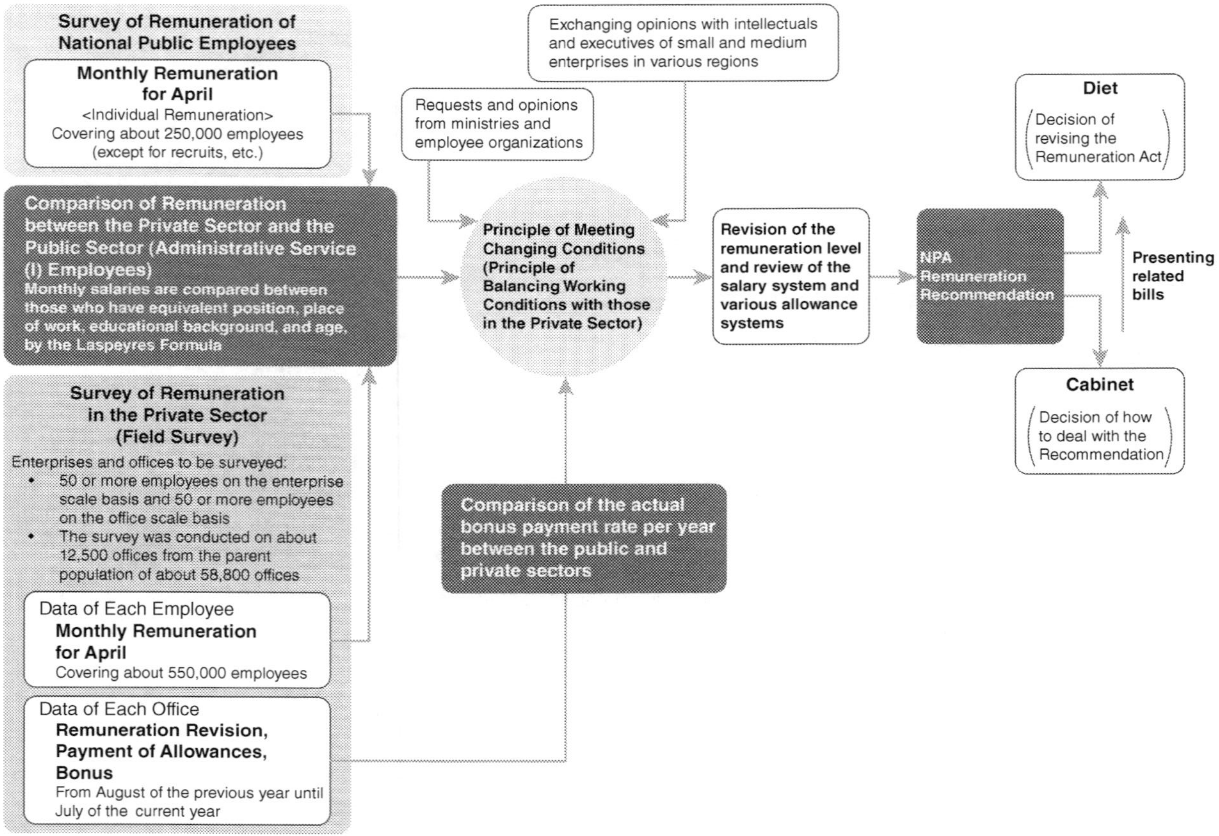

FIGURE 1.3 Process of remuneration recommendation

Source: National Personnel Authority (2020, p. 15).

Mid-career Recruitment

In April 1998, the National Personnel Authority Regulations 1–24 (special provision for hiring private human resources to stimulate public service) came into effect, and a flexible mid-career hiring system was established to hire private human resources with a high degree of expertise and extensive experience that cannot be obtained through trainings within the organization. This has made it possible to recruit the following human resources through selection: (1) persons who are recognized as having advanced and specialized knowledge/experience through professional work experience outside the organization (e.g., lawyer, certified public accountant);

(2) persons who are recognized as being potentially useful to public affairs through experience in practical work outside of organization (e.g., IT relations, fund management) to meet current demands, in terms of administration; and (3) persons who are recognized as being potentially useful to public affairs through various activities and experiences in fields outside of public affairs (e.g., NPO members).

Hiring Fixed-Term Employees

In November 2000, the law concerning the recruitment of fixed-term administrative grade employees and the special provision of remuneration (Act on Officials with Fixed Term of Office) came into effect. A system has been put in place to hire fixed-term employees with a specialized knowledge/experience useful to public affairs and to pay salaries suitable for persons who have a high degree of specialized knowledge/experience.

Consequently, it became possible to hire talented personnel from the private sector, for fixed terms when: (1) engaging the person, who has highly specialized knowledge/experience or excellent insight for a job that particularly requires the utilization of the person's highly specialized the knowledge/experience or the excellent insight, for a certain period of time; (2) it is difficult for a certain period of time to secure a staff who is qualified to be engaged in the relevant work within a department because it takes a considerable period of time to train staffs with specialized knowledge/experience; and (3) the period, during which the specialized knowledge/experience of the person concerned can be effectively utilized in the relevant work, is limited because the specialized knowledge/experience is related to a rapidly advancing technology and the inherent nature of the specialized knowledge/experience.

Public-Private Personnel Exchange

In March 2000, the law on personnel exchanges between the national government and private companies (Act on Personnel Exchange between the Government Sector and Private Enterprises) was enacted, and a new bidirectional personnel

36 Motomichi Otani

exchange system between the national government and private enterprises was established. This system ensures mutual understanding between the national and private enterprises through personnel exchanges between national institutions and private enterprises while safeguarding fair operation of public affairs under fair procedures that guarantee transparency and openness. The purpose is to deepen and stimulate organizations and personnel development. It is composed of two systems, each with a maximum term of five years: one is an exchanging dispatch wherein a national public employee is dispatched to a private company for a certain period of time and engages in the business as an employee of the private company while holding the status of a national government employee; another one is interchanging recruitment wherein a retired private company employee is hired immediately by a national institution, with a fixed term and similar responsibilities.

Performance Assessment and Promotion

The National Public Service Act was revised in 2007 and a new personnel evaluation system was introduced that considers employees' abilities and performance. The evaluation of national public employees' abilities is carried out on an annual basis, with biannual performance evaluations. Employees' abilities are assessed through a competency scale, while their performance is measured by management by objectives. The results of these evaluations are reflected in employees' salaries and promotions and are also considered in training and other aspects of personnel development (National Personnel Authority 2020, pp. 12–13).

Those who are authorized to make appointments select suitable employees for promotion within the organization. The way in which employees are promoted differs depending on whether they are career-track employees or non–career-track employees. Since career-track employees are expected to serve in senior staff positions in the future, they are trained as generalists in order to cultivate a broad-based range of knowledge and perspectives. Accordingly, they experience many transfers over the short span of one to two years.

These employees are generally promoted at the same time based on the year in which they joined the civil service, usually until they reach the level of section chief or director (*kachō*) at around the age of 45 (though this varies by ministry). This is done to maximize motivation; keeping consistencies in promotions allows individual employees to feel that they too will have a chance at success.

In the case of each ministry, although promotion past the rank of director will continue to deputy director-general (*shingikan*), director-general (*kyokuchō*), and permanent vice-minister (*jimujikan*), there are sufficient posts up to the rank of director for all employees who join in a given year, but posts at the rank of deputy director-general and higher are more limited in number. For this reason, attaining posts at the level of deputy director-general and above requires emerging victorious from fierce competition.

Losers must take their leave from the office organization in the form *amakudari* ("descent from heaven"). The reward for those who win in such "up or out"

Performance Evaluation

The evaluator evaluates the achievement of the evaluatee shown in the course of duty during the appraisal period of half a year.

Example of goal setting [Unit Chief at HQ]

Content of task	Goal	Degree of difficulty	Degree of importance
Compilation of an opinion report draft	To sort out the points at issue by ▼ (month) in order to achieve a certain conclusion for the outline of the □□ Basic Policy at the △△ conference with the goal of compiling an opinion report draft.		◎
Review of ◆	· ·		
Implementation of ■	· ·	△	

(Note 1) 3-5 goals are usually set.
(Note 2) In the column for 'Degree of difficulty', ◎ would mean a difficult goal, and △ an easy one.
(Note 3) In the column for 'Degree of importance', ◎ would mean the goal is particularly important, and △ it is relatively unimportant.

Competency Evaluation

The evaluator evaluates the ability of the evaluatee shown in the course of duty during the appraisal period of one year.

Example of evaluation items [Division Director at Regional Office]

<Planning of implementation measures>
To plan implementation measures which meet the local demands of administration based on the organization's policy.

① Understanding of administrative demands: to correctly understand the local demands of administration and the problems associated with each case.

② Awareness of results: to have a clear image of the expected results and to plan the optimum implementation measures with due consideration for options including challenges of taking new measures.

Other evaluation items include "ethics", "judgement", "explanation/coordination", "operation of business" and "leadership in organization/human resource development".

Basically, evaluation in 5 grades (S, A, B (average), C, D) [absolute evaluation]

FIGURE 1.4 Basic framework of the personnel evaluation system

Source: National Personnel Authority (2020, p. 12).

38 Motomichi Otani

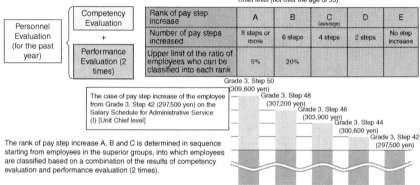

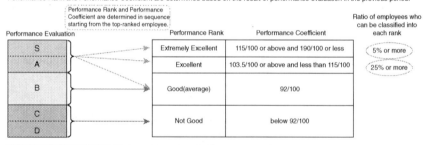

FIGURE 1.5 Utilization of evaluation results

Source: National Personnel Authority (2020, p. 13).

struggles is the rank of permanent vice-ministers, the highest post a bureaucrat can achieve. Normally, only one person in any given cohort can reach this rank (cohort sizes vary from ministry to ministry but are generally around 20 employees).

Since non-career track employees are expected to serve as staff in charge of providing practical support, they are trained as so-called specialists who are familiar with the practices of a specific field. For this reason, the scope of the transfers they experience is limited. In many ministries, such transfers will take place repeatedly inside specific bureaus, and these bureaus are frequently given substantive authority for managing personnel affairs.

Non-career-track employees do not experience fierce competition for advancement like those on the career-track, and it is possible for them to work as specialists until the age of retirement. While the highest-ranking post attainable by a non-career-track employee in this ministry is director, very few individuals are able to reach this role.

In this way, whereas personnel management for career-track employees regards promotion as an incentive for motivation, personnel management for non-career-track employees regards employment security and professionalism as incentives for motivation.

The structure of the entire personnel management system for national public employees is shown in the figure by superimposing promotion management of previously mentioned career-track employees and non-career-track employees. This is called "Double Piece Model" (Inatsugu 1996, pp. 30–6; Otani 2021, pp. 181–3).

The phenomenon known as *amakudari* is a customary personnel practice for career-track employees in which bureaucrats that are forced out of the government organization as a result of fierce "up or out" competition for promotion elect to take early retirement, whereupon they find reemployment as executives with external agencies or private firms. As seen in the advancement model, the practice is incorporated into personnel affairs for career-track employees and could even be called a kind of de facto reemployment service provided by government ministries.

The suggested benefits of this practice include "the stimulation of government agencies," whereby the retirement of older employees makes it possible to appoint younger staff; "wage compensation," whereby lower wage levels during a bureaucrat's active career are supplemented by higher wages after retirement; and "public-private partnerships," whereby former bureaucrats are able to facilitate the exchange of information and mutual understanding between the public and private sectors by moving into private industry.

On the other hand, several adverse impacts have also been mentioned: bureaucrats gain access to high salaries and high-level posts, can receive repeated retirement payouts by repeating the *amakudari* process more than once (a practice known as *watari* or "migration"), and cozy ties are formed between the sending ministries and the *amakudari* destinations.

For this reason, regulations concerning *amakudari* have been strengthened as a part of recent national public service system reforms, with the result that the

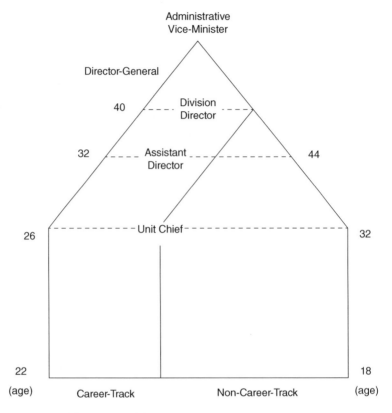

FIGURE 1.6 Double piece model

Source: Inatsugu (1996, p. 35).

circumstances surrounding the practice have undergone dramatic changes (Mabuchi 2020, pp. 319–35; Otani 2021, pp. 183–4).

Training

The National Personnel Authority provides training common to all ministries, and each ministry handles training specific to its own duties. Training that targets employees of all ministries includes programs tailored to specific ranks, those involving the dispatch of employees to external organizations, and those based on specific themes.

Programs tailored to specific ranks include initial training for new employees, "third-year follow-up" sessions for those who are in their third year, as well as programs for section chiefs, assistant directors, and directors. There are also seminars that target higher-ranking officials.

The initial training is a three-day camp program that takes place several days after public employees are hired. The purpose of this camp is to instill in new employees the ethical values and the sense of mission required as servants for the entire nation and make them deepen their understanding of one another so that they will be able to work together as members of the government on various policy measures. In addition, one or two months after they are hired, employees will go through a five-week training session to strengthen their awareness as servants of the entire nation and to acquire the basic skills and knowledge they need to carry out various measures. This includes one week of field training in local governments, nursing facilities, and other venues.

The dispatch training includes a long-term overseas fellowship program in which ministry employees are sent to graduate schools outside Japan, a short-term overseas fellowship program at foreign government institutions or multinational organizations, and a domestic fellowship program at graduate schools in Japan.

Theme-based programs include career training for female employees and harassment awareness training and staff management training for those in supervisory positions (National Personnel Authority 2020, pp. 5–6).

Senior Civil Service (Senior Management)

Among senior positions in each ministry, the three highest ranks of minister, senior vice-minister, and parliamentary secretary are reserved for politicians. The highest post for career public employees is administrative vice-minister, followed by directors-general of each bureau, deputy directors-general, and directors. The positions from deputy-director general all the way up to administrative vice-minister are called "designated" positions. These positions are filled through internal promotions rather than external appointments.

As mentioned previously, the major features of Japan's national public service personnel system are its "closed career system" and "ministerial personnel management." As a result of these personnel systems, the loyalty of national public employees is directed not to the country but to their home ministries. For this reason, in cases in which the interests of the country run contrary to the interests of their home ministries, we tend to see sectionalism – officials privilege the interests of their home ministries over those of the country, despite being national public employees. Therefore, in 2014, the Cabinet Bureau of Personnel Affairs was established in the Cabinet Office in an effort to maintain loyalty to the central government by unifying personnel affairs for senior government officials in each ministry.

The Deputy Chief Cabinet Secretary serves as the director of the Cabinet Bureau of Personnel Affairs, while approximately 600 senior officials from various ministries belonging to the rank of deputy director-general or higher are subject to the new centralized personnel management system. Individuals who have undergone "eligibility screening" to determine whether they possess the abilities and qualifications required to serve as senior-level public employees will be placed on a roster of candidates for senior executive-level positions. While individual ministers with appointive power appoint officials by examining the suitability of candidates listed on this roster, in practice, appointments are decided in "consultations over

42 Motomichi Otani

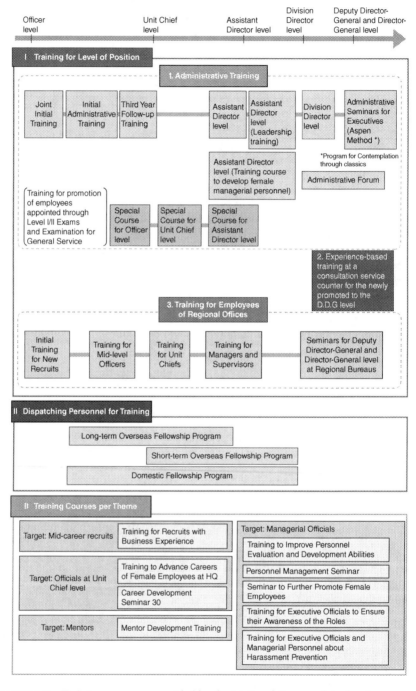

FIGURE 1.7 Training programs provided by the National Personnel Authority

Source: National Personnel Authority (2020, p. 5).

appointment and dismissal" carried out between the Prime Minister and the Chief Cabinet Secretary.

While it is expected that this will strengthen the Prime Minister-led character of personnel affairs for senior public employees and facilitate the promotion of policies advocated by the administration of the day, it is predicted that the tendency of bureaucrats who care about their own futures to be overly sensitive to the mood of the Prime Minister's office will also be strengthened.

This is also a question of whether we should prioritize political neutrality or political responsiveness on the part of national public employees. The conventional limitation on political appointments in Japan's national public service system was established due to public employees' fears of politicians and their attempts to secure political neutrality. However, such high importance is placed on the political neutrality of bureaucratic agencies due to the fact that it is difficult for them to be influenced by politicians, and the possibility of "bureaucracy-led" policy is increasing.

For this reason, support for "political leadership," which asserts that elected politicians should control national public employees, has been on the rise. If such political leadership progresses, national public employees will start striving to faithfully realize the policies of politicians, increasing their political responsiveness. However, while political responsiveness is important, excessive responsiveness is also a problem. The possibility that bureaucrats will gauge the mood of politicians and make excessive "conjectures" has also been highlighted by recent scandals (Izumo 2017; Ashitate 2019; Otani 2021, pp. 186–7).

References

Ashitate, H. (2019) 'Kanbu jinji to seiji-kainyu seido' [Executive appointments and political intervention system] in M. Otani and K. Kawai (eds) *Gendai Nihon no Koumuin Jinji* [Civil Service in Contemporary Japan: How Recent Government Reforms Changed the Public Personnel System], (pp. 79–95), Tokyo: Daiichi Hoki.

Inatsugu, H. (1996) *Nihon no Kanryo Jinji System* [Public Personnel System in Japan], Tokyo: Toyo Keizai, Inc.

Izumo, A. (2017) 'Naikaku-jinji-kyoku secchigo no kanryo jinji' [Introducing competency review system to higher civil service: Political influence and changes in departmental career patterns], *Journal of the Faculty of Political Science and Economics, Tokai University*, 49: 1–23.

Mabuchi, M. (2020) *Gyouseigaku Shinban* [Public Administration], 2nd edn, Tokyo: Yuhikaku.

Ministry of Internal Affairs and Communications (2021) *Chihou-Koumuin Kyuuyo Jittai Chousa Kekka no Gaiyou 2021* [Outline of the Results of the Fact-finding Survey on Compensation of Local Government Employees 2021], Tokyo: Ministry of Internal Affairs and Communications.

Morizono, S., Yoshida, K. and Onishi, M. (eds) (2015) *Chikujou Kokka-Koumuin-hou* [Annotation to the National Public Service Act], Tokyo: Gakuyo Shobo.

National Personnel Authority (ed) (2006) *Koumuin Hakusho 2006* [White Paper on Public Employees 2006: FY2005 Annual Report], Tokyo: Nikkei Printing, Inc.

National Personnel Authority (ed) (2020) *Profile of National Public Employees in Japan*, Tokyo: National Personnel Authority.

National Personnel Authority (ed) (2022) *Kokka-koumuin jinji profile* [Profile of National Public Employees], Tokyo: National Personnel Authority.

Otani, M. (2021) 'Kokka-koumuin no jinji kanri' [Personnel management of national government employees] in S. Nishioka and Y. Hirokawa (eds) *Gyouseigaku* [Public Administration] (pp. 170–87), Tokyo: Bunshindo.

2

SOUTH KOREA

Juhyun Nam

Context and Overview

Administrative reform has been required in any era of time, but the current era might be the period that requires the reform most strongly. The emergence of diverse technologies such as blockchain, big data, and AI demands the development of capacity to fully utilize those technologies. The recent COVID-19 pandemic highlights capabilities to tackle unexpected risks and to secure redundancies in management. All these challenges apply not just to the private sector but also to the public sector, and the case of the Korean government is not an exception. Emphasizing the proactive governance, the Korean government has been conducting various administrative reforms in the personnel management field. To prepare further reforms, it is critical to understand the fundamental structure of the reform subject. This chapter introduces major institutional structures and issues of personnel management of South Korea.

Major contents of administrative reform in Korea are not much different from those of global administrative reform. The New Public Management (NPM) administrative reform, which was proceeded in the Western developed countries, has also been a big stream of reform in the Korean government's personnel system since the late 1990s. In the wake of the economic crisis, a full-scale government personnel reform began, and the strong and centralized bureaucratic tradition has been gradually changed into a Western-style professional civil service (Kim 2000). The current personnel administration might be the product of the change, or the result of the intermediate phase, and that change is still going on. Later, the chapter briefly explains the civil service system in South Korea by seven major issues, including central Human Resource Management (HRM) unit, recruitment, civil service classification and status, openness of positions, performance assessment and promotion, training, and senior civil service.

DOI: 10.4324/9781003326496-4

46 Juhyun Nam

Civil Service System

Central HRM Unit

Ministry of Personnel Management (MPM) is the second independent HR government agency in the S. Korean government history. In 2014, the ministry is established under the Office of Prime Minister (at central government level) which is responsible for designing and implementing personnel policies including recruitment, human resource management, remuneration, welfare, pension, and ethics of the civil service. The purpose of this institution is to reinforce fair, transparent, and balanced innovation throughout the civil service system.[1] As of May 2022, it consists of eight bureaus and 25 divisions and two affiliated organizations including the National Human Resources Development Institute (NHI) and the Appeals Commission. The total number of employees is 594, which consists of 403 in the head office and 191 in affiliated organizations (Ministry of Personnel Management 2022, pp. 107–9).

For about 70 years after the establishment of the government, central personnel agencies have been transformed to improve the efficiency of national human resources management and the fairness of government personnel to cope with the development stages of Korea. However, for most of that time, it was a part of a general administration to support government affairs as a general administration agency, rather than governmental professional HR agency to meet the new expectations from the public and trends.

Government Administration was the first agency charged with public personnel functions with inauguration of the Republic of Korea Government in 1948, under the main idea of recruiting and managing the best HR to assist and lead the national development while Korea was struggling to rise from the ashes of war. In 1955, personnel functions moved to the Administrative Bureau of the State Council and to the Administrative Office of the State Council in 1960. In 1963, Personnel Bureau was established under the Ministry of Government Administration. Personnel Commission and Appeals Commission were also created then. Civil Service Commission (CSC) established by the Kim Dae-jung Government in 1999 was the first independent personnel institution. However, it was later incorporated into the Ministry of Public Administration and Security (MOPAS) in 2008 under the government restructuring program during the financial crisis and former CSC was reborn as an independent organization in 2014, as currently Ministry of Personnel Management (MPM).

In the case of local government officials, the competent ministry is the Ministry of the Interior and Safety, which is in charge of the local government administration, and has a separate legal system[2] different from the state public officials. The personnel policy of local government officials is to operate with some modifications based on that of the state officials. There are also differences in the operation of personnel policies by individual municipalities.

Recruitment

The recruitment of top talent to government is known to have significantly contributed the Korea's rapid economic growth. Most notably, the primary and most essential principle of recruiting is that all applicants are subjected to fair competitive examination. The best talents selected through these rigorous test have served as the driving force for rapid national development.

There are two types of recruitment examinations: first, majority of new recruits are being selected from the fresh graduates. And secondly, experienced professionals are recruited. In the past, the government's personnel system was based on the premise that most of the manpower needed would be hired as university graduates and they worked as career civil servants. However, the recruitment of more experienced professionals has been expanding in the government since the 2000s.

Recruitment exams for grades 5 (deputy director of division, junior managerial level), 7 and 9 (general staff) are administered every year through written tests (once or twice) and interviews. Based on strict fairness, the recruitment exam has long contributed to the formation of competent bureaucracy. In principle, Korean nationals are recruited, but foreign nationals are allowed only in certain sectors (except for national security, foreign investment attraction, trade and industrial policy, education, culture, welfare, urban planning, etc.).

Experienced professionals are also recruited to fill positions that require a high level of expertise. This system recruits professionals with career credentials and academic degrees in a specific field and is implemented regularly or when necessary for all grades, including Senior Civil Service (director general level in charge of bureau in the central government and over). Since 2010, the proportion of career position recruitment has been higher than that of open competitive examination. As of 2014, career employment accounted for 53.3% of total employment (Park 2017, p. 38). In order to be hired as an expert of Grade 5 in the government, a professional must have at least 10 years of professional experience or a Ph.D. and recruitment to Grade 7 requires a minimum of three years of experience or a master's degree.

The Korean government operates an official website called the Cyber National Official Examination Center (www.gosi.kr) for the civil service recruitment examination. The website discloses and transparently provides information on the schedule of recruitment examinations, the number of candidates selected, application submission, test questions and answers, and different test data to the public.

Recently, it takes a long time from job posting to appointment after the final pass because of lots of applicants. For example, in the case of open competitive recruitment for Grade 5, applications are submitted in February, followed by the first multiple-choice test in March, the second essay-type exam in June, and the interview in September. The final results will be announced in October. Successful candidates will be appointed as new civil servants in April of next year and will be assigned to each ministry after foundation training for four months and on-the-job training in the central and local government for one year. Recently, the MPM has

48 Juhyun Nam

tried to shorten the recruitment process. However, it is difficult to solve the problem because it takes a large-scale public recruitment method that is conducted once a year and there are too many applicants.

Except for career employment, the candidate's background such as education, gender, and age are not taken into account in the examination process, and only the results of the written and interview tests determine whether candidates pass or fail. Academic requirements for examination have been abolished since 1973, and the maximum age for examinations has been also abolished since 2009. Most tests are operated by the MPM to increase fairness. Blind recruitment interviews are used to minimize interviewers' bias due to factors such as gender, education, appearance, and age. Personal information about the examiners is strictly secured, and external experts participate in the interview process to ensure fairness. In addition, MPM operates a new program that restricts job rotation of recruitment experts instead of providing incentives such as monetary compensation and promotion to them.

Civil Service Classification and Status

As of 2021, there are about one million public servants in Korea, with about 750,000[3] in the central administration and 380,000 in the local administration (Ministry of the Interior and Safety 2021). Public servants comprise the following different categories[4]:

- General service (career service): public officials engaged in general administration, technology, and research
- Special service (career service): public officials serving as judges, prosecutors, diplomats, teachers, police, and fire-fighting officers
- Political service (non-career service): public officials who are elected officials or require the approval of the National Assembly to be appointed
- Special administrative service (non-career service): public officials designated by statutes like secretaries, policy advisors to the Minister, staff of the National Assembly, planning and coordination director of the National Intelligence Service, and other public officials designated by statutes as in special administrative service

The General Service consists of public officials in Grade 3–9 and senior officials belonging to the Senior Civil Service (SCS). The Special and Political Service each has its own grade system according to the Court Organization Act, the Prosecutor's Office Act, the Foreign Service Officials Act, the Police Officers Act, the Public Educational Officials Act, etc.

In principle, the State Public Officials Act stipulates matters concerning the retirement of public officials. The general service recruited through open competition is guaranteed to work until retirement age. The retirement age of general service is 60 years; however, an extension of the retirement age is being discussed recently. Exceptions to the retirement age of general public officials apply to teachers, prosecutors, university professors, etc. The retirement age of teachers, prosecutors, and university professors is, respectively, 62, 63, and 65 years. Police and soldiers (career military) have a separate retirement age system where the retirement time varies depending on the position and promotion. The 60-year-old retirement, long-term employment guarantee policy of government, of public

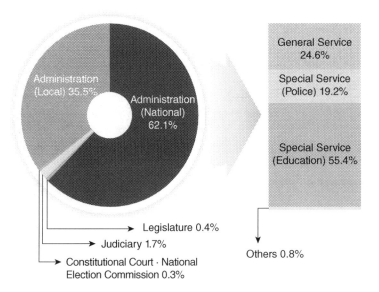

FIGURE 2.1 Composition of civil service
Source: retrieved from www.mpm.go.kr/english/system/publicOfficials/.

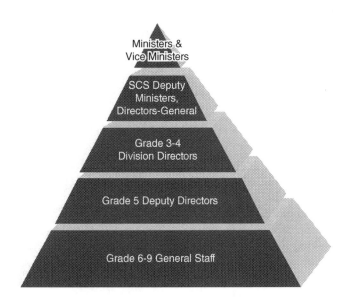

FIGURE 2.2 Civil service rank system of central administration
Source: retrieved from www.mpm.go.kr/english/system/publicOfficials/.

50   Juhyun Nam

servants has been an important motive for securing competitiveness of Korean bureaucracy as the job security in the private sector has worsened or unstable. Because the competition is quite tough these days, many applicants graduate from the top universities even though Korean government never requests any academic background except some professional posts.

On the other hand, continuing work of specialist and minister's policy advisers does not have a guaranteed retirement age as they are working under the contract basis. Specialist with the contract term will usually retire at the term of the contract. The contract is usually set within five years. Depending on the work performance, they can be reappointed through competition or converted to general service. Since the minister's policy advisers are politically appointed, they share their fate with the retirement of the minister. Personnel management of specialists in the government differs from those of general service in promotion, adjunct system, and transfer of duties because they are premised on their position.

Openness of Posts/Positions

"Open position system" has been in operation since 2000. This system, along with a performance-based pay, was the most disruptive personnel reform policy of the CSC since the economic crisis of the late 1990s. However, the opening of public office in the Korean government, in principle, is to give fair opportunities to all those who meet the requirements for the position. It meant that not only suitable persons outside the public office but also incumbent civil servants can be appointed to the positions through a fair selection process. In addition, there was not much inflow of experts from the private sector to public office due to lack of understanding of public service work, lack of publicity, and difference in salary level. As a result, only a limited number of positions become filled by external experts, and there have been criticisms on the lack of openness of public office. For this reason, the MPM designates particular positions where incumbent career service civil servants cannot be appointed, and only external experts can be appointed to these positions. These specific positions are mainly the fields such as IT technology, cultural arts, and public relations, where the private sector has a larger pool of experts. The term of office for the open position is for three years with the possibility of extending it to five years if the performance is exceptional. Moreover, if he or she achieved outstanding result after completing the total employment period of five years, it is possible to switch to a general service with tenure to retirement age.

However, it is pointed out that there are still many limitations in overcoming the closedness of the public sector because many current civil servants are still employed in these open job positions. For this reason, all departments' open position selection examinations are now conducted by an independent "Central Selection Committee" established by the MPM. The committee consists of all members of the public, including experts in related field. Also, the MPM is running a national talent database of professionals working in various fields for more active government headhunting service[5] (MPM 2018a).

In recent years, the transfer between ministries, personnel exchange with other ministries, has expanded with the recruitment of private experts from the government. An official website (www.gojobs.go.kr) provides job matching services within government. Government officials are encouraged to move from one department to another by providing financial incentives and promotion points. These measures are aimed at reducing the harmful effects of sectionalism and allowing government officials to work with more diverse experiences and broader perspectives. However, in many cases, ordinary civil servants are still hired through competitive examination for Grade 5, 7, and 9 on a large scale and are promoted up to managerial level by job rotation and career within their ministries. Most of them continue to work for lifetime in one ministry and get promoted there.

Performance Assessment, Promotion

Public officials are regularly evaluated for their work performance. Public officials of grade 4 or higher, including senior civil servants and directors, are annually evaluated with regard to individual and departmental performance, and competence associated with job performance. After setting performance targets and indicators through consultation with evaluator, they sign a performance agreement regarding individual and department duties and are evaluated based on this agreement at the end of the year. The results of the performance evaluation affect in grading for yearly performance salary and used in various personnel management processes as promotion and personnel screening.

Public officials of grade 5 or below receive a semiannual evaluation regarding work performance and job competency. The evaluator has a face-to-face talk with the official receiving a performance evaluation, periodically checks and records the status of work done, and evaluates the official based on the results. The results of performance evaluations affect promotion screening and grading for performance bonuses and are also used in HR operations such as job transfers and training.

According to the results of performance evaluations, public officials of level 5 or higher are paid a performance-based annual salary (accumulative), and public officials of level 6 or below are paid a performance-based bonus (at least once a year, lump-sum). The performance-based pay system was introduced in 1999 in the form of performance annual salaries for director-general or higher level (SCS), and performance bonuses for director or lower level (Grade 3 or below). Since then, the range of public officials receiving performance-based annual salaries has gradually expanded to include grade 5 public officials in 2017.

The results of evaluations are used as reference for performance pay according to four ratings (S, A, B, and C). Also, senior officials above the division director level cannot receive performance bonuses if they fall in the bottom 10% of the performance evaluation results. This result is cumulative annually and may make a big difference over the years. In case of SCS, qualification screening process can be operated according to the performance result.

Meanwhile, the relatively strict evaluation standard set by the MPM is applied to the performance evaluation of senior positions, and the discretionary judgment of each Ministry is allowed in the evaluation of working-level public officials below grade 6 and the amount of their performance pay. For example, the number of evaluation grades is 3 or more, and there is discretion in the amount of performance pay.

The State Public Officials Act stipulates that a person can be promoted if work performance evaluation, career, and other abilities are demonstrated. The Decree on the Appointment of Public Officials sets a specific minimum number of working years required for promotion for each grade.[6] Division director (Grades 3~4) can also be promoted to SCS only if they pass the evaluation of competency assessment of appraising the six core leadership competencies which required to the SCS. The assessment center for the competency test is operated by the MPM.

Training

The MPM provides various off-and-online training and education environment where public officials can develop their professionalism and expertise based on leadership pipeline. As a professional leadership development institute under the MPM, the National HRD Institute (NHI) carries out education program for national public officials. Besides the NHI, the government operates a separate civil service training institute for more professional training of special knowledge such as taxation, the provincial law, and so on under each ministry. In addition, each ministry and individual civil servant can utilize private education and training institutions. The location of the national HRD institute has been changed and developed since the establishment of government. The first institution, the National Officials' Training Institute (NOTI), was founded in 1949 in Seoul and it was expanded and reorganized as the Central Officials' Training Institute (COTI) in 1961. The organization was relocated in Gwacheon in 1981 and it was reorganized as a current NHI and its main campus was relocated in Jincheon according to the balanced national development plan in 2016.[7]

Newly hired civil servants must complete foundation job training course in the NHI or other ministry training institutes. The initial training period depends on the kinds of the civil service grade and job position. They are 3–4 weeks training for new civil servants in Grade 7 and 9 and 18 weeks for new officials in Grade 5, respectively. In addition, public officials of Grade 4 or above are required to receive competency training to strengthen their leadership as candidates for manager-level or director-level promotion.

Also, civil servants below Grade 4 must complete 100 hours of job training course each year. They can design customized curriculum and utilize various public and private educational institutions. In addition, some selected civil servants can have the opportunity to study or work for training at foreign universities or institutions with government scholarship. It offers up to two years of long-term training or several weeks of short-term training to provide study abroad. The concrete detail of civil service training program is as follows.

The NHI also provides global training programs for foreign government officials by the means of development assistance or specific request from the respective countries. Due to the implications of Korea's rapid growth experience

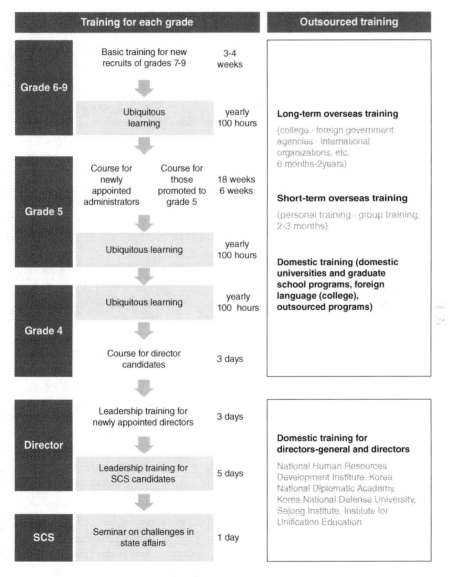

FIGURE 2.3 Training program of civil service

Source: Retrieved from www.mpm.go.kr/english/system/humanResource/.

54 Juhyun Nam

for developing country officials, this global curriculum has been more activated in recent years. In 2018, for example, 15 worldwide training courses were held, and 536 foreign officials were trained at the institution, well exceeding expectations at the start of the year (National Human Resources Development Institute 2018).

Senior Civil Service (Senior Management)

Senior Civil Service (SCS) system in Korea was introduced in 2006 to place high-ranking officials at the deputy minister or director-general levels in the right places at agencies across the government, beyond partitions between ministries and to encourage openness and competition between the civil service and the private sector, as well as among the ministries (State Public Officials Act 2–2). In fact, earlier attempts were made to introduce an integrated SCS system in Korea. The first trial dated back to Kim Young-sam's administration in the mid-1990s and the second trial was taken as civil service reform after the IMF bailout in Kim Dae-jung's administration in the late 1990s (Kwon and Kwon 2010, p. 2). However, the previous attempts have been concluded with the creation of positions/grades for the middle manager level and the introduction of alternative reform programs such as open position system and performance-related pay system (Nam 2016, pp. 159–60).

As of 2019, about 1,568 senior civil servants are classified and managed as the Senior Civil Service. Among them, the numbers of Job Grade 1 of deputy minister level and Job Grade 2 of director general level respectively occupy 255 (16.3%) and 1,137 (72.5%). There were 1,447 male (92.3%) and 121 females (7.7%) in SCS.[8] And, some of these posts are open to the private sector to encourage top professionals to work in the civil service. Also, through a job position system, the government is encouraging inter-ministerial competition among public officials in different ministries in principle.

A person who wants to become a senior civil servant must first go through a rigorous leadership competency assessment. The assessment is run approximately 70 times a year. A total of 909 evaluations were conducted from 2006 to the end of 2018, and 1,197 of the 5,442 candidates failed to pass, resulting in a 78.0% pass rate.[9]

Through using the professional tools such as group discussion, role play or in-basket method, an assessment is made as to whether a candidate has the credentials and abilities required of senior civil servants. Six core competencies for assessment (problem recognition ability, strategic thinking skills, change management skills, performance-orientedness, client satisfaction, and coordination and integration skills) are measured through four assessment exercises (1:1 role performance, 1:2 role performance, in-basket technique, and group discussion), which allow appraisers to see whether the appraisees have the qualifications and abilities required of senior civil servants. In the next step, those candidates who pass the leadership evaluation are subject to personnel screening conducted by the Appointment

Screening Committee of the MPM, and successful candidates who pass this screening are finally selected for the posts to be filled in the next appointment period.

Senior civil servants are paid a differential remuneration according to the grade of duty and performance evaluation results. The performance pay was introduced in 1999 in the form of performance annual salaries (accumulative) for director-general or higher level (SCS). The salaries of SCS members vary widely from person to person as the salary increase rate varies according to the results of the performance evaluation because it is accrued every year. In addition, political factors may be involved in deciding the increase rate of senior civil service pay. In particular, it sometimes freezes depending on the economic circumstances of the country. The measure is due to the perception that high-ranking officials have a shared responsibility for the country's economy.

Senior civil servants with poor performance evaluations are subject to qualification screening to determine whether they should continue to perform duties as senior civil servants. However, it rarely happens and the reason is often said that before the appointment of SCS, a disqualified person is dropped at the competence assessment, and low performers may choose to resign before being referred to the screening committee.

Concluding Remarks

The Korean bureaucracy has evolved with the history of national formation and economic development. The authority of public officials was strong, and the top talents who recruited by the civil service examination system have been involved in major government decision-making.

However, with the democratization process in the 1980s and the Asian economic crisis in the late 1990s, the perception that the government civil service system should be more efficient arose. Accordingly, administrative reform has been promoted to limit the excessive authority of government officials and to implement a Western-style professional civil service system. In this process, it was most important to remove patronage, secure fairness, and introduce performance-based system. These reform initiatives yielded results to some extent and aided in the modernization and improvement of the Korean human resources (HR) system.

However, regardless of the achievement, the Korean government is facing new challenges. In order to create a successful administration even in the face of declining population and low national economic growth, reforming personnel policies should be continued. The current government HR system is not fundamentally different from the HR of top-tier companies in principle; however, it has been noted that government is gradually losing its competitiveness and the gap with private sector has been widening at a faster rate than anticipated.

For reference, in the corporate HR, the change to a job-oriented system has been rapidly introduced and the compensation packages are diversified due to the turnover of top talents. In addition, employee-friendly HR innovation is being carried out in a way that emphasizes employee experience and organizational

56 Juhyun Nam

culture. On the other hand, the civil service system in Korea is relatively rigid and cannot keep up with the pace of recent changes or seems to be blind to important and new reform topics after the democratization and efficiency of the bureaucracy.

The implication is that the traditional seniority-based and fairness-oriented personnel management needs to be reconsidered from the perspectives of millennials and Z-generations' new and forward-looking demands. Such a need is extending to the public sector, and the influence of the trend is not negligible. Considering these challenges, the Korean government needs to continue its reform efforts in the HR area to secure, develop, and excite competent human capital. Agendas such as a flexible and human-centric HR management system, as well as the pursuit of work-life balance through the use of smart technologies, might, for example, be important drivers of Korean government HR innovation in the post-pandemic era.

Notes

1 MPM's Korean name includes the concept of "innovation." The ministry is the only Korean central administrative agency to have a name for innovation.
2 It means the Local Public Officials Act.
3 Among them, there are about 181,000 in general service and about 569,000 in special service. www.org.go.kr/psncpa/pbsvnt/selectAll.do.
4 Source: State Public Officials Act, Article 2.
5 The government headhunting service proceeds with the process of recommending the best candidate for the government position through analyzing the job requirements of the market survey, identifying talent with the national talent database, and contacting the target candidate. It is in charge of Human Resource Information Director of MPM.
6 The minimum years of promotion required for each level are 3 years for Grade 4, 4 years for Grade 5, 3.5 years for Grade 6, 2 years for Grade 7 and 8, and 1.5 years for Grade 9 (Article 31). However, there is an exception that performance proficiency may lead to special promotion even if the minimum working period is not fulfilled (Article 35–2).
7 Currently, Jincheon-Gwacheon Campus dual system was established according to campus-specific development strategy. Jincheon Campus is a center for foundation training and public leadership training by position, and Gwacheon Campus is specialized as a global leadership center in charge of global training program for foreign civil servants (National Human Resource Development Institute 2018, p. 6).
8 The data was retrieved at the official website of MPM (www.mpm.go.kr/mpm/info/infoBiz/bizBoard/?boardId=bbs_0000000000000120&mode=view&cntId=41).
9 www.mpm.go.kr/mpm/info/infoBiz/compAppr/compAppr01/.

Useful website

www.mpm.go.kr (The official website of Ministry of Personnel Management)
www.nhi.go.kr (The official website of National HRD Institute)
www.moleg.go.kr (The official website of Ministry of Government Legislation)

References

Kim, P. (2000) 'Administrative reform in the Korean central government: A case study of the Dae Jung Kim administration', *Public Performance & Management Review*, 24(2): 145–60.

Kwon, Y. and Kwon, K. (2010) 'Study on the introductory process of the Korean senior civil service system', *Korean Public Personnel Administration Review*, 9(2): 1–30.

Ministry of the Interior and Safety (2021, December 31) 'The number of civil servants', available at: www.org.go.kr/psncpa/pbsvnt/selectAll.do (accessed 16 May 2022).

Ministry of Personnel Management (2022, May 31) '2022 Statistical yearbook', available at: www.mpm.go.kr/mpm/lawStat/infoStatistics/hrStatistics/hrStatistics03/ (accessed 25 August 2022).

Ministry of Personnel Management (2018a) *2017 Annual Report*, Sejong: Ministry of Personnel Management.

Nam, J. (2016) *The Patterns and Dynamics of the Civil Service Pay Reform in Korea*, Doctoral dissertation, London School of Economics and Political Science.

National Human Resources Development Institute (2018) 'HRD annual report 2018', available at: www.nhi.go.kr/sharing/data/annual/List.htm.

Park, C.-M. (ed) (2017) *State Bureaucracy in East Asia: Tradition and Change*, Seoul: Pakyoungsa.

3

TAIWAN

Bennis Wai Yip So

Introduction

Basic Profile

The civil service system of Taiwan was founded on the *Kuomintang's* (KMT, Nationalist) rule in Mainland China, as the Republic of China, in the 1930–40s and then transplanted into Taiwan after the World War II. Due to its unique political system, which consist of five separate branches of powers – executive, legislative, judicial, examination, and supervisory, the civil service system is separately administered under the jurisdiction of the Examination Yuan (established in 1930) that is independent of the executive branch, that is, the Executive Yuan (see Figure 3.1). The civil service system is characterized by a centralized personnel management system. The same set of rules and a uniform system are applied to all civil servants. The current basic personnel framework was launched from 1987, commonly called the "new personnel system."

Career civil servants in Taiwan refer to nonpolitical appointees working in state authorities and public organizations. They enjoy legal protection as permanent officials of the state in contrast to other nonpolitical staff who are employed by state agencies. All career civil servants, except for several particular services such as police, customs, judiciary, and public transport, fit into a single common 3-rank and 14-grade ranking system: grades 1 to 5 lie in the elementary rank; grades 6 to 9 lie in the junior rank, and grades 10 to 14 lie in the senior rank. The civil service is not divided into the central and the local categories. Civil servants working in the central and local governments enjoy an equal legal status and mutually transferable. However, the central government agencies have more higher-grade positions and most senior-rank positions are concentrated in the central level.

DOI: 10.4324/9781003326496-5

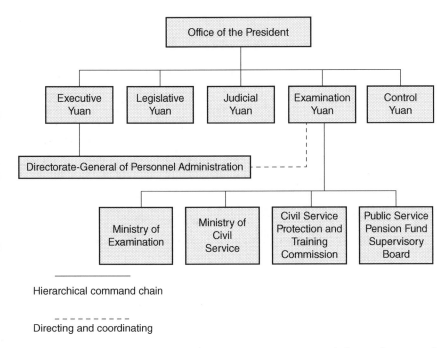

FIGURE 3.1 Structure of central government in Taiwan (special focus of personnel authorities).

The career civil servant workforce now numbers more than 360,000, of which approximately 250,000 work for the government administration. The rest works in public hygiene and medical service institutes, publicly owned enterprises (not all staff members in the enterprises are civil servants), and works as administrative staff in public schools (excluding teachers). More than 50% of the workforce now serves in the central level.

In general, the civil service system of Taiwan can be categorized as a "career-based system" in the sense that civil servants tend to be hired at the beginning of their career and then working for the state becomes their lifelong career. The system recruits civil servants mainly through an entrance examination and seldom allows or encourages mid-career entry into the service (OECD 2005).

Background and Recent Trend of Development

The traditional Chinese imperial bureaucratic management features prominently in the civil service system in Taiwan, especially its single uniform ranking system, and recruitment and selection system through civil service entrance examinations (CSEEs). The founding father of the Republic of China, Sun Yat-sen, highly appreciated the examination system of imperial China. The examination can be devised to remedy the defect of democracy in which, Sun argued, elected officials may not be qualified for government positions. According to Sun's ideal, all government officials, whether elected or not, must pass a public service examination before assuming office.

In 1930, this Sun's idea (he already passed away in 1925) was realized by setting up the Examination Yuan under the KMT government in Nanjing. The constitution of the Republic of China promulgated in 1947 further legitimized its status as the top personnel authority, independent of the executive branch. Article 85 of the constitution clearly stipulates: "In the selection of public functionaries, a system of open competitive examination shall be put into operation. . . . No person shall be appointed to a public office unless he is qualified through examination." Although the use of the CSEEs was ultimately confined to the selection of career civil servants, the examination conventionally only refers to those organized by the Examination Yuan. In addition, the authority of the Examination Yuan was extended to the sphere of public personnel policy-making and management, and to all examinations for professional and technical qualification.

Civil servants in Taiwan can refer to both elected officials/political appointees and career officials. Before democratization, career officials could be simply promoted to political positions. Career civil servants were not supposed to be politically neutral. Due to its single uniform ranking system, all civil servants enjoy opportunities to be promoted from the bottom to the top grade (Hwa 2001).

On the other hand, the civil service system has been absorbing elements or practices from Western countries during its modernization. It experimented with the position classification system that was transplanted from the United States in the 1960–80s, even though it was abandoned in 1986 (more detail later). Its disciplinary mechanism shares some elements in the counterparts from Germany, Britain, and the United States. Since the establishment of the new personnel system alongside the democratization in the 1990s, the civil service system has been further institutionalized. This was exemplified by the enactment of the civil service protection act in 1996, by which a comprehensive mechanism and procedures for protecting civil servants' status and various legal rights against administrative and political infringements (copied from Germany) were established.

The Examination Yuan has been trying to uphold prestige and reputation of the CSEEs by minimizing other staffing channels for nonpolitical positions. From 1991, all new entrants of government technical staff, who had been widely open to anyone with relevant education qualifications and relevant work experiences, had to be recruited from the CSEEs. From 1997 onward, government agencies were no longer allowed to directly recruit permanent "government employees" who had not passed the CSEEs and could be promoted to elementary-rank positions.

Interestingly, while the Examination Yuan was establishing institutions to enhance the degree of legal protection of civil servants and to "purify" the staffing channels in the 1990s, the trend of public sector reforms in the West was deregulating and flexibilizing the public personnel management that implied lesser protection of legal status of civil servants and diversification of public employment (OECD 1990; Bossaert 2005). Hence, the public personnel policy in Taiwan does not proceed in congruence with or even proceed against the western trend.

In addition, although the 1990s, during the democratic transition, witnessed some significant reforms noted earlier, the separation of personnel authority from the executive branch in general has caused slow progress in civil service reforms, because all significant personnel reforms must be approved by both the Examination Yuan and the national legislature, that is, Legislative Yuan. This was at the same time exacerbated by the democratization. Since the endings of the office terms of the Examination Yuan (six years per term before 2020) and the President (four years per term) were not simultaneous,[1] there was possibly a two- or four-year gap that the party affiliations between the ruling government and the heads of the Examination were divided. Since the first assumption of power by the Democratic Progressive Party (DPP) in 2000, there had, for the first time, appeared two such gaps (September 2000~August 2002 and September 2016~August 2020) (see Table 3.1). These gaps represented an embarrassing period that the cooperation and coordination between the government and the Examination Yuan became problematic. It might lead to a policymaking void. No new or ambitious policy would be put forward (So 2019).

The inefficiency of the personnel reforms can be exemplified by the case of the enactment of the civil service neutrality act for regulating the political behavior of career civil servants. Personnel officers in the Examination Yuan had already realized the significance of civil service neutrality as soon as the rise of electoral politics in the 1980s. The first bill of the law was drafted in 1994. Although there were some controversies at the very beginning of the review of the bill in the Legislative Yuan, subsequent several versions of the bill varied a little from one another. The same bill was submitted three times. The law had not been approved during the first rule of the DDP (2000–2007) until the re-assumption of power by the KMT, and it was finally approved in 2009, 13 years after the first direct election of the President in 1996 (So 2013).

TABLE 3.1 Juxtaposition of government's and Examination Yuan's office terms

Government's Office Term	2000–2004	2004–2008	2008–2012	2012–2016	2016–2020
President	Chen Shui-bian (DPP)		Ma Ying-jeou (KMT)		Tsai Ing-wen (DPP)
Examination Yuan	9th	10th	11th		12th
Examination Yuan's Office Term	1996–2002	2002–2008	2008–2014		2014–2020
Appointed by	KMT	DPP	KMT		KMT

62 Bennis Wai Yip So

Civil Service System

Central HRM Unit

The Examination Yuan is a top and independent personnel authority to take charge of public personnel policies and administration in Taiwan. Four authorities are affiliated with the Examination Yuan: the Ministry of Civil Service (MCS), the Ministry of Examination (ME), the Civil Service Protection and Training Commission (CSPTC), and the Public Service Pension Fund Supervisory Board (see Figure 3.1). They respectively take charge of rules and regulations for governing public personnel system and management, and supervision of personnel management of government agencies; civil service examinations; legal protection and training of civil servants; and monitoring of public service pension fund.

The Examination Yuan is a collegial decision-making body composed of a head, a deputy head, previously 19 minister-level commissioners before 2020, and the ministers of MCS, ME, and CSPTC (Remark: the deputy head chairs the Public Service Pension Fund Supervisory Board). The commissioners are usually prestigious specialists or scholars from various fields in light of various categories of examination, and their work should be independent of any political party. All of the heads and commissioners were appointed by the President for a fixed six-year term (with approval of the Legislative Yuan) before 2020. The ministers of the MCS, the ME, and the CSPTC are directly appointed by the President.

In December 2019, the Legislative Yuan approved an amendment of the organic act of the Examination Yuan, reducing the number of commissioners from 19 down to 7 to 9 (the number of incumbent commissioners is 9 now), and the office term for the heads and commissioners of the Examination Yuan is reduced to four years. That means the office terms of both the President and the Examination Yuan will come to the same. From 2020 onward, all top leaders of the Examination Yuan must be appointed by the incumbent president. The cooperation and coordination between the government administration and the personnel authority in personnel policies should be supposedly improved.

As Taiwan adopts a continental law system, all rules and regulations governing the civil service system must be in the form of codified law. All the rules and regulations are first drafted by the Examination Yuan's subordinate ministries or the CSPTC and then submitted to the Examination Yuan for discussion and approval. Any significant policymaking that entails law-making or amendment must be then reviewed and approved by the Legislative Yuan.

Besides the Examination Yuan, there is another central personnel authority set up under the Executive Yuan – the Directorate-General of Personnel Administration (DGPA). It was set up in 1967 to take charge of the personnel administration of government agencies under the Executive Yuan. The DGPA is not the field administration of the Examination Yuan, but it was directed by the Examination Yuan before 2020. The DGPA also plays a coordinator between the Executive Yuan and the Examination Yuan for personnel policies. In addition, the DGPA also takes charge of some administrative decision-making that are not concerned with law-making, including the management of government workforce strength, and adjustment of civil service compensation and welfare.

A "line management" is applied to personnel officials in all government agencies and public organizations. All personnel officials are appointed and deployed by superior personnel authorities instead of the top executives of government agencies or public organizations. The DGPA manages all personnel officials under the Executive Yuan; others are under the jurisdiction of the Ministry of Civil Service. This arrangement is designed to avoid the abuse of power of the chief executives and to well protect the rights of civil servants.

Simply speaking, the authorities of Examination Yuan, as top personnel authorities, cover the institutional building and reforms of the civil service system, qualifying civil servants by organizing examinations, and the civil service protection, training, and retirement management. Other aspects of personnel management are left to government agencies and public organizations, but they are indirectly monitored and directed by the personnel line management.

Recruitment

All career civil servants must be recruited from CSEEs that are organized by the Ministry of Examination under the Examination Yuan. The CSEEs are divided into three levels: elementary-level examinations for entrants to Grade 1 positions; junior-level for entrants to Grade 3 positions; and senior-level for entrants to Grades 6, 7, or 9 positions. Apart from the above general CSEEs, separate special examinations in line with these three levels are organized for recruiting staff for some particular services such as police, customs, and judiciary, for certain local government vacancies, and for the disabled and aborigine.

All citizens who are aged 18 or above are eligible for taking elementary-level examinations. No education level is required. Only high school graduates or above are eligible for taking junior-level examinations. College graduates or above are eligible for taking senior-level examinations for Grade 6 positions, master's degree holders or above for Grade 7 positions, and doctoral degree holders for Grade 9 positions.

All kinds of examinations are usually held once a year. Apart from the levels and the divide between general and special CSEEs, the examinations consist of a variety of categories that are organized for recruiting staff for corresponding professional groups of civil servants. Instead of directly applying for a position, applicants take a specific category of the examinations. Those who pass a specific category of the examinations are centrally assigned to a job position of the corresponding professional group. The job assignment prioritizes candidates with higher scores with reference to their agency preference.

The CSEEs are legally allowed to adopt a wide range of selection methods for recruitment, including written test, oral examination, physical test, psychological test, and screening of applicants' credential, publication, and invention. In practice,

64 Bennis Wai Yip So

the elementary level, the junior level, and the senior level for entrants to Grade 6 positions under the general CSEEs, and the special examination for recruiting civil servants for local governments now only adopt written tests. Other general and special CSEEs adopt more than one method, usually including an oral examination.

The merit-based recruitment is guaranteed foremost by the centralization of the CSEEs that are solely organized by the independent authority, the Examination Yuan. Political officials and public managers exercise no right or discretion to select the entrants. Anonymous marking is applied to all written tests. Subjective judgment or bias in the selection procedures is minimized. Hence, any abuse of power and favoritism can be avoided. However, the CSEEs mainly test academic and legal knowledge of examinees through multiple-choice questions and essay writing. Job-related skills are seldom tested in the examinations (Shih 2003; So 2015).

Civil Service Classification and Status

The civil service classification system underwent three systemic overhauls in 1954, 1969, and 1987. In 1954, right after the retreat of the KMT government from Mainland China, the civil service system adopted a rank-in-person system with three ranks (elementary, junior, and senior ranks), each of which contained three grades. All positions are broadly divided into administrative and technical categories. The overhaul in 1969 tried to replace it with the U.S. position classification system. The position classification system horizontally and scientifically divided job positions into 159 class series and vertically adopted a 14-grade ranking system. Each position was classified into one specific class series and one specific grade. Almost any recruitment and job promotion had to pass through an examination.

The experimental reform failed due to the rigidity of the classification system, which did not allow deployment as flexible as the original rank-in-person system did. A new system that integrated the original rank-in-person system with the position classification system into a unique system called "joint rank-in-person and in-position" was launched in 1987 and has been functioning up to now (Hsu 2006). The civil servants classified into this system now accounts for about 54% of the total career workforce. The rest belongs to unclassified workforce that tends to serve in a fixed service, such as police and customs.

The current system merged the 14-grade system into the traditional three-rank system, as noted at the beginning of this report. Job positions are classified into numerous professional groups. All professional groups are broadly divided into two categories: administrative and technical. Similar professional groups form a professional cluster. Positions affiliated with various professional groups span one to three grades. A free transfer to any positions of the same grade in the same professional group, or in various groups but in the same cluster, or related professional groups in diverse clusters is allowed.

As of January 2020, the administrative category contains 25 professional groups that form 9 clusters; the technical category contains 32 professional groups that form 16 clusters. It is designed to allow more open transfers among various professional groups in the administrative category. Professional groups in the technical category tend to be closed to one another, but they are allowed to transfer to related administrative professional groups.

The career civil servants enjoy a lifelong employment status. Their rank and grade, and their basic salary level are legally protected. The deprivation of the civil service status of an official (typically related to a severe disciplinary offense) and imposing other severe sanctions (e.g., salary downgrade or reduction) are not allowed without passing through stringent legal procedures.

By contrast, government fixed-term contract employees, which now number more than 30,000, are directly hired by government agencies. They will never become permanent staff unless they pass one of the CSEEs. They do not share most legal rights of career civil servants. They cannot enjoy the pension of civil service. No grade and rank is accorded to them. Hence, they enjoy no job promotion opportunity. They need to renew the employment contract annually (So 2016).

Openness of Positions

If there are vacancies available, a government agency can open the positions either to external recruitment (confined to the grades of the entry levels) through the CSEEs, or to internal recruitment through promotion or transfer within the agency, or transfer from other agencies. Public managers can choose only one of the above three channels to fill a vacancy.

For the transfer from other agencies, all incumbent classified civil servants can apply for the positions that are open to other agencies only if they are qualified for the positions. Such an active job transfer is a popular way nationwide for civil servants to advance their career in Taiwan. There is no restriction imposed on the transfers between central and local governments, and between different lines of ministries or departments. However, a restriction on free transfers was imposed on new entrants, disallowing those from the general CSEEs to transfer to other agencies under different ministry or department lines in their first three service years. Recruits from special examinations face stricter restrictions on transfers. For those who entered through the special examination for local government vacancies, entrants cannot be transferred to other agencies in their first three service years and to other agencies outside their affiliated region in their second three service years, which is essentially a 6-year limitation on transfers (So 2018).

There is no arrangement or program of external mobility between the government and the private sector. Secondment from nongovernment organizations (mainly from the academic field) is possible, especially for political positions and personal staff of chief executives.

Performance Assessment and Promotion

Performance appraisal of civil servants is legally divided into three types: The first is "yearly appraisal" that is done regularly at the end of a year for assessing the

66 Bennis Wai Yip So

performance in that year; the second is "ad hoc appraisal" that is done at any time for assessing any significant merit or demerit generated by a civil servant; the third is "incomplete yearly appraisal" that is also done at the end of a year for assessing the performance of a civil servant who has been working in an agency for less than one year but more than six months.

The criteria of the (incomplete) yearly appraisal are formally composed of four dimensions: work performance (65%), conduct (15%), knowledge (10%), and talent (10%). The result of the assessment is rated in four levels of grades: A, B, C, and D. The assessment of the ad hoc appraisal results in according either a "double merit" or a "double demerit." Due to the inflation of grade A rating, since 2001 a cap measure has been put on the appraisal rating in each agency. In principle, only 50% of all staff in an agency should be rated grade A, and the maximum ratio must not be more than 75%. The ratio usually reaches the maximum for most agencies (Chen et al. 2011).

The assessment result is closely tied to the compensation and promotion of a civil servant. The exceptionally worst result is leading to dismissal. In the case of yearly appraisal, those who get grade A are awarded an extra one-month salary as a performance bonus; those who get grade B are awarded an extra half-month salary as a performance bonus. In these two cases, one-step higher salary increment is granted. For those who get grade C, no performance bonus is awarded and no salary increment is granted. Grade D is the worst rating, only out of misconduct of a ratee, and leads to dismissal. In the case of incomplete yearly appraisal, the rules are the same, except that no salary increment is granted. In the case of ad hoc appraisal, those who are accorded a "double merit" are immediately awarded an extra one-month salary as a performance bonus and one-step higher salary increment is granted. "Double demerit" is also leading to dismissal.

If one gets grade A in two consecutive yearly appraisals or gets one grade A and two grade Bs in three consecutive yearly appraisals, one is qualified for promotion of his/her position grade within the same rank. If a position spans more than one grade, she/he automatically gets promoted to one higher grade. Those who are accorded a "double merit" can enjoy a priority to be promoted to a higher job position.

Apart from the appraisal, one can be qualified for the promotion of his/her rank through a rank promotion examination organized by the Ministry of Examination and/or rank promotion training (more detail in the next section). For the promotion from elementary to junior rank, one (a grade-5 officer) must pass both the promotion training and the rank promotion examination for qualifying his/her status to be an officer in the junior rank. If one only passes the rank promotion training without passing the rank promotion examination, she/he can only get promoted as high as a grade-7 officer or grade-8 officer for a master's or higher degree holder. For the promotion from junior to senior rank, one (a grade-9 officer) must pass either a rank promotion training or a rank promotion examination for the qualification. Now the promotion from junior to senior rank is mostly qualified by the training rather than the examination.

The above qualification is only a pre-requisite for job promotion. Those qualified have to wait for vacancies available in the agencies they serve or in other agencies. If there is a vacancy, as noted earlier, the position can be open to external recruitment (for entry-level positions), transfer from another agency, or internal promotion or transfer. As noted earlier, one vacancy can only be open to one of the above three channels. The procedures for the former two channels have been reported earlier. If a vacancy is filled by an internal transfer (from the same-grade position), the decision is directly made by the chief executive of the agency.

For the internal promotion, it is divided into two situations. For managerial positions, the promotion decision can be directly made by the chief executive of an agency or (in the case of the position of chief executive or deputy chief executive) the chief executive of the superior agency. Otherwise, the decision should be made by a selection committee that fills the vacancy by selecting candidates from the subordinate staff. The selection committee would make a candidate list by ordering all subordinate staff into layers according to their position grades and seniority. The committee would select a candidate first from the highest layer and then, if no suitable candidate, next layer. There are some criteria for the selection, including their annual appraisal rating, seniority, education level, training experiences, and outstanding performance.

Training

There are two training institutes offering general training programs for civil servants. One is the National Academy of Civil Service (NACS) affiliated with the CSPTC; another is the Civil Service Development Institute (CSDS) affiliated with the DGPA. The NACS mainly offers training programs for new entrants, for rank promotion, and for senior civil service. The CSDS offers on-the-job general training programs for mid- to senior-level civil servants under the Executive Yuan (including local governments), and, as a personnel authority, it specifically offers training programs for personnel officers under the Executive Yuan.

In addition, many central ministries and local governments have their own training institutes. The former mainly offers job-related professional training courses for their staff and then the latter on-the-job general training courses. Some training institutes offer pre-entry training programs for some particular workforces, such as Taiwan Police College for police, and Institute of Diplomacy and International Affairs for diplomatic officers (see all training institutes affiliated with central government agencies in Table 3.1).

Most new entrants recruited from the CSEEs need to receive a basic training program offered by the NACS. For those who are recruited from the senior-level examination, they should receive a 5-week common training program. For those who are recruited from the elementary-level and the junior-level examinations, they should receive their respective basic training programs for 3 weeks. For the rank promotion training programs, the elementary-to-junior rank training lasts for 5 weeks and the junior-to-senior for 4 weeks.

68 Bennis Wai Yip So

TABLE 3.2 Training institutes of central government agencies in Taiwan

Training Institutes	Affiliation
National Academy of Civil Service	Civil Service Protection and Training Commission
Civil Service Development Institute	Directorate-General of Personnel Administration
The Institute of Diplomacy and International Affairs	Ministry of Foreign Affairs
Social Welfare Workers' Training Center	Ministry of Health and Welfare
Judges and Prosecutors Training Institute	Ministry of Justice
Cadre Training Academy	Investigation Bureau, Ministry of Justice
Training Institute for Correctional Officers	Agency of Correction, Ministry of Justice
Professional Training Center, Ministry of Economic Affairs	Ministry of Economic Affairs
Training Institute, Ministry of Economic Affairs	Ministry of Finance
Environmental Professionals Training Institute	Environmental Protection Administration
Education, Training & Testing Center	Coast Guard Administration, Ocean Affairs Council
Aviation Training Institute	Civil Aeronautics Administration, Ministry of Transportation and Communications
Training Institute, Directorate General of Highway Bureau	Directorate General of Highway Bureau, Ministry of Transportation and Communications
Commission on Training	National Audit Office
Training Center, National Security Bureau	National Security Bureau
Training Center, Directorate General of Budget, Accounting and Statistics	Directorate General of Budget, Accounting and Statistics
Taiwan Police College	National Police Agency, Ministry of the Interior

Senior Civil Service (Senior Management)

Senior-rank civil servants from Grade 10 to Grade 14 can be considered as members of senior civil service in principle. However, there is no separate establishment of senior civil service, the management of which is distinct from the mid- and junior-level civil service. Despite that, the NASC does offer a special training program focusing on policymaking and leadership for the senior civil servants.

There was a special CSEE for externally recruiting Grade-10 civil servants from 1968 to 1993. This special examination was aimed to recruit highly educated people into the government. However, the special examination was condemned as a corrupt practice, being tailor-made for specific candidates, so it was abolished in 1994. Since then, Grade-10 civil servants have been available from the internal promotion only (Tsai 2009).

In 2010, the Examination Yuan attempted to establish a separate senior civil service. Managerial positions of Grade 12 and above, excluding those in local governments, judiciary, national security, and foreign affairs departments, were planned to be involved in this special management system. These accounted for about 700 positions. However, this proposal was not supported by the Executive Yuan so that it has not been realized yet (So 2019).

Note

1 The office term of the President had been six years, but it was reduced to four years from 1996 onward under the constitutional amendment in 1992.

Useful sources and websites

Examination Yuan Website: www.exam.gov.tw/en/

Ministry of Examination Website: https://wwwc.moex.gov.tw/english/home/wfrmEnglish.aspx

Ministry of Civil Service Website: https://eng.mocs.gov.tw/

Civil Service Protection and Training Commission Website: www.csptc.gov.tw/en/cl.aspx?n=1018

References

Bossaert, D. (2005) *The Flexibilisation of the Employment Status of Civil Servants: From Life Tenure to More Flexible Employment Relations? Survey for the 44th Meeting of the Directors General Responsible for Public Administration of the EU Member States*, Brussels: EUPAN.

Chen, D.-Y. et al. (2011) 'Norm of seniority or performance appraisal? An analysis of the performance appraisal system in Taiwanese public sector', *Journal of Civil Service* (in Chinese), 3(1): 53–91.

Hsu, Y.-S. (2006) *Theory and Structure of Joint Rank-in-Person and in-Position Classification System: Review of Current Public Personnel System* (in Chinese), Taipei: Commercial Press.

Hwa, L-J. (2001) 'The public administration of the Republic of China on Taiwan', in A. Farazmand (ed) *Handbook of Comparative and Development Public Administration*, 2nd edn (pp. 397–408), New York: Marcel Dekker.

OECD (1990) *Flexible Personnel Management in the Public Service*, Paris: OECD.

OECD (2005) *Trends in Human Resources Management Policies in OECD Countries: An Analysis of the Results of the OECD Survey on Strategic Human Resources Management*, Paris: OECD.

Shih, J. N. (2003) 'The civil service examination in Taiwan: An assessment and challenges ahead', *Taiwanese Political Science Review* (in Chinese), 7(1): 157–207.

So, B. W. Y. (2013) 'Civil service neutrality in Taiwan: Is it neutrality with or without dichotomy?' *Issue & Studies*, 49(1): 39–70.

So, B. W. Y. (2015) 'Exam-centred meritocracy in Taiwan: Hiring by merit or by examination?' *Australian Journal of Public Administration*, 74(3): 312–23.

So, B. W. Y. (2016) 'Flexible internal labor market of civil service in Taiwan: Decentralized job mobility fueled by a centralized career-based system', *Journal of Democracy and Governance*, 3(1): 111–38.

So, B. W. Y. (2018) 'An exploratory study of government internal labor market in Taiwan: Balance of interest between individuals and organizations', *Journal of Civil Service* (in Chinese), 10(1): 21–58.

So, B. W. Y. (2019) 'The unique development of civil service system under a unique public personnel system in Taiwan: Should we let it go on?' *Policy and Personnel Management* (in Chinese), 10(1): 1–24.

Tsai, L.-W. (2009) 'The reform and development of the staffing of senior civil service', *Personnel Administration* (in Chinese), 169: 36–53.

4

SINGAPORE

James Low[1]

Background

Singapore is a small city-state of about 710 km^2 in Southeast Asia, straddling the strategic trade routes between the Indian Ocean and South China Sea. Without any natural resources, the island that is sandwiched between the Malay peninsula and the Indonesian archipelago, imports all the necessities to sustain its 5.6 million population. Although multi-ethnic in composition, Singaporeans live in relative harmony. Citizens enjoy a per capita income of S\$81,222 (US\$59,746; DOS 2019) and one of the highest standards of living in the world (Mercer 2019), afforded by a thriving economy. The global financial center, bio-medical hub, and manufacturer of high value electronics generated a GDP of S\$491 billion in 2018 (US\$361 billion; DOS 2019). Unemployment in late 2019 amidst the trade tensions between China and the United States was 2.3%; the annual average over the previous five years hovered around 2.0% (MOM 2019).

Singapore's transformation is typically attributed by scholars to the strategic foresight and disciplined determination of its political leadership (Turnbull 2009; Dtysdale 1984; Lam and Tan 1999; Tan 2007; Ng 2010). Political visions, critical as they were and without downplaying their importance, had to be translated into policies – and this depended on the bureaucracy (Low 2016a). Significant credit for Singapore's modernization is due to its Public Service, which turned the strategic foresight of the political leadership into reality.

The Singapore Public Service has its origins in the bureaucracy set up by the British when they colonized Singapore in 1819 (Seah 1971; Lee 1977). When Singapore became a self-governing state in 1959, it inherited a Westminster parliamentary system of government; the bureaucracy localized and reoriented itself toward nation-building under the newly elected local government (Low 2018). When Singapore was part of Malaysia between 1963 and 1965, the system of government

DOI: 10.4324/9781003326496-6

72 James Low

and the bureaucracy remained largely unchanged. By 1965 when independence was thrust upon Singapore, the Public Service quickly adjusted to the functions of a sovereign state (Chan 1991). Meritocracy as a key personnel management principle (Quah 1972, 1996) and a commitment against corruption (Quah 1978, 1989, 2003) allowed the Public Service to ramp up the country's economic and social development (Quah 1987) through the 1970s and 1980s. Dividends from development in turn raised the quality of human capital and that of the Public Service. By the 1990s, the Singapore Public Service had become well regarded for its "competence, efficiency and integrity" (Jones 1997). Determined not to be lulled by its laurels into complacency, the Public Service undertook reforms under the banner of Public Service for the 21st Century (PS21). Beyond harnessing corporate managerial practices and competition principles to induce efficiencies, as part of the global New Public Management trend, PS21 set the Singapore Public Service on a trajectory of continuous change to remain relevant in its operating environment.

The Singapore Public Service today comprised 145,000 officers in 16 ministries and over 60 statutory boards (PSD 2019a). It is "extremely efficient" (WEF 2019) and one of the least corrupt by international standards (Transparency International 2019). Unlike counterparts on some postcolonial states, Singapore's bureaucracy has never interfered in the political arena. In Westminster tradition, the Singapore Public Service serves the elected government-of-the-day. Unique even to civil services of developed countries, the Singapore Public Service has gone beyond efficiency and integrity to position its officers to "anticipate, welcome and execute change" (PSD 2022). High performing, clean, and faceless behind the political masters, the Singapore Public Service is quintessentially professional by Westminster standards.

Civil Service System

Central HRM Unit

The Public Service Division (PSD), in the Prime Minister's Office (PMO), is the central personnel management agency of the Singapore Public Service.

Article 110 of the Constitution (2019) confers the Public Service Commission (PSC) the authority "to appoint, confirm, emplace on the permanent or pensionable establishment, promote, transfer, dismiss and exercise disciplinary control over public officers." The PSC is an independent organ of state. Its members are appointed by the President of Singapore. For operational efficiency and to help agencies better respond to the needs of the citizenry, the "Public Service (Special and Senior Personnel Boards) Order 2010" of the Constitution devolves some of the authority and responsibilities of the PSC to the ministries through a system of personnel boards, with PSD maintaining oversight and parity across the ministries. The PSC retains responsibility for appointing and promoting senior officers in the grades of Deputy Secretary and Chief Executive Officers (CEOs) of statutory board and above.

PSD is considered a ministry, notwithstanding the "division" in its nomenclature. The most senior civil servant heading the PSD is the Permanent Secretary, who reports to the Minister in-charge of the Public Service. PSD was established within the Ministry of Finance in 1983 (Low 2018). It consolidated all human resource management (HRM) functions which until then were distributed across different agencies of the Public Service. In 1994, PSD was transferred to the PMO.

Today, most of the HRM functions are delegated to the ministries and statutory boards. These agencies have autonomy in recruitments, appointments, performance appraisals, promotions, and training of their respective officers. PSD concentrates on setting HR policies to support the personnel management work of the ministries and statutory boards.

For greater efficiency, some routine HRM functions are devolved to VITAL, the shared services arm of the Public Service (VITAL 2019). VITAL aggregates common corporate services such as HR, finance, and procurement across the Public Service to achieve economies of scale and improve service quality. Some of the HR functions VITAL manages include payroll and claims administration, learning services such as course registration, training records management and training statistics analysis, and travel management services involving air tickets, hotels, and travel insurance.

Recruitment and Openness of Posts/Positions

Hiring decisions in the Singapore Public Service consider whole person qualities and the job-fit of the applicant to the positions applied.

Job vacancies in the Public Service are advertised on the job portal Careers@ Gov. Anyone interested in a career with the Public Service can browse through the portal to explore the positions available, the agencies these vacancies are located in, the job descriptions, the requirements needed for the jobs, and other related details. Officers already serving in the Public Service can also apply to fill these vacancies. All applicants, including existing Public Service officers, undergo similar recruitment processes and evaluation criteria.

Job applicants are assessed on the basis of the relevance of their work experience, skills, professional qualifications, and credentials needed for the job. For applicants with no prior work experience, their academic performance and participation in co-curricular activities, internships, and other activities outside of formal education are evaluated as a proxy for the skills and attributes that the job may require. These include problem-solving skills and leadership qualities. In all cases, hiring agencies look for applicants' personal attributes that embody the Public Service values of Integrity, Service, and Excellence.

Officers already serving in the Public Service may be posted or seconded – or temporarily assigned – to another agency as part of operational requirements or professional development.

74 James Low

Civil Service Classification and Status

Until 2017, officers in the Singapore Public Service were organized into four divisions. This legacy of the British colonial bureaucracy placed officers with degrees in Division I, officers with diplomas and GCE A level (high school) certificates in Division II, and those with secondary and primary education in Divisions III and IV, respectively (Low 2018). In 2017, PSD stopped grouping officers according to their education levels to emphasize that officers' career progression will not be limited by academic qualifications (*Straits Times*, 5 January 2017).

Officers in the Public Service can be appointed to different schemes of service, depending on their roles and career tracks. For instance, officers may undertake specialist roles such as police officers and economists and be placed on specialist schemes of service. Officers may also be placed on the generic scheme of service and be put in different roles in ministries. All the schemes of service have their respective grades and career progression structures.

In line with the national movement to recognize skills beyond paper qualifications, both graduates and nongraduates can be appointed on the same grade if they are both found qualified for the job. To illustrate the shift, the Civil Service has progressively merged career tracks to allow for more seamless progression of officers regardless of their academic qualifications. For example, the Education Scheme of Service, which employs the largest number of public officers, has revised its scheme to a single salary structure where both graduates and nongraduates are remunerated and can progress along the same structure.

While there are variations between the different schemes of service, salaries in the Public Service are based on the principle of market competition. Salaries are benchmarked against the private sector to attract and retain talent. This allows the Public Service to fill the broad range of functions across the Service.

Officers who are appointed to the permanent establishment have to serve a minimum probation period of one year before they are considered for confirmation. This probation mechanism allows the ministries to assess their suitability for a longer-term career with the Civil Service. At the same time, this gives officers sufficient time to figure out their job-fit with the Service.

Some positions are contract appointments, as the jobs are only needed for specific periods.

The Singapore Public Service does not have a policy of guaranteeing lifelong employment in the Public Service. All officers, regardless of their seniority, are expected to maintain a high standard of conduct. Officers found guilty of misconduct will be dealt with accordingly and, depending on the severity of the misconduct, possible penalties range from reprimand to dismissal.

Performance Assessment and Promotion

Performance management in the Singapore Public Service is comprehensive and rigorous. From the organization's perspective, one of the purposes of performance appraisal is to "uncover and take stock of talent within the organisation, to know the strengths and weaknesses of our officers . . . [and] to deploy and develop our officers" (PSD 2009).

Officers undergo performance appraisals every year. Managing performance is a joint effort between the supervisor and the officer. The performance management cycle involves work planning between officers and their supervisors, regular reviews and feedback, evaluation, development, and rewards and recognition according to results of performance assessment. Supervisors and officers are expected to meet regularly, not just once or twice a year, to continuously review work targets and priorities, provide timely feedback and discuss development needs.

Performance appraisal is conducted based on the qualities in the AIM framework: Analytical and intellectual capacity, Influence and collaboration, and Motivation for excellence. These three clusters expanded into seven sets of detailed qualities to guide the appraisal of officers.

One of the outcomes of appraisal is the officer's salary: the amount of merit increment to the monthly salary, and the amount of a one-time annual performance bonus.[2] Officers who are assessed to have consistently performed well and assessed to be ready for bigger jobs may be promoted. Conversely, where an officer is evaluated to have performed below expectations, the officer may receive a lower or no merit increment and performance bonus. For officers assessed to have not met the expectations of their job grades, their supervisors would need to explore with the officers the reasons for their performance. Could the reasons be due to any mismatch in ability, job fit, organizational fit, attitude, or aspirations? Depending on the nature of the reasons, officers may be counseled on ways to improve, or to seek a transfer to other departments or agencies, or exit the Public Service. Officers who disagree with decisions made by the personnel boards can appeal to the PSC, as the final board of appeal. The PSC helps ensure that officers, regardless of their seniority, are treated fairly and consistently.

Apart from performance, public officers are also assessed based on their Currently Estimated Potential (CEP). The CEP concept was adapted from Shell in 1983 and refers to an "estimation of the highest appointment or level of work an officer can ultimately handle competently" (PSD 2009; Quah 2010). CEP "influences how far an officer can go . . . how quickly he/she may advance up the career ladder, with high potential officers being promoted more quickly if they demonstrate performance consistent with or exceeding these high expectations. As a result of this approach, the best officers can rise up to be Permanent Secretaries [the highest public service appointment] in their forties" (Saxena 2011).

Training

There are two broad categories of training in the Singapore Public Service: in-house training and centralized training.

With the wide range of functions carried out by the 16 ministries and more than 60 statutory boards, training in the Public Service can be specialized and particular to the respective agencies (Low 2018). Induction in uniformed organizations, for example, will immediately emphasize regimentation; training for new teachers focuses on pedagogical skills. Such specialized training is typically undertaken in-house by the agencies.

Each agency conducts its own in-house induction program to integrate its new officers into its particular organizational environment. Induction programs can span between one to two days, to one to two weeks, at the discretion of the respective agencies. Thereafter, on-the-job training at the department or unit level is the primary mode to familiarize new officers with the nature of the job, working processes, and departmental culture.

Centralized training cutting across the Public Service is conducted at the Civil Service College (CSC). These include functional training in core domains such as finance, HR, procurement, regulation, and so on. Centralized training helps to ensure uniformity of processes and consistency of standards in these functions across the Public Service.

Centralized training and the CSC have long been used to foster ethos and lead reforms in the Singapore Public Service (Low 2018). For example, induction training for all Public Service officers familiarize them with the values of the Public Service. As part of the Public Sector Transformation reforms, training is used for "Preparing every officer for the future: Every public officer will learn and reskill and adapt to changes. Every officer will pursue innovation and be open to new ways of working" (PSD 2019b).

As part of the country's Smart Nation drive, many courses have been rolled out to equip officers with digital literacy. The CSC has launched the LEARN mobile app to allow officers to learn anytime, anywhere (PSD 2019c). Training programs at the CSC also orient officers toward serving the public with "Integrity, Service, Excellence" (values of the Singapore Public Service).

Leadership development is another aspect of centralized training at the CSC. The main mode of executive development at the CSC is the milestone programs. Milestone programs are a series of intensive courses scheduled at key points – or milestones – in an officer's career (Low 2016a). Some of the milestone programs at the CSC include:

- the Learn to Lead Programme for first-time managers (CSC 2019a);
- the Empowered to Lead Programme for middle managers (CSC 2022b);
- the Directors' Developmental Experience and Senior Management Programme for director-level officers (CSC 2022a, 2022d); and
- the Executive Leadership Programme and Leaders in Administration Programme catering to officers who are assuming key leadership positions (CSC 2022c).

Apart from leadership development, these milestone programs – at times spanning several weeks – forge a sense of camaraderie and shared élan among the participants. By fostering shared perspectives on policy issues among leaders brought together from across the Public Service, milestone programs cultivate a whole-of-government orientation among officers from different agencies. Such whole-of-government perspectives can "ease communication and coordination among agencies" especially at times of crisis (Low 2016b).

Senior Civil Service (Senior Management)

The Administrative Service and senior officers of the respective sectoral domains and professional services form the leadership corps of the Singapore Public Service. The PSC is the authority for appointing officers to the Administrative Service, as well as appointing and promoting officers to the senior management ranks (equivalent to Deputy Secretary and Statutory Board CEO and above). The PSC also considers candidates for appointment as Statutory Board CEOs.

In 2013, to broaden the identification of talent and diversity of leaders, the Public Sector Leadership Programme (PSLP) was started to groom sectoral and specialist leaders in five sectors: central administration, economy building, infrastructure and environment, security, and social (PSD 2014). Together, the Administrative Service and PSLP form the key central talent pipelines. In 2018, there were 330 Administrative Service officers and 880 PSLP officers (PSD 2018).

There are two phases in the PSLP. Under the PSLP General Phase, officers are tried out in at least two positions in different sectors before consideration for absorption into the Administrative Service, or appointment to the PSLP Sectoral Phase. Officers from other schemes of service who exhibited outstanding performance and potential, as well as suitable mid-career candidates from outside the Public Service, could similarly be assessed for suitability for Administrative Service or PSLP.

Senior professional officers head their respective specialist services. Professional officers such as teachers, economists, police officers, and so forth serve in the same specialist services and rise up the ranks of their respective services. For instance, the most senior professional officer in the Education Service is the Director-General of Education, and the most senior police officer is the Commissioner of Police. At PSD which is the central personnel management arm of the Public Service, there is a chief human resource officer.

Notes

1 All views in this chapter are the author's and do not represent the Civil Service College. For correspondence, email James_Low@CSCollege.gov.sg.
2 Salary increments also take into consideration the performance of the national economy, performance of the organisation, and the performance of the officer's department.

References

Chan, H. C. (1991) 'Political developments, 1965–1979', in E. Chew and E. Lee (eds) *History of Singapore* (pp. 157–81), Oxford: Oxford University Press.

Civil Service College (CSC) (2019a) 'Learn to lead programme', available at: www.cscollege.gov.sg/programmes/pages/display%20programme.aspx?epid=kdjiue5mv8cm5j65eup3bvw54o (accessed 29 April 2019).

Constitution of the Republic of Singapore (2019) available at: https://sso.agc.gov.sg/Act/CONS1963?ValidDate=20170401&ProvIds=P1IX- (accessed 12 April 2019).

CSC (2022a) 'Directors' developmental experience', available at: https://register.csc.gov.sg/registration?courseId=303085&classNum=0 (accessed 18 May 2022).

CSC (2022b) 'Empowered to lead programme', available at: https://register.csc.gov.sg/registration?courseId=301294&classNum=0 (accessed 18 May 2022).

CSC (2022c) 'Leaders in administration programme', available at: https://register.csc.gov.sg/registration?courseId=301529&classNum=0 (accessed 18 May 2022).

CSC (2022d) 'Senior management programme', available at: https://register.csc.gov.sg/registration?courseId=301534&classNum=0 (accessed 18 May 2022).

Department of Statistics (DOS) (2019) 'Singapore in figures, 2019', available at: www.singstat.gov.sg/-/media/files/publications/reference/sif2019.pdf (accessed 9 November 2019).

Dtysdale, J. (1984) *Singapore: Struggle for Success*, Singapore: Times Books International.

Jones, D. S. (1997) 'Public service for the 21st century – PS21', in C. F. Kee and T. L. Thaver (eds) *Everyday Life, Everyday People* (pp. 76–80), Singapore: Ministry of Education and National University of Singapore.

Lam, P. E. and Tan, K. Y. L. (1999) *Lee's Lieutenants: Singapore's Old Guard*, Australia: Allen & Unwin.

Lee, B. H. (1977) *The Singapore Civil Service and Its Perceptions of Time*, Honolulu: University Microfilms International.

Low, J. (2016a) 'Milestone programmes for the administrative service in the Singapore public service', in A. Podger and J. Wanna (eds) *Sharpening the Sword of the State: Building Executive Capacities in the Public Services of the Asia-Pacific* (pp. 181–212), Canberra: ANU Press.

Low, J. (2016b, December) 'Singapore's whole-of-government approach in crisis management', *Ethos*, 16: 14–22.

Low, J. (2018) *Inception Point: The Use of Learning and Development to Reform the Singapore Public Service*, Singapore: World Scientific.

Mercer (2019) 'Quality of living city ranking', available at: https://mobilityexchange.mercer.com/Insights/quality-of-living-rankings (accessed 9 November 2019).

Ministry of Manpower (MOM) (2019) 'Summary table: Unemployment', available at: https://stats.mom.gov.sg/Pages/Unemployment-Summary-Table.aspx (accessed 9 November 2019).

Ng, I. (2010) *The Singapore Lion: A biography of S. Rajaratnam*, Singapore: Institute of South East Asian Studies.

Public Service Division (PSD) (2009, November 2–3) 'Effective performance management in the Singapore civil service', Conference on Improving Public Service Performance in the OECD Countries in Times of Crisis, available at: Siteresources.worldbank.org/ . . . /Resources/Day2-Panel2-Hoe-Soon-Tan.ppt (accessed 16 April 2019).

PSD (2014) 'Speech by Mr Peter Ong, head of civil service at the inaugural public service leadership dinner', available at: www.psd.gov.sg/pressroom/speeches/speech-by-mr-peter-ong – head-of-civil-service-at-the-inaugural-public-service-leadership-dinner (accessed 29 April 2019).

PSD (2018) 'Speech by Mr Leo Yip, head, civil service at the public service leadership dinner 2018', available at: www.psd.gov.sg/pressroom/speeches/speech-by-mr-leo-yip – head – civil-service-at-the-public-service-leadership-dinner-2018 (accessed 29 April 2019).

PSD (2019a) 'Developing careers', available at: www.psd.gov.sg/what-we-do/developing-careers (accessed 5 April 2019).

Singapore **79**

PSD (2019b) 'Transforming the public service to build our future Singapore', available at: www.psd.gov.sg/what-we-do/transforming-the-public-service-to-build-our-future-singapore (accessed 14 May 2019).

PSD (2019c) 'Speech by Mr Chan Chun Sing, minister for trade and industry and minister-in-charge of the public service at committee of supply 2019', available at: www.psd.gov.sg/press-room/speeches/speech-by-mr-chan-chun-sing – minister-for-trade-and-industry-and-minister-in-charge-of-the-public-service-at-committee-of-supply-2019 (accessed 30 April 2019).

PSD (2022) 'Organisational chart', available at: www.psd.gov.sg/AboutUs/Organisation-Chart/ (accessed 24 August 2022).

"Public Service (Special and Senior Personnel Boards) Order 2010." *Constitution*, available at https://sso.agc.gov.sg/SL/CONS1963-S824-2010?DocDate=20180727 (accessed 14 May 2019).

Quah, J. S. T. (1972) *Origin of the Public Service Commission in Singapore*, New Delhi: Indian Institute of Public Administration.

Quah, J. S. T. (1978) *Administrative and legal measures for combating bureaucratic corruption in Singapore*, Singapore: Chopmen.

Quah, J. S. T. (1987) 'Public bureaucracy and policy implementation in Singapore', *Southeast Asian Journal of Social Science*, 15(2): 77–95.

Quah, J. S. T. (1989) 'Singapore's experience in curbing corruption' in A. J. Heidenheimer, M. Johnson and V. Levine (eds) *Political Corruption: A Handbook* (pp. 841–53), New Brunswick: Transaction Books.

Quah, J. S. T. (1996) 'Decentralising public personnel management: The case of the public sector in Singapore', in S. Kurosawa, T. Fujiwara and M. A. Reforma (eds) *New Trends in Public Administration for the Asia Pacific Region: Decentralisation* (pp. 492–506), Tokyo: Local Autonomy College, Ministry of Home Affairs.

Quah, J. S. T. (2003) 'Singapore's anti-corruption strategy: Is this form of governance transferable to other Asian countries?' in J. B. Kidd and F. J. Richter (eds) *Corruption and Governance in Asia* (pp. 180–97), Basingstoke: Palgrave Macmillan.

Quah, J. S. T. (2010) *Public Administration Singapore Style*, Singapore: Emerald Group Publishing.

Saxena, N. C. (2011) *Virtuous Cycles: The Singapore Public Service and National Development*, Singapore: United Nations Development Programme.

Seah, C. M. (1971) *Bureaucratic Evolution and Political Change in an Emerging Nation: A Case Study of Singapore*, PhD thesis, Victoria University of Manchester, Manchester.

Straits Times, 5 January 2017.

Tan, S. S. (2007) *Goh Keng Swee: A Portrait*, Singapore: Editions Didier Millet.

Transparency International (2019) 'Corruption perceptions index 2018', available at: www.transparency.org/files/content/pages/2018_CPI_ExecutiveSummary.PDF (accessed 23 November 2019).

Turnbull, C. M. (2009) *A History of Modern Singapore, 1819–2005*, Singapore: National University of Singapore Press.

VITAL (2019) 'Who we are', available at: www.vital.gov.sg (accessed 14 May 2019).

World Economic Forum (WEF) (2019) 'Singapore crowned world's most open and competitive economy', available at www.weforum.org/agenda/2019/10/competitiveness-economy-best-top-first-singapore-secret-consistency/ (accessed 9 November 2019).

5

HONG KONG

Wilson Wong and Raymond Hau-yin Yuen

Context and Overview: The Hong Kong Civil Service

Hong Kong was formerly a British Colony, and the city has become a Special Autonomous Region (SAR) of China after the transfer of sovereignty in 1997 under the "One Country, Two Systems" (OCTS) framework, supposedly enjoying high autonomy under the Basic Law, which is its mini-constitution. The politico-administrative regime of Hong Kong has been founded, developed, and inherited from its colonial history under the British administration. Hong Kong government has been described by Lau (1982) as a "de facto independent and self-governing state." However, in the last two decades after the transfer of its sovereignty, many core features of the administrative state including its civil service system have been challenged by market-based reforms and the new constitutional and political order under the increasing influence of China (Wong 2003; Wong and Xiao 2018). With regard to the latter, political control of the civil service and the emphasis of its political loyalty in the form of obedience to the ruling government and patriotism has been tightened at the expense of the autonomy, professionalism, and other acclaimed core features of the civil service. The recent social unrest namely the Water Revolution in Hong Kong which opposed the legislation of the Anti-Extradition Bill has further led to the efforts of the Hong Kong government to reinforce this trend. This is consistent with the new policy of China, the sovereign power after 1997, to exercise overall jurisdiction over Hong Kong as Hong Kong people show more resistance toward further and fast integration with the mainland. One of the key examples of the deepening politicization of the civil service is the Hong Kong police force. With police brutality as one of the main foci drawing outcry and criticism around the world in the Water Revolution, the police is viewed as no more than an agent of the state in violation of many core principles traditionally governing the civil service including public accountability, creditability, trust, and respect for the law and citizen rights.

DOI: 10.4324/9781003326496-7

Contrary to the western democratic model in separation of powers, Hong Kong has an "executive-led" system rooted into the tradition of administrative state (Wong 2013). The government enjoys an asymmetric power over the legislature in policymaking and governance, while an ongoing process of democratization has empowered the role of legislature in public governance. Hong Kong has been long-term regarded as an "administrative state" with the executive power dominated by senior bureaucrats. Bureaucrats were acting as a de facto policymaker during the colonial era until 2002. The executive power is highly centralized and supported by "a unified civil service run by a meritocratically selected and small-circled administrative elite" (Burns 2004; Miners 2000; Scott 2006; Painter 2005; Wong 2009).

In general, the colonial governance with the civil service as the core is featured by a minimalist, noninterventionist state with a strong corporatist tradition. Although the government to a high extent delivered effective governance, while it refrained from active socioeconomic intervention, the authoritative regime was able to maintain the legitimacy through systematic elite integration. Despite the absence of procedural political legitimacy, the ability of the bureaucracy to maintain political stability and economic prosperity, coupled with fast and strong economic growth, gave the state high political performance legitimacy (Sing 2001; So 2002).

Nowadays, the government of Hong Kong is composed of various types of organizations which are at the same time tightly managed by a central system of financial and administrative controls. More than 50 "government departments and agencies" are operating under the supervision of various policy bureaus. Although the "civil service system" is central to the Hong Kong government, it does not compose the entire "public sector" in Hong Kong. It is important to highlight that civil servants in Hong Kong only refer to those employed on "civil service terms of service" in government bureau and departments, other employees of statutory public organizations subsidized by government budget are not civil servants, such as the doctors in public hospitals managed by the Hospital Authority, and also the urban planner employed by the Urban Renewal Authority (HAB 2004).

In the original design of the post-1997 political order, the Beijing government intended to retain the imprint of the colonial civil service system, as it is highly regarded for managing the colony's affairs and entrenching a number of measures, which ensured continuity and stability in this regard. However, the old institutional arrangements have not been successfully coped with the more complex socioeconomic situations that arise after 1997 (Wong 2003, 2013). While Hong Kong civil service keeps its core tradition after the sovereignty transfer, it faces new trends and challenges with new competing values emerged contesting the civil service traditions in the past two decades, and it inevitably undermined the role and influences of the civil service in policymaking and management. These challenges include the followings:

Democratization, dysfunctional political system, and raising citizen expectations: The political arena in Hong Kong has become more and more pluralistic, while the dominance of bureaucracy in decision-making has been broken down in facing the increasingly diversified social interests. The civil society

82 Wilson Wong and Raymond Hau-yin Yuen

becomes more active in demanding good governance and engaging in policy advocacy. Also there is a rising demand on the progress of democratization and the quality of public services. Against this backdrop, the executive-led colonial system failed to deliver effective governance and democratic representation to maintain the needs of legitimacy and efficiency, leading to the SAR Government governance crisis (Lee 1999; Wong 2009). The political system has been gradually disarticulated; it failed to rationalize the relationship between politicians and bureaucrats with the tensions mounted between the executive and legislature (Scott 2000) and integrate competing and sectoral social interests (Wong 2009). The postcolonial government of Hong Kong is featured by disjointed polity, institutional incongruity, and disconnection between policy and politics. Paradoxically, the SAR government attempts to strengthen the executive-led political system as a solution to the problems, which only further worsens them (Cheung 2004, 2007).

Politicization and political appointment system: While the bureaucracy is sharing its power with society under the force of democratization, it is simultaneously losing its power and autonomy to the non-democratically elected and China-appointed politicians through the process of politicization. The bureaucratic dominance in policymaking and public governance remained until the introduction of the Principal Official Accountability System (POAS) in 2002 under the administration of Chief Executive Tung Chee-hwa. POAS can be considered the most remarkable political reform that had been implemented since the Handover (Cheng 2004; Loh and Cullen 2005). Under the new political appointment system, there are 15 policy bureaus that work under the supervision of the Chief Executive; the head of the policy bureau is called the policy secretary. These politically appointed secretaries are responsible for policymaking and monitoring, and are accountable for their performance in the relevant policy domain, replacing the civil servants, mainly the administrative officers, as top policymakers. The senior civil servant, also known as the administrative officer grade, can now only serve as permanent secretaries, and a layer below the political appointees and their policy role is undermined and confined to provide advice and consultancy to their political master. The executive council becomes the top decision-making body of the government and it resembles the cabinet in Westminster System.

The new top political layer can impose political pressures on the civil service in its operation. At the same time, since the Chief Executive is appointed by the central government of China, politicization of the civil service also simultaneously reflects the heightening of the influence of China over Hong Kong and its civil service. With the goals of enhancing political control and ensuring political loyalty, there is a growing penetration of political influence from the top level of the civil service to all other levels in the hierarchy. For example, amidst the social movement of Water Revolution, the government proposed all civil servants should declare its loyalty to the ruling government which also implied that they could be discharged for actions perceived as disloyal. This does not only threaten the professionalism, autonomy, and political neutrality of the civil service, it also represents a gradual decline of the ideals of the civil service and eventually downgrade it to a political tool of the ruling government.

"Hollowing-out" of the state and new public management: There has been an increasing pressure for the government to adopt a wide range of managerial practice in modernizing the civil service system (Common 2005) and establish new bodies such as executive agencies and public corporations outside the traditional structure of government (HAB 2003). The purpose of reform is generally twofold: first it emphasizes to empower the manager with more discretion to make all the important personnel decisions including hiring, dismissing, rewarding, and promoting with greater flexibility, the most prominent and impactful reform is the adoption of non-civil service contracts (NCSC) in labor-intensive departments; secondly, it aims to promote a result-oriented, pro-business, private-sector management culture for governing the bureaucracy. The comprehensive civil service reform program launched in 1999 in five main areas: entry and exit, pay and conditions of service, conduct and discipline, performance management, training and development, bringing significant challenges to the merit principles central to the governing of the civil service.

Civil Service System

Central HRM Unit

Name, Location in Government, and Organizational Type of Central HRM Unit

The Civil Service Bureau (CSB) is the central HRM unit of the Hong Kong Government, CSB is one of the 15 major policy bureaus in the Government Secretariat. The head of the CSB, with an official title as the Secretary for the Civil Service, is one of the Principal Officials appointed under the Political Appointment System and a Member of the Executive Council. Unlike other politically appointed policy secretaries for bureaus, the Secretary for the Civil Service is appointed from the senior administrative officer from the civil service, who may choose to return to the civil service when his term expires. The Secretary for the Civil Service is responsible to the Chief Executive (CE) for civil service policies as well as the overall management and development of the civil service, including such matters as appointment, pay and conditions of service, staff management, manpower planning, training, and discipline. His primary role is to ensure that the civil service serves the best interests of the community and delivers various services in a trustworthy, efficient, and cost-effective manner.

Tasks and Functions

As the central HRM unit of the Hong Kong Civil Service, the Civil Service Bureau is mainly responsible to determine overall human resource policies and practices of the civil service. In the central level, it executes personnel policies including succession planning for directorate level officers, direct management of generalist grades, carrying out integrity checking, hearing staff appeals and grievances, etc. The power of creating non-directorate posts is delegated to the policy branches and departments. The Civil Service Bureau still retains the role to supervise and advise other policy bureaus and government departments on the implementation of its human resources policy. The policy bureau oversees the human resources plan of its subordinated departments, reviews proposals for directorate post creation, and undertakes manpower planning, appointment and promotion, and appraisal of directorate officers together with CSB. The departments and executive agencies manage its HRM system in consultation with CSB and its policy bureau, prepare annual departmental human resource plan, and administer departmental rules and regulations. For instance, the heads or directors of department are required to determine "Guide to Appointment" and job descriptions of specific civil service positions, and they are responsible to submit "Forecast of Occupancy of Directorate Posts" to the parental policy bureau and the civil service bureau for succession planning too.

Beyond the Civil Service Bureau, the Legislative Council, as the legislative branch of the government, also plays an important role in scrutinizing the civil service. On the one hand, the Public Accounts Committee considers reports of the Director of Audit on the accounts and the results of value-for-money audits of the Government and other organizations which are within the purview of public audits; on the other hand, the Finance Committee and its Establishment Subcommittee controls the personnel ceiling of the civil service by approving the request from government in opening new positions in directorate level. Civil service establishment in non-directorate level is managed by the Head of Department and departmental establishment committee through the Notional Annual Midpoint Salary (NAMS) System.

Recruitment

Definition and Eligibility

According to the Basic Law, all new civil service recruits appointed on or after July 1, 1997, must be permanent residents of the Hong Kong Special Administrative Region, except for foreign nationals who may be employed as advisers by discretion of the government; moreover, the principal officials must not have right of abode in a foreign country. As an equal opportunity of employment, the government appoints civil servants based on the principle of open and fair competition, and the candidates have to go through a competitive process on the basis of merit and are appointed only if they possess the qualifications and capabilities required for the job. Entry requirements for civil service posts in general are set on the basis of academic or professional qualifications, technical skills, work experience, language proficiency, and other qualities as required. The merit-based recruitment of civil service in entry level is guaranteed by centralized examination conducted by the Civil Service Bureau and the subsequent selection interview by corresponding department and executive agency.

Competitive Examination

The Civil Service Bureau administers the centralized written examination called the "Common Recruitment Examination" (CRE); it includes the language competence tests on Chinese and English language and also an aptitude test on the candidates' reasoning abilities. The CRE result is a prerequisite for applying most of the civil service positions; the candidates must meet the threshold of language proficiency of all degree or professional grades, some of these grades also require a pass in the aptitude test. Moreover, a "Basic Law Test" was introduced to align with the CRE since 2008, the result of this test will also be taken into consideration in assessing the suitability of a candidate. Starting from July 2022, all candidates for civil service jobs must pass the "National Security Law Test" in order to be considered for appointment.

In addition to the CRE, a Joint Recruitment Examination (JRE) will be held separately for the recruitment of entry ranks of civil service grades in various government bureaus and departments, including Administrative Officer, Executive Officer, Labour Officer, Trade Officer, Management Services Officer, and Transport Officer. Recruitment of these grades is varied across years, subjected to the manpower needs of the year. The JRE focuses to examine the applicants' analytical and written communication abilities through scenario case analysis, which is considered to be critical in performing the job duties in these grades.

Direct Application

Vacancies in the basic rank of a majority of civil service grades, or where promotion is not possible or where there is a special need, are open for direct application. The corresponding bureau and departments can determine the entry terms and qualifications with reference to a CSB guide to appointment. Applicants who possess the required levels of result in Common Recruitment Examination are eligible to apply for the position. The application will then be reviewed by the corresponding department, and potential candidates will be shortlisted to attend the selection interview. Selected candidates are required to undertake medical examination and integrity checking before the formal appointment. Physical and fitness tests are also required for disciplined services.

Monitoring

Meanwhile, there are both internal and external watchdogs for external advice and monitoring to guarantee the merit-based recruitment at the entry level. For instance, the Public Service Commission is an independent statutory body, the chairman and member of the commission are appointed by the Chief Executive

86 Wilson Wong and Raymond Hau-yin Yuen

who gives advice on appointments, promotion, and discipline matters of civil service policy and management, and it also monitors all appointment and promotion of civil servants on point 26 of the Master Pay Scale or above and seeks to safeguard the impartiality and integrity of the appointment and promotion systems in the civil service. The public service commission should also be consulted to ensure that fairness and broad consistency in the level of disciplinary punishment are maintained throughout the civil service.

Civil Service Classification and Status

Functional Level and Grade

The Hong Kong civil service is inherited from the British tradition with a Board Classification system. Positions in the civil service system are grouped into grades and ranks according to basic similarities based on common yardstick and consistent values. "Grade" refers to the type of position, for example, Police Inspector. "Rank" refers to the level of the position within the organizational hierarchy of the specific grade, for example, Senior Police Inspector and Chief Police Inspector.

The Hong Kong civil service is broadly categorized in two groups, that is, the generalist grade and departmental grade. The "Generalist Grades," including "Administrative Officer," "Executive Officer," and clerical and secretarial grades officers, are under the direct management of a central authority of the Civil Service Bureau. Civil servants in these grades are the pillars of interdepartmental coordination and communication, they will be transferred from department to department based on administrative need. It emphasizes on efficiency in streaming internal administrative arrangement including selection process, training programs, pay scales, examination, rotation, etc. It is important to highlight the unique policy and leadership role taken by the "Administrative Officer" grade in the government bureau and departments. Unlike most of the other grades, the administrative officer is the elitist group of the civil service, they are recruited from open examination and merit-based interviews, and only the top (less than 1% of the cohort of application) candidates will be selected to join the grade. The administrative officer grade is expected to be the "conscience" of the civil service who are obligated to safeguard and promote the public interest, and they are multitalented professionals to communicate with the public and formulate policies to meet the changing needs of social and economic development.

The second group is called "Departmental Grades," including professional officers, technocrats, and disciplinary forces such as Police Inspector, Health Inspector, Education Officer, Taxation Officer, Environmental Protection Officer, and Government Social Worker. These grades are managed directly by their parent departments. Civil servants in these grades generally spend their entire career within one

Employment Status and Conditions/Job Security

Before the major civil service reform in 1999, a majority of the civil servants were appointed on permanent and pensionable terms in the basic and entry ranks, with a very small proportion of civil servants, usually in junior rank of departmental grades, being employed with "Non-Civil Service Contract" (NCSC) with a duration of several months to one year to meet occasional and seasonal needs of public service such as the postal officers and public lifeguards. Generally, permanent employment offers a very stable career for civil servants, unless the civil servants committed an offense serious enough to warrant dismissal. However, such a stable career pathway stifled the exchange of talents with the private sector and made the civil servants being less than fully motivated. It also discourages able potential application.

Since the 1999 Civil Service Reform, a greater flexibility has been injected into the civil service entry system; a security of tenure for new appointees in basic rank has been replaced by agreement (contract) terms aligned with the promise of structured career and long-term employment in promotional ranks, usually being described as a "Three Plus Three Contract" system. Under the new entry system, recruits will normally be appointed to basic ranks in civil service grades on a longer probationary period of three years, compared to two years previously; then another three-year contractual terms will be offered if their performance is satisfactory, before they are further considered for appointment on the prevailing permanent and pensionable terms. The new arrangement did not affect the disciplinary services and those civil servants who are already in post. Moreover, direct recruits to supervisory ranks will normally be appointed on three-year agreement terms. These recruits will be required to serve on agreement terms for at least three years before they can be considered for appointment on the new permanent terms. This new contract system for entry was modified and streamlined in 2010, and now entry recruits will normally be appointed to basic ranks in civil service grades on three-year probationary terms, before they are considered for appointment on the prevailing permanent terms.

Meanwhile, the government introduced the Non-Civil Service Contract (NCSC) Scheme in 1999, and it offers the Permanent Secretaries and Department Heads a flexible means of employment to enable them to respond promptly to their respective Bureaus and Departments' changing operational and service needs. The government contends that the NCSC staff are initially employed under specific conditions, including the positions (i) are time-limited, seasonal, or subject to market fluctuations; (ii) requiring staff to work less than conditioned hours; (iii) tapping the latest expertise in a particular area of the labor market; and (iv) the mode of service delivery is under review or likely to be changed. In practice, the use of NCSC terms has been increased significantly after the year

2000, to the extent that it even replaces the regular and established long-term positions in delivering a wide range of core public services. According to the policy paper by the Civil Service Bureau tabled on Legislative Council Panel on Public Service (2018), there were 10,380 full-time NCSC staff as of June 30, 2017. Compared with the historic peak of 18,537 as of June 30, 2006, there had been a reduction of about 8,200 positions (or around 44%). The government report shows that 3,673 staff have been employed with NCSC term for five years or more. Moreover, 8,520 full-time NCSC positions were identified by the relevant policy bureau and departments as involving work with significant permanent nature that should more appropriately be handled by civil servants. In June 2017, somewhat 68 government bureaus and departments were listed as employing NCSC staff, it covers a wide range of policy domains; Hong Kong Post (1,818), Leisure and Cultural Services Department (1,293), and Education Bureau (1,201) are the top three government agencies in NCSC staff employment.

Openness of Posts/Positions

Internal and External Recruitment

In Hong Kong civil service, normally only positions in the basic rank of different grades are open to external recruitment, or with the possibility of in-service recruitment. Beyond the appointment in the political offices, civil servants are generally recruited only from the entry level, external recruitment is usually available for the ad hoc positions requiring strong industrial and professional background to carry out specific tasks and projects.

Internal and External Mobility

According to the official website of the Civil Service Bureau, the total number of the Civil Service was 171,458, with a 2.3% increase over the previous year in March 2018. There were 14,626 new appointments to the Civil Service in the year 2017–18; as for the new appointments, 8,437 (57.7%) are entry or basic rank from generalist and departmental grades in master-pay scale, 1,957 (13.4%) were from the Police Force, and 2,689 (18.4%) of them were from General Disciplined Services, including immigration officer and correctional officer, etc. There were 8,616 civil servants leaving the Civil Service (5.1% of the total strength at the beginning of the financial year), out of which 6,660 (77.3%) were retired, and 1,333 were resigned (15.5%).

Internal mobility in civil service is very limited, and neither transfer nor promotion across grades in the civil service system is plausible. Civil servants in departmental and professional grades are staying in the same agency or related agencies for their entire career, while those in the generalist grades are rotating across different units and departments to meet the changing working demands.

TABLE 5.1 Number of officers leaving the service

	2016–2017	2017–2018	2018–2019	2019–2020
Number of Leavers	7 793	8 616	8 557	8 311
(as % of strength at the beginning of financial year)	(4.7%)	(5.1%)	(5.0%)	(4.8%)
(as % of the average of strength at the beginning and end of financial year) *(Note 7)*	(4.7%)	(5.1%)	(4.9%)	(4.7%)

Sources: "Statistics" from the official website of Hong Kong Civil Service Bureau. Retrieved on 28 April 2022.

TABLE 5.2 Officers leaving the service during 2019–2020 – By wastage types and terms of appointment

Wastage Type	Terms of Appointment					
	Local[1]	Overseas[2]	Common[3]	New[4]	Total	(%)[6]
Retirement	6 096	1	18	22	6 137	(73.8)
Resignation	137	1	4	1 429	1 571	(18.9)
Completion of Agreement	384	14	0	6	404	(4.9)
Death	93	0	0	37	130	(1.6)
Dismissal	4	0	0	10	14	(0.2)
Termination of Service	0	0	0	15	15	(0.2)
Other Reasons[5]	8	0	0	32	40	(0.5)
Total	6 722	16	22	1 551	8 311	(100.0)
(%)[7]	(80.9)	(0.2)	(0.3)	(18.7)	(100.0)	

Sources: "Statistics" from the official website of Hong Kong Civil Service Bureau. Retrieved on 28 April 2022.

Notes:

[1] "Local" refers to the set of terms offered to a local officer appointed before the introduction of common terms.

[2] "Overseas" refers to the set of terms offered to an overseas officer appointed before the introduction of common terms.

[3] "Common" refers to a common set of terms of appointment and conditions of service applicable to new appointees to the Civil Service on civil service terms and conditions who are offered appointment on or after January 1, 1999, and before June 1, 2000.

[4] "New" refers to new sets of terms of appointment and conditions of service applicable to new appointees to the Civil Service on civil service terms and conditions who are offered appointment on or after June 1, 2000.

[5] Other reasons include completion of apprenticeship, resolution of agreement by mutual consent, etc.

[6] (%) denotes percentage to total. (These figures may not add up exactly to the total due to rounding.)

[7] This percentage is sometimes called "Central Wastage Rate." This relates all leavers from the Civil Service during the year to the average number of civil servants during the year.

External mobility rate is also very low. First, the staff wastage rate is 5.1% of the whole civil service in the year 2017–18 (compared to 4.7% in 2016–17), and there were totally 8,616 personnel leaving the civil service. However, a majority of the leaving cases are due to retirement (77.3%) and completion of contact or agreement (5.2%); only 15.5%, a total of 1,333 resigned from their

TABLE 5.3 Principal officials who were former civil servants (1997–2021)

Year	Chief Executive	Super-Secretaries	Bureau Secretaries
1997	0/1 (CH Tung)	2/3	17/17
2002	0/1 (CH Tung)	1/3	6/11
2007	1/1 (Donald Tsang)	2/3	9/12
2012	0/1 (CY Leung)	2/3	4/12
2017	1/1 (Carrie Lam)	1/3	7/12
2021 (after Reshuffle)	1/1 (Carrie Lam)	1/3	8/12

Sources: Hong Kong Yearbooks and Hong Kong Government Website. retrieved on 28 April 2022

jobs (Tables 5.1 and 5.2). The number of dismissal and termination of service are trivial.

Secondly, it is important to highlight the continuous trend to select and appoint ex-civil servants, especially retired permanent secretary, to serve as the chief executive, super secretaries (Chief Secretary for Administration, Financial Secretary, and Secretary for Justice), and secretaries of policy bureaus at the beginning of each new administration, since the introduction of political appointment system in 2012 (Table 5.3). This can be explained by a lack of robust political party system for grooming political talents to take up the policymaking role in the government, while the senior administrative officers become the "natural alternative" with their extensive practical experiences and broad exposure across policy domains in the government.

Performance Assessment and Promotion

Performance Assessment: Types, Tools, Criteria, and Frequency

In Hong Kong civil service, performance management is an objective and continuous assessment on an individual's performance against previously agreed work objectives, mainly through annual staff reports. As a critical HRM function, it plays a strategic role to enhance both individual efficiency and effectiveness and channel staff efforts toward departmental goals. It also serves as a critical tool for both developmental and administrative purposes; on the one hand, it focuses on the assessment of the appraisees' performance strengths and weaknesses, and identifies areas and opportunities for staff training and development; on the other hand, it improves communication between managers and staff and clarifies objectives to assist management to plan postings, transfers, and promotions.

In practice, performance management in Hong Kong civil service is an ongoing process, involving continuous communication between managers and staff on performance across the phrases of "Performance Planning," "Continuous Coaching and Development," "Interim/Mid-year Review," and "Performance Appraisal," with the appraisal reports normally completed annually. A top-down approach is adopted for "target-based" and "competency-based" performance assessment. The head of the department/executive agency is responsible to design the appraisal systems and also to ensure the fairness, transparency, and objectivity for its implementation. The immediate supervisors of the appraisee serve as the appraising officer and conduct the evaluation directly with the inputs from the relevant higher-level managers. The peers, subordinates, and clients/customers of the appraisee have no role in the evaluation exercises. The final report of individual appraisals will usually be moderated by the departmental "assessment panels" before an actual grade of performance is assigned for the appraises. It aims to ensure the consistency of assessment standards among different appraisers in the same grade by undertaking moderating and leveling work among appraisal reports. The assessment panel is also responsible for monitoring performance and identifying under-performers and outstanding performers for appropriate actions of rewards and sanctions.

Incentives

Promotion is the major incentive for rewarding competent officers, by selecting officers from a lower rank to fill vacancies in higher ranks in the same grade. Promotion is merit-based. Officers are selected for promotion on the criteria of character, ability, experience, and any qualifications prescribed for the higher rank, with the provisions of both paperboard and interview. It aims to ensure the highest performing candidates who are best able and ready to perform the more demanding duties at a higher rank. Seniority will be given weight only when no eligible officer stands out as the most meritorious and suitable for promotion. Acting arrangement with a certain probation period will generally be prescribed. All eligible officers are considered on an equal basis and will be appointed to act in the prospective higher position prior to a formal promotion to the higher position. However, in reality, the prospect of promotion for civil servant is largely limited by the structural constraint of existing grade establishment; the problem of low upward mobility is evidently shown by the fact that more than a half of the civil servants are in top pay increment band of its rank, of which a majority of them are coming from the junior rank of its grade. There has been a keen competition for promotion after the freezing of civil service recruitment in the year 2000. The situation has been gradually improved along with increase in civil service recruitment in the recent decade.

Good performers are rewarded mainly in the form of letters of appreciation and commendations; however, outstanding performance will not directly lead to any pay increase or monetary benefits. Officers who have exemplary performance in position will be given due recognition through letters of award and appreciation, or through various commendation schemes such as inter alia, the Secretary for the Civil Service's Commendation Award Scheme, the Commendation Letter Scheme, the Long and Meritorious Service Travel Award Scheme, etc. However, there is a lack of tool or discretion for the managers to promote high performance of subordinates through pay increase. Civil service pay in Hong Kong is strictly based on the "grade" and "rank" according to various types of "pay scales." Pay increase is mainly in the form of either increment within the current pay bank or promotion to a high rank. According to Civil Service Regulation (CSR), "an office may be granted an increment only if conduct and diligence in the year under review have been satisfactory," this provision was amended in 2000 to cover "overall performance at work." In practice, officers normally advance one increment a year within their respective rank scales until they reach the maximum point of the scales. Even the rule and practice on the award of increments has been tightened, in general the award of increments is still more associated with seniority not performance. On average, 60% of the civil servants are in top of pay increment band of its rank, and a majority of them are in junior rank. Moreover, in order to cope with the problem of over-grading in performance appraisal, a majority of the department and executive agencies also implemented the policy of "forced choice appraisals," it only allows the appraiser give rations of "excellent" and "outstanding" grade to only a certain percentage of all appraises in the same cohort.

The Civil Service Bureau also piloted "Pay for Performance" scheme in October 2001. A nonconsolidated Pilot Scheme has been implemented in six departments, including Buildings Department, Electrical and Mechanical Services Department, Government Flying Service, Home Affairs Department, Department of Justice, and Rating and Valuation Department. It allows the director of these departments should involve their staff to design, develop, and administer their own schemes and decide on the detailed assessment criteria for bonus allocation; the rewards will be granted to team rather than individual, based on the performance of individual divisions/sections/offices of a department or different work teams within a section/office; the reward is one-off in nature and will not be built into base pay. Eventually the government abandoned the proposal of pay-for-performance system due to a mixed outcome of the pilot scheme.

Sanctions

The Civil Service Bureau emphasizes the civil servants being accountable to procedural requirements and the hierarchical command from unit heads and immediate supervisors. Civil servants will be liable to disciplinary action if they (1) fail to observe any government regulation or official instruction; (2) misconduct themselves in any manner; or (3) by their actions, bring the Government service into disrepute. Generally, while the provision of disciplinary procedure is centralized to the Civil Service Bureau, the authority to hand sanction cases was decentralized to the head of department/executive agency after the Civil Service Reform in 1999. It significantly reduced the proceeding time of disciplinary actions. Secrétariat on Civil Service Discipline (SCSD) in the Civil Service Bureau is responsible to advise on preliminary investigation and collation of evidence of alleged misconduct, case work on disciplinary actions, providing logistic support on disciplinary hearings and serving as the resource center on precedent disciplinary cases. Based upon the initial judgment, both formal disciplinary proceedings and informal disciplinary actions, including official warning, in either verbal or written form, would be issued to the alleged civil servants. Also, the process of disciplinary actions is checked and monitored by several government departments and watchdogs; the

Department of Justice will be consulted at various stages to ensure the disciplinary proceedings are properly conducted; the Public Service Commission will be consulted on the level of punishment on every case; and for the cases of corruption, such as the allegation on "unauthorized acceptance of advantages/entertainment from persons with official dealings," and "use of official information for personal gain," the Independent Commission Against Corruptions (ICAC) will recommend the cases for disciplinary or administrative actions according to the "Prevention of Bribery Ordinance" and the norm of "Assets control disproportionate to the official income."

Compared to misconduct behaviors, the mechanisms to handle sub-standard performers in civil service is focusing more on "rehabilitation" rather than punishment. In practice, an officer who scores the fourth-level overall rating (i.e., "moderate") will be closely monitored by the working department or executive agency; under-performers will be counseled and offered assistance to bring their performance up to the expected level. If the problem persists, under-performers can be forced to retire according to Section 12 of the Public Service (Administration) Order; the Chief Executive can require persistent sub-standard performers to retire in the public interest with the disclose grounds from the relevant inquiry or proceedings. However, dismissal cases, due to misconducts, are rare, and forced retirement of sub-standard performers is particularly very minimal, the disciplinary system in Civil Service emphasizes to ensure the rights of the alleged civil servant to be well informed with reasons of disciplinary actions and the rights to question evidence and witness. As such the disciplinary proceeding is not efficient to impose immediate sanction and it usually takes a long processing time up to two years.

Training

The Civil Service Training Institute and Programs

On-the-job training is emphasized in the civil service, particularly among the "generalist" grades including the "Administrative Officer" and "Executive Officer." The direct workplace supervisor is responsible to guide the subordinates to learning through practice in acquiring the expertise, skills, and knowledge to perform the job duties. On top of this, the Civil Service Bureau determines the overall training and development policy framework for the civil service and renders support toward individual bureaus and departments to run their own vocational program or training activities to equip their staff with updated job-specific skills and knowledge. While the power of selecting and approving training applications is delegated to individual bureaus and departments, the Civil Service Training and Development Institute (CSTDI) under the CSB is responsible to design and coordinate different training and development programs designed to enhance performance and to support the core values and functions of the civil service. Meanwhile, four core areas are identified to cater the common training needs of all civil servants, they are "senior executive development," "national studies programmes," "human resource management consultancy service," and "promotion of a continuous learning culture."

First, "Senior executive development" focuses to enhance the capabilities of officers at the managerial level to sharpen their managerial and communication skills through various leadership development programs, thematic workshops and seminars, and the Secretariat Attachment Scheme in local or overseas context. Second, "National studies programmes" offer civil servant comprehensive understanding on the Mainland-Hong Kong relation under "One Country Two System." It also aims to familiarize civil servants with the mega-trends of political, socioeconomic development in Mainland China and elaborate on the latest national policies that may potentially have impacts on Hong Kong. The CSTDI collaborates with reputable institutes in Mainland, including Tsinghua University, Peking University, Zhejiang University, Nanjing University, Wuhan University, Jinan University, Sun Yat-sen University, Foreign Affairs University, the Chinese Academy of Governance, etc., to organize a wide range of short courses, thematic studies, and staff exchange programs. The CSTDI also invites scholars and relevant experts to organize regular local program on national affairs and the Basic Law. Third, the CSTDI also provides consultancy service to government departments and executive agencies for improving their competences in human resource management, and it also disseminates best practices in human resource development in the areas of training needs analysis, learning strategies, development of competency profiles, performance management systems, etc. Finally, CSTDI also maintains a comprehensive e-learning platform called "Cyber Learning Centre Plus" (CLCP); it offers a wide range of diversified learning resources, training information, and reference materials for continuous self-learning of civil servants.

Comparing the Singaporean civil service where it emphasizes centralized, formal, and regular training for civil servants at entry-level with updated skills and cutting-edge knowledge in a systematic manner, there is clearly a gap to fulfill in Hong Kong. A new Civil Service College aimed to enhance training for civil servants to ensure "the full and accurate implementation of the one country, two systems' principle", was established in December 2021.

Senior Civil Service (Senior Management)

"Senior Civil Service" in Hong Kong

There is no officially defined "senior civil service" in the Hong Kong Government. Hierarchically, the civil servants in "directorate" level remunerated under the "Directorate Pay Scale D1 to D8" (or equivalent, with D8 being the highest rank) could be identified as senior civil servants as they are usually the top-ranked officers who occupy key leadership positions in government bureaus or executive departments.

A majority of the "directorate" officers are the senior officers in departmental grades who are promoted to its top rank, that is, the principal officers. They are appointed at the entry level and incrementally promoted through seniority and screened by performance appraisal. Furthermore, a significant proportion of officers in the directorate level are from the "Administrative officer" grade, who assume a formal role with authority in shaping the policymaking process and coordinating policy implementation across departments and executive agencies. The Administrative Service is a small elite cadre (724 in the year 2018) of multiskilled professional administrators who play a key role in the Government of the Hong Kong Special Administrative Region; they "monopolize" all policymaking posts in the government and many top posts in executive departments (adding the relevant government organization chart).

Administrative officers are generalist grade recruited and managed directly by the Civil Service Bureau. Like most of the professional grades, they are initially appointed with three years probational period, then subsequently considered for appointment on the prevailing permanent terms. However, as a generalist grade, members of the Administrative Service are not staying in the same department throughout their career, they are posted by the Civil Service Bureau around a wide variety of posts laterally in different bureaus and departments at a regular interval, usually in two to three years; they are mainly deployed on the coordination and formulation of Government policies and programs, overseeing their implementation and controlling the resources involved. Through regular post rotation, it cultivates a board policy vision with managerial experiences for administrative officer and prepares them to take up the higher supervisory role in the policy bureau. Outstanding administrative officers who demonstrate leadership potential will be promoted by the Civil Service Bureau across the directorate levels up to the top job of "permanent secretary" of the policy bureau. In fact, top administrative officers were serving policy secretaries as de facto policymakers before the introduction of political appointment system in 2002. Nowadays, the "permanent secretary" is still playing a prominent role in advising politically appointed policy secretaries and assisting the formulation of government public policy.

In practice, the administrative grade is also the major source of the policy cabinet under the political appointment system because of their privilege with extensive experiences in government policy and management; more than a half of bureau secretaries across the government since 2002 were ex-civil servants, and most of them are former senior administrative officers. Under the political appointment system, even the administrative officers are obligated to follow the policy direction set by politically appointed policy secretary; however, they are chosen and dismissed neither by the Chief Executive nor the policy secretary of bureau. In principle, the Civil Service Bureau evaluates the performance of administrative officers independently and decides the lateral posting or promotion for the administrative officers, however, as the Secretary of Civil Service is appointed by the Chief Executive, the decisions of civil service management may also be affected by the preference of the Chief Executive. In other words, the civil service system has been gradually politicized in the sense that the civil servants may show political loyalty and obedience to the political appointees, even at the risk of violating commands from their immediate civil service supervisors, in order to fast-track their own careers: especially if they are also interested in political appointments in the future.

In fact, since the introduction of political appointment system in 2002, many senior administrative officers in the directorate level were subsequently appointed by the new administration as the policy secretary.

Useful sources and websites

Hong Kong Yearbook 2021. www.yearbook.gov.hk/2021/en/
Hong Kong Government Website: www.gov.hk/en/residents/
The Civil Service Bureau: www.csb.gov.hk/eindex.html
Hong Kong Fact Sheets: www.gov.hk/en/about/abouthk/factsheets/

References

Burns, J. (2004) 'Administrative reform in a changing political environment: The case of Hong Kong', *Public Administration and Development*, 14: 241–52.

Cheng, C. Y. (2004) 'The quest for good governance: Hong Kong's principal officials accountability system', *China: An International Journal*, 1(2): 249–72.

Cheung, A. B. L. (2004) 'Strong executive, weak policy capacity: The changing environment of policy-making in Hong Kong', *Asian Journal of Political Science*, 12(1): 1–30.

Cheung, A. B. L. (2007) 'Executive-led governance or executive power 'hollowed-out': The political quagmire of Hong Kong', *Asian Journal of Political Science*, 15(1): 17–38.

Common, R. (2005) 'Administrative changes in the Asia-Pacific: Applying the political nexus triad', *International Public Management Journal*, 7(3): 347–64.

HAB (Home Affairs Bureau) (2003) 'Review of the role and functions of public sector advisory and statutory bodies', *LC Paper*, No. CB(2)1713/02–03(01), Hong Kong: Home Affairs Bureau.

HAB (Home Affairs Bureau) (2004) 'Review of advisory and statutory bodies Hong Kong', available at: www.legco.gov.hk/yr03-04/english/panels/ha/papers/ha0213cb2-1263-03e.pdf (accessed 25 July 2014).

Lau, S. K. (1982) *Society and Politics in Hong Kong*, Hong Kong: The Chinese University Press.

Lee, E. W. Y. (1999) 'Governing post-colonial Hong Kong: Institutional incongruity, governance crisis, and authoritarianism', *Asian Survey*, 39(6): 940–59.

Legislative Council Panel on Public Service (2018, January 15) 'Public service non-civil service contract staff', available at:
https://www.csb.gov.hk/english/info/files/common/Panel_Paper_Non_Civil_Service_Contract_Staff_20180115_e.pdf

Loh, C. and Cullen, R. (2005) 'Political reform in Hong Kong: The principal officials accountability system', *Journal of Contemporary China*, 14: 153–76.

Miners, N. (2000) *The Government and Politics of Hong Kong*, Hong Kong: Hong Kong University Press.

Painter, M. (2005) 'Transforming the administrative state: Reform in Hong Kong and the future of the developmental state', *Public Administration Review*, 65(3): 335–46.

Scott, I. (2000, January) 'The disarticulation of Hong Kong's post-handover Political System', *The China Journal*, 43: 29–53.

Scott, I. (2006) 'The government and statutory bodies in Hong Kong: Centralization and autonomy', *Public Organization Review*, 6: 185–202.

So, A. (2002) 'Social protests, legitimacy crisis, and the impetus towards soft authoritarianism in the Hong Kong SAR', in S. K. Lau (ed) *The First Tung Chee-hwa Administration: The First Five Years of the Hong Kong Special Administrative Region* (pp. 399–418), Hong Kong: The Chinese University Press.

Sing, M. (2001) 'The problem of legitimacy for the post-handover Hong Kong government', *International Journal of Public Administration*, 24(9): 847–67.

Wong, W. (2003) 'From a British-style administrative state to a Chinese-style political state: Civil service reforms in Hong Kong after the transfer of sovereignty', in *Working Paper, Center for Northeast Asian Policy Studies (CNAPS), Brookings Institution*, Washington, DC: Brookings Institution.

Wong, W. (2009) 'The civil service', in W. Lam, P. L. Lui and W. Wong (eds) *Contemporary Hong Kong Government and Politics*, Expanded 2nd edn, Hong Kong: Hong Kong University Press.

Wong, W. (2013) 'The search for a model of public administration reform in Hong Kong: Weberian bureaucracy, new public management or something Else?' *Public Administration and Development*, 33(4): 297–310.

Wong, W. and Xiao, H. (2018) 'Twenty years of Hong Kong and Macao under Chinese rule: Their absorption under "one country, two systems" (with)', *Public Money and Management*, 38(6): 411–18.

6

VIETNAM

Ngo Thanh Can

Context and Overview: The Civil Service in Vietnam

Vietnam has had four types of civil service systems since more than 100 years ago. The first is civil service of Vietnam Feudal system, the second is civil service of French colonial system, the third is civil service of the South of Viet Nam during the Vietnam war, and the fourth is the current civil service system. The civil service deals with state activities and tasks and manages civil servants to carry out the state activities and tasks.

Vietnam public administration machinery. According to the Constitution of 2013, the Vietnamese political system consists of three parts: the Vietnam communist party, State, and Sociopolitical associations. The communist party is the leadership of the State and society. Across all organizations, agencies, and bureaus there is a communist party unit, responsible for making sure the organization goes in the right direction to achieve communist visions and goals.

The sociopolitical associations consist of six associations: Vietnam Front Fatherland Association, Vietnam Trade Unions, Vietnam Youth Unions, Vietnam Women Unions, Vietnam Farmer Association, and Vietnam Ex-soldier Association.

The Vietnam State has three branches: legislative, executive, and judicial branches. For the legislative bodies, there are four levels: National Assembly, Provincial People's Council, District People's Council, and Commune People's Council. For the judicial bodies, there are three levels: The Super People's court, Provincial People's court, and District People's court. For the executive bodies, there are four levels: the central, provincial, district, and commune levels. At the central level, there are organizations and agencies as follows: The Government, Ministries (18), Ministerial equivalents (4), and Under government agencies (8).

DOI: 10.4324/9781003326496-8

There are three levels at local: Provincial People's Committee with 20 departments, District People's Committee with 12 Divisions, and Commune People's Committee. There are 63 provinces (five central cities and 58 provinces), 713 districts (rural districts, urban districts, and cities in the province), and 11,162 communes. In 2021, it was restructured to reduce eight districts and 557 communes. There are 708 districts and 10,605 communes.

Vietnam public administration institutional. There are several laws dealing with civil service area, such as the Constitution of 2013, the Law on Local Government of 2015, the Law on Legal Documents Issue of 2015, the Law of Anti-corruption of 2018, the Law of Cadres and Civil Servants of 2008, and the Law of Public Servants of 2010.

In the present, there are some main principles for state management of civil service to make sure state agencies are running well as below:

> To ensure the leadership of Party and Management of State; To ensure the principle of democracy-concentrate, individual responsibility and clear decentralize; To consider the combination of job title, position, and staff size in order for the management of civil servants; To employ, evaluate, classify civil servants base on political quality, moral and performant competence; To carry out gender equality and to ensure equality, fairness, transparency, democracy.[1]

Vietnam civil servants. There are some concepts of persons who work for the State and government in the Vietnam civil service. It needs to clarify some definitions, such as cadre, civil servant, and public servant.

Cadres are elected to keep their position in the party organizations, State machinery, and sociopolitical associations, for example, the President, ministers, chairperson of People's Council, and chairperson of People's Committee.

Civil servants work for party organizations, State machinery, and sociopolitical associations, for example, Vice-Minister, Director of the department in a ministry, and a staff working for District People's Committee.

Public servants work for public schools, public universities, public hospitals, and research institutes, such as teachers, lecturers, medicine doctors, and researchers.

Vietnam's civil servants are divided into five grades: 1. Senior expert grade, group A; 2. Principal expert grade, group B; 3. Expert grade, group C; 4. Clerk, Technical grade; and 5. Worker grade, group D. Each grade has main criteria: training qualification (political theory and state management), working experience, performance competence, and foreign language skills (Ngo 2018, p. 67)

Vietnam civil service is generally improving in order to better meet the requirements of civil service, enabling it to focus on serving people and enterprises. Over the past 20 years, Vietnam has implemented two Master programs on public administration reform (PAR). The first is the PAR Master Programme phase 2001–2010, and the second is the PAR Master Programme phase 2011–2020. Vietnam's central government, local government, and public officials put a lot of effort and resources into achieving the PAR goals and objectives. The successes and results of the implementation of the PAR plans were to support the legal framework for innovation, get a better economy, improve the human resource, reduce the government structure, and make it better in action.

Various PAR projects have led to successes such as the institutional reform project, Government machinery reform project, improving quality of public officials' projects, public financial reform projects, and so on. In spite of this, there were some problems, difficulties, weaknesses, and shortcomings in the implementation of the PAR. Those problems, difficulties, weaknesses, and shortcomings had caused from some reasons, such as dissatisfaction of people in the PAR, not much support for enterprises' business, and other resistances. So, looking at the results of PAR implementation, it can be said, some goals of PAR were not successful as desired as the Government and the people expected (Ngo 2013).

For the next coming years, the PAR Master Programme phase 2011–2020 carried out much better than the previous one. One of the good experiences was the lesson learned from last PAR MP 2001–2010. The Vietnam Government, local government, and public officials tried their best to carry out PAR MP 2011–2020 successfully with the big successes of the institutional reform project, the administrative procedure reform, the government machinery reform, the public finance reform project, the improvement of public officials' quality project, and the public administration system modernization project. In 2021, the Vietnam government issued the PAR MP 2021–2030 with six contents: the institutional reform, the administrative procedure reform, the government machinery reform, the public finance reform, the civil service reform, and the e-government and digital government development.

Nowadays, Vietnam's civil service reform reaches significant objectives: "Building a civil service with professional, responsible, transparency, flexible and effective." At the same time, with the transition of HRM from career system to job system, from traditional public administration to new public management, the Vietnam government is carrying out anticorruption policies.

Civil Service System

Central HRM Unit

General Information on HRM Unit

Vietnam is a unique state, not a federation state, and the Ministry of Home Affairs (MOHA) is a central ministry in charge of human resource management at the national government level. The MOHA is one of the 22 ministries and ministerial-level agencies.

The structure of the national government is as follows:

TABLE 6.1 Structure of the national government

The Primary Minister
Vice-Primary Ministers

1. Ministry of National Defense
2. Ministry of Public Security
3. Ministry of Foreign Affairs
4. Ministry of Justice
5. Ministry of Finance
6. Ministry of Transportation
7. Ministry of Construction
8. Ministry of Education and Training
9. Ministry of Agriculture and Rural Development
10. Ministry of Industry and Trade
11. Ministry of Planning and Investment
12. Ministry of Health
13. Ministry of Science and Technology
14. Ministry of Natural Resources and Environment
15. Ministry of Information and Communications
16. Ministry of Home Affairs
17. Ministry of Labor, War Invalids and Social Affairs
18. Ministry of Culture, Sport and Tourism
19. *Government Office*
20. *Government Inspectorate*
21. *State Bank of Vietnam*
22. *Commission on Ethnic Minority Affairs*

Source: https://chinhphu.vn/cac-bo-co-quan-ngang-bo-co-quan-thuoc-chinh-phu

The current numbers of civil servants and public servants are as below:

TABLE 6.2 Numbers of civil servants and public servants

Number of civil servants	*(person)*
Civil servants from district level and up, 2020.	250,774
Cadres, civil servants at commune level, 2020	234,617
Public servants, 2020	1,671,635

Source: The Government Report No. 128/BC-CP, April, 19.202,1 on Review, evaluation of PAR Master Programme in period 2011–2020.

The number of civil servants in 2021[2] in the public administration system (not including of Ministry of National Defense and Ministry of Public Security) is 249,650 in total; 106,836 in Ministries and Ministerial Equivalents; 140,508 in local authorities at provincial and district levels; 1,068 in representative agencies in abroad; and 552 in reservation in detail.

Organization Chart of Ministry of Home Affairs – MOHA

The Ministry of Home Affairs is responsible for helping the government manage the areas dealing with civil services, such as civil servants, government structure, human resource management, religious affairs, and state archives. There are 13 departments, three agencies, two training institutions, a research institute, and the

Journal and the Office in the MOHA. The structure of MOHA is the diagram given below:

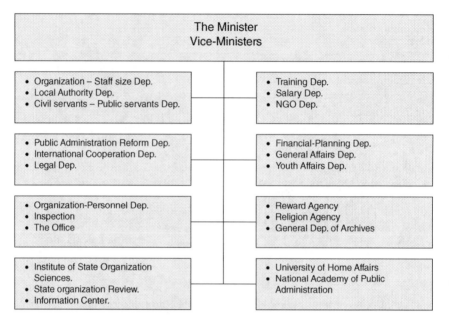

FIGURE 6.1 The structure of the Ministry of Home Affairs

Source: www.moha.gov.vn/gioi-thieu/co-cau-to-chuc.html

Tasks and Functions of the MOHA

The MOHA assists the government in guiding, examining, and implementing regulations of public employee administration. Other ministries have functions in managing employees in their scope.

The government unifies the management of cadres and civil servants in the state agencies from the central to the local level; builds and trains a contingent of state officials and public servants being clean, qualified, capable, and loyal to the State; decides and directs the implementation of policies for recruitment, training, utilization of employees, wages, commendation, discipline, and retirement; and prescribes and directs the implementation of specific policies for cadres of commune level.

The MOHA is responsible[3] for the organizational structure of state administration; local government organizations, management of administrative boundaries; officials, public servants, and state employees; NGOs; state archives and state administration of public services; training for civil servants; state management of religious affairs; and state management of youth affairs. In the field of public personnel administration, the MOHA has the following functions.

(1) The MOHA guides and supervises the policy implementation of cadres and civil servants who hold leading and managerial positions of ministries,

ministerial-level agencies, and government agencies, aggregates information and reports to the Prime Minister on how leading and managerial cadres and civil servants within the authority of the Prime Minister implement government policies and plans, and guides and supervises the implementation of planning and building program on cadres and civil servants.

(2) The MOHA guides and supervises the implementation of the legal provisions of the Government and the Prime Minister on recruitment, utilization of workforce, managing working position, rank appointments, transferring and promotion, change titles of career positions, evaluation, appointment, reappointment, the resignation, dismissal, discipline, termination, retirement, ethics, cultural communication of cadres and civil servants.

(3) The MOHA guides and supervises the implementation of the provisions of the Government on the titles and criteria of cadres and public servants holding leading deputy ministers and ministries positions and equal. It regulates ranks and codes of civil servant ranks, issues, guides, and supervises the implementation of regulations of professional standards of civil servants and guides the structure of civil servants and portfolios civil servants.

(4) The MOHA organizes rank promotion competitions from the specialist class and equivalent to the principal-specialist or equivalent rank; from the principal specialist rank or equivalent to the senior specialist or equivalent rank. It also builds a database of public employees.

(5) The MOHA guides and supervises the implementation of training programs and training plans for public employees. It also guides regulations of the government in organizing training institutes of ministries and ministerial-level agencies.

(6) The MOHA builds human resources planning in the field of Home Affairs and to guide and supervise implementing the regulations of the Government and Prime Minister on salary policies and system including minimum salary, salary scale, salary schedules, and allowances.

Ministries and ministerial-level agencies have power in public employee administration in the scope of decentralization, and they organize examinations to recruit civil servants. Ministries and ministerial-level governments can implement other contents such as utilization, transfer, training, and promotion. However, public employees in other ministries and ministerial-level governments must take examinations organized by the MOHA for promotion, for example, from principal specialists to senior specialists.

Recruitment

Civil servant recruitment is followed by *The Government Decree No. 138/2020/ NĐ-CP, on 27 November 2020 on recruitment, usage and management of civil servants* and *The Government Decree No. 115/2020/NĐ-CP, on 25 September 2020 on recruitment, usage and management of civil servants, public servants.*

104 Ngo Thanh Can

Process of Recruitment Civil Servants

Recruitment of civil servants is a multiple-stage process conducted in an inter-related sequential manner to ensure objectivity, fairness, and accuracy. According to the Law on Cadres and Civil Servants 2008 and by-laws instructing recruitment implementation, the recruitment process comprises the following steps: (1) Determining recruitment demand based on quantity and criteria of each recruitment position; (2) Establishing recruitment regulations, and then, announcing recruitment demand including information on quantity, criteria of each recruitment position, time, and place to submit portfolios of applicants. Then following up to collect and review registration portfolios; (3) Organizing competitive and/or non-competitive examinations; or in some cases, recruiting by consideration: for those who commit to work for five years in remote, mountainous, and difficult areas; (4) Consolidating examination results and announcing results of recruitments, complaint solving or verification (if required), then, issuing recruitment decision; (5) people who have recruited works on probation, then after reviewing and evaluating their performance, they will be appointed as civil servants.

Applicants to civil service recruitment examinations have to take four mandatory subjects: general knowledge test, professional test, computer skills test, and foreign language test. In the general knowledge test, applicants must take a writing test on political and machinery apparatus of the Communist Party of Vietnam, the State, sociopolitical organizations; state administrative management; guiding principles, directions and policies of the party, and legislation of the State on the recruiting field or sector.

In the professional test, applicants take two tests: one writing test and one multiple-choice test about the working major required by the job position. For the position requiring foreign language or information technology to be the primary profession, the professional test will be about foreign language or information technology. The determination of formats and contents of professional tests in the case where foreign language or information technology is required as the working major is vested in the jurisdiction of the head of the recruiting agency, and the appropriateness of formats and contents must be ensured.

In the foreign language test, applicants take a written test or an interview in one language among English, Russian, French, German or Chinese, or other foreign languages under the job position requirement determined by the head of recruiting agency. In case that job positions require the use of the language of an ethnic minority, the ethnic minority language test replaces the foreign language test. The determination of the format and contents of ethnic minority language tests is vested in the jurisdiction of the head of the recruiting agency.

In the computer skills test, applicants take an on-computer practicing test or a multiple-choice test relevant to the requirements of job positions, and the head of the recruiting agency determines the test format and contents.

Applicants for a specific group of civil service should take two rounds of examinations. Three subjects are tested in the first round: general knowledge test with

60 items (60 minutes); foreign language test with 30 items (30 minutes); computer skills (Office IT) test with 30 items (30 minutes). Applicants who pass the first round will take the second-round examination: oral examination (30 minutes) or written examination (180 minutes).

Recruitment Criteria and Selection Procedures

In recruitment announcement, there are recruitment criteria as follows: Article 36 of Law on Cadre and Civil servants, 2008: "*Applicant who has all conditions as follows, can apply for recruitment without difference in nationality, gender, social classes, religion:*

a) *A Vietnamese Citizen;*
b) *18-year-old and up;*
c) *Application form, CV;*
d) *Certificates and Degrees that meet with the requirement of the vacancy job, position;*
e) *Good political characters and morals;*
f) *Good health for performance;*
g) *Other conditions for the vacant job.*"

Generally, there are some criteria for civil servant grades that need recruitment as below: requirements of competence such as knowledge, skills, attitude, and job qualification. There are some criteria for civil servants: political theory certificate; state management certificate; professional qualification; foreign language certificate; and IT, computer skill certificate.

Applicants who pass the recruitment exams need to be on probation in the office. The time of probation[4] is as below: 12 months for civil servant C and six months for civil servant D.

For a political appointment, Cadres are selected by-elections. Voters elect members of the National Assembly and National Assembly elect members of the government. For provincial levels, members of the people council are elected by people, voters. And members of the people committee are elected by the people council, as seen in the below diagram.

Based on recruitment conditions of the law and requirements of vacant jobs, the head of the management agency can consider accepting applicants without recruitment exams in some particular cases as follows: applicants who receive a bachelor's degree from university as a number one rank student (the first one); applicants who get bachelor's degree and a postgraduate degree from universities abroad with excellent ranks; applicants have a bachelor's degree with at least five years of working experience in the same working area of vacant job. In this case, there are two rounds for recruitment. In the first round, agencies check, review, and match all conditions and criteria of applicants to meet with all requirements of the vacant job. Applicants pass the first round if everything is fine. In the second round, applicants should take an oral exam to check their competence.

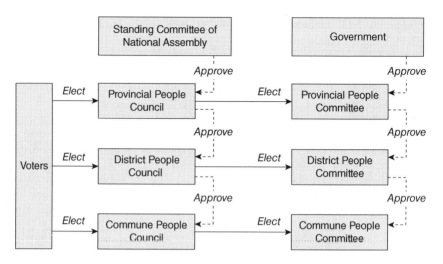

FIGURE 6.2 The local administrative organizational levels

Source: Ngo, T. C. (2016) 'The administrative organization', *Theory and Practice*: 419.

In recruiting leaders or managers, firstly, agencies must get permission from the management civil servant authority. Secondly, applicants who meet with requirements of the position have an oral exam and present a proposal to the exam council.

There are some problems with attracting talented people to public organizations. First, the salary of civil servants is not high. According to the Ministry of Home Affairs, the basic salary of public officials is VND 1.49 million (US$64) per month. This amount is much less than Vietnam's minimum monthly salary that ranged from VND 2.92 million (US$125) to 4.18 million (US$179) (Kiet 2020). Second, working conditions in public organizations, sometimes, are not suitable to either attract or retain highly qualified candidates.

Civil Service Classification and Status

Civil Service Classification in Terms of Functional Level and Grade

According to the Law on Cadres and Civil Servants 2008 and Law on Public servants 2010, the public personnel in Vietnam is grouped into cadres, civil servants, public servants, and commune cadres and commune civil servants.

Cadres are elected or assigned to a fixed-term position while civil servants work on a permanent basis. Cadres are elected officials (leaders of the Communist Party, National Assembly, ministers, chairman of People's Committees at provinces, districts, and communes). Cadres and civil servants can work for the party, sociopolitical organizations, and administrative agencies.

Civil Servants are officials in state organizations – National Assembly, The President Office, People's Court, People's Procuracy and Government (Deputy minister and below down to District level), party and social organizations (Fatherland front, Youth Union, Women Union, Farmer Union, and Ex-Soldier Union), police and military units, and managers of SOEs. Based on their appointed ranks, civil servants are classified into: SE – Senior expert grade; PE – Principle expert grade; E – Expert grade; T – Technician/clerical staff grade; and W – Worker and cleaner. Civil servants are also categorized into different groups.

i)   Class A, including those appointed to the senior-specialist or equivalent rank;
ii) Class B, including those appointed to the principal-specialist or equivalent rank;
iii) Class C, including those appointed to the Specialist or equivalent rank;
iv) Class D, including those appointed to the technician or equivalent rank or employee rank.

Based on working positions, civil servants are classified into: (i) civil servants holding leading or managerial posts; ii) civil servants not holding leading or managerial posts.

Public Servants are officials in public service such as universities, schools, hospitals, cultural centers, etc.

Commune Civil Servants are heads of police units and military units, statisticians, land administrators, accountants, legal officers, and social-cultural officers. For the commune police, there has been a new policy since 2018. All communes have three official policemen – a head of the police unit, a deputy head of the police unit, and one police.

Civil Servants' Employment Status or Employment Condition (e.g., Permanent/Lifelong Employment vs. Fixed-Term/ Temporary Employment, and Statutory Employment vs. Contractual Employment)

Civil servants must meet with the criteria in Decision No. 414/TCCP-VC, 29/6/1993, issued by the Government Commission on Organization and Personnel (Ministry of Home Affairs now). Civil servants' criteria include tasks, knowledge, competence and education, training requirements, such as educational qualification, and state management training certificate. The standards for cadres and managers at all levels are stipulated in Party Regulation No. 89 –QD/TW, 04/8/2017 on the standard framework for leaders and managers. The standard framework for leaders and managers at all levels includes 1. Political ideas; 2. Moral, lifestyle, organization consciousness; and 3. Education qualifications: professional qualification, political theory qualification, state management qualification, IT qualification, and foreign languages.

Cadres, civil servants, and public servants have to meet with the following criteria: political theory certificate; state management certificate; professional qualifications; foreign language certificate; IT, computer skill certificate.

108 Ngo Thanh Can

In general, cadres are in the positions for five years (the term of office). Civil servants are permanent employees, and it is generally lifelong employment. Public servants are contractual employees with two kinds of contracts. The first is a fixed-term contract. Newcomers (after recruitment) have two times fixed-term contracts for one year. Then, public servants have an unfixed-term contract. They can work for schools, universities, hospitals, etc., as long as they can and as long as their institution wants their work.

Information on Job Security for Civil Servants

The Law on Cadre and Civil Servants 2008 provides several civil servants' rights, such as: "making sure all conditions for performance of the tasks: 1. Giving authority (is empowered) in performance of tasks, 2. Making sure all conditions for performance of tasks, 3. Providing all information dealing with their tasks and their authority, 4. Being trained for strengthening their competence, 5. Being protected by the law in the performance of the tasks."[5]

By the law, cadres and civil servants have salaries and allowance from the State. Civil servants in remote areas, mountainous areas, and in some special jobs have a priority policy for the allowance and salary. When cadres and civil servants have extra works, they have an allowance for extra working time. They can have money for extra work, nighttime work, business out of office, and others by regulations. They have free time: holidays, national days, and new year holidays.

Cadres and civil servants are guaranteed training, learning, science study, business, and social activities. They have a priority policy on housing, transportation, social insurance, and health insurance. Civil servants or cadres who get injured or die while performing their duties are entitled to priority benefits to the likes of war-invalids or soldiers, patriotic-war-dead.

Openness of Posts/Positions

Posts Open to Recruitment

All posts are open to internal and external (outside of the civil service) candidates in general, but some special posts that need some professional skills and knowledge, like some posts in international affairs or inspection, are limited to applicants who have professional expertise.

For the cadres, generally, most of the applicants on the list for voting are internal nominees. Some posts are rotation bases from other administrative levels, such as people from the center to provinces, provinces to districts, or district levels to communes.

For the civil servant recruitment in local governments, most applicants are residents in the local area with internal recruitment. However, provinces can have posts that are open to internal and external applicants currently.

Mobility Within the Civil Service (Among Central Departments/ Ministries) and External Mobility (Outside of the Civil Service)

In Vietnam, by the law, for mobility within the civil service, there are transfer, appointment, rotation, and secondment among central departments and ministries, and among central ministries, and local authorities.

Commune civil servants could move within only commune levels. Commune civil servants must take exams for recruitment for entry into district levels.

For external mobility in leadership positions, there are transfer and rotation of the leaders and managers between central ministries, local authorities, and state enterprises. The government has policies for transfer, rotation, and secondment of leaders and managers before their appointment to higher positions with certain periods (three to five years and more) of transfer, rotation, and secondment time.

Most mobility cases are in civil service, for example, from party units to government agencies, from the government to the party units, or sometimes, mobility within party units, the government, and political – socio associations. Some external mobility cases are mobility between party units, the government, and state-owned enterprises.

Performance Assessment and Promotion

Performance Assessment

Based on evaluation results, public employees are put into the four following types[6]:

i) Excellent accomplishment of tasks (Excellence performance)
ii) Good accomplishment of tasks (Good performance)
iii) Accomplishment of tasks with limited capability (Task's Completion, but limited competence)
iv) Non-accomplishment of tasks (No completion of the task).

For civil servant performance evaluation, there are six criteria for performance assessment: 1. Observance/obey to the guideline and policies of the Party and laws; 2. Political qualities, ethics, lifestyle and working style, and manners; 3. Specialized or professional capabilities and qualifications; 4. Task performance progress and results; 5. Sense of responsibility and collaboration in work; and 6. Attitude in serving the people.

If civil servants hold leading and managerial positions, besides the above criteria, they shall be evaluated based on the following:

1. Results of operation of agencies, organizations, or units they are assigned to lead and manage;
2. Leading and managerial capabilities; and
3. The capability of mobilizing and uniting civil servants.

110 Ngo Thanh Can

Annual evaluations on civil servants are conducted before the appointment, planning, transferring, training, and at the end of rotation or secondment period.

The evaluation results of civil servants shall be filed in their personnel records and notified to the evaluated civil servants. Civil servants who accomplish their tasks for two consecutive years with limited capability or who accomplish their tasks with limited capability in a year and fail to accomplish their tasks in the subsequent year may be assigned to other jobs. Relevant authorities, organizations, or units will not allow any civil servant who has failed to accomplish tasks for two consecutive years.

The appraisal process of civil servants is as follows:[7]

Step 1: Self-evaluation by a written report of civil assessment;
Step 2: Civil servants present a self-evaluation report in an all-staff meeting. Each staff can give comments on civil servant's performance, and a clerk takes minutes;
Step 3: Standing members of cell communist party give comments on civil servant's performance;
Step 4: Based on all comments of the staff meeting, leaders and managers decide to give comments on each civil servant's performance assessment and decide to classify;
Step 5: Leaders and managers inform the results of evaluation's civil servants to civil servants.

The process of appraisal for leaders and managers is as follows:

Step 1: Self-evaluation by a written report of civil assessment;
Step 2: Leaders and managers present a self-evaluation report in an all-staff meeting.
Each person in the meeting can give comments on the leader's performance, and a clerk takes minutes;
Step 3: Standing members of cell communist party have a meet and give comments on leader's performance;
Step 4: Based on all the comments in the party meeting, a higher authority decides to give comments on the leader's performance assessment and decides to classify;
Step 5: Leaders and managers inform the results of evaluation's leaders and managers.

In fact, there are some problems with the evaluation of civil servants. In the staff meeting, staff's comments on one person usually depend on their behaviors rather than their performance; staff's comments come from their relationship, not from civil servant's competence or results of performance. In the civil servant evaluation, civil servants are ranked as the excellent accomplishment of tasks (Excellence performance) that limited number up to 20%. So, if the number of civil servants ranked as Excellence performance is more than 20%, they are selected by voting for a number of 20% only. That problem can reduce the civil servants' work motivation.

Rewards, Commendations, and Disciplines

Civil servants who perform well receive rewards depending on the levels of the results of performance. Incentive methods used for good performance are as follows:

- Certificate of satisfactory progress from the Prime Minister;
- Certificate of satisfactory progress from Ministers, Certificate of satisfactory progress from Chairman of Provincial Committee;
- Commemoration of the leader of the agency or institution;
- Salary increase;
- Consideration of promotion.

Sanction methods that are taken in case of poor performance are as follows:

- Giving reprimands
- Strong warnings on bad performance
- Decreasing salary down
- Demotion
- Dismissal of position.

(By the Law on Cadres and Civil servants 2008, Government Decree No. 56/ND-CP 2016)
The cadres and civil servants who have two years with "Non-accomplishment of tasks" of performance evaluation can be dismissed from civil service. For the cadres, if they have problems with performance, such as not good health for performance, not good competence for performance, or not meeting with task's requirements, they can get permission for dismissal and discharge from the job.

Career Advancement

There are some career advancements done through open competition (competition open to external and internal applicants): leaders of department levels (in ministries and provincial committees), leaders of project management units, advisors, and consultants at high levels.

i) *Career advancements have been done by the recruitment council which sets up by ministers or chairpersons of the provincial People Committee.* First, applicants have to present their development proposals at the recruitment council meetings as part of the recruitment process of career advancement. Secondly, the council members give comments and decisions for pass or no-pass. For example,

112 Ngo Thanh Can

for some essential jobs like directors or deputy directors of departments in ministries or province levels, nominees take examinations administered by the recruitment council.

ii) *Career advancement done by election.* First, the authority introduces applicants with an open method to demonstrate that they meet the criteria of the job. Secondly, applicants are selected by voting. For example, some positions like advisors and consultants of National Assembly Units can be elected.

iii) *Career advancement done by appointment by the leader (Prime Minister).* In this case, firstly, applicants are introduced by authority with an open way to show that the applicants meet all criteria of the job. Then second, applicants are appointed by the leader (Prime Minister). For example, some jobs like advisors, consultants of government can be appointed.

Promotion Criteria

There are two types of promotion in the Vietnam civil service system: the first is a promotion from lower to higher positions, and the second is a promotion from lower civil service grade to a higher one.

i) *Promotion criteria to higher positions.* Applicants have to meet the criteria as suitable with vacant positions: political theory certificate; state management certificate; professional qualification; foreign language certificate; IT, computer skill certificate, and their commendation. Applicants who meet requirements of the vacant position could go through the following appointment process.

ii) *Promotion criteria to higher civil servant's grades.* Applicants must meet higher civil servant grade criteria: political theory certificate; state management certificate; professional qualification; foreign language certificate; IT, computer skill certificate, and working years. Applicants who meet the higher civil servant grade criteria could take promotion civil servants grade examinations.

Training

Civil Servant's Training System

Vietnam has a system of training institutes for government employees with different roles. Ho Chi Minh National Academy of Politics and National Academy of Public Administration play leading roles in training mid- and high-ranked public personnel.

The Ho Chi Minh National Academy of Politics is directly managed by the Party Central Committee and the government and puts under the direct and regular leadership and instruction of the Political Bureau and the Secretariat of the Party Central Committee. The Ho Chi Minh National Academy of Politics is a national center for training middle- and high-ranking leaders and managers, and political theory science researchers of the political system. The National Academy of Public Administration (NAPA) is a national training center for mid- and high-ranked civil servants on public administration and state management. The NAPA also implements training programs for some positions from vice-ministers to heads of departments of ministries. Besides two national training centers, each ministry has its training institutes. These institutes train public personnel at the lowest rank and heads of an office of a ministry's department.

Training institutes in ministries for training and development of civil servants are presented as below: Central training institutes are Ho Chi Minh National Academy of Politics (training in Politic Theory) and National Academy of Public Administration (training in State Management). Ministries have training institutes, provinces have training schools, and districts have training centers. The training institute system is as follows:

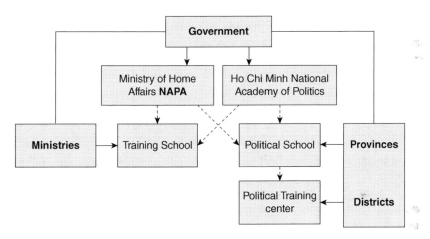

FIGURE 6.3 The training institute system

Source: Ngo T. C. (2014), Training and Development in Public Sector, p. 92.

Training Programs Offered by the Institutions

In Vietnam, training programs are diversified. Firstly, there are training programs for public personnel at different grades of civil servants. These programs include training contents[8] for senior specialists or equivalent ranks; principal specialists or equivalent ranks; specialists or equivalent ranks; and technicians or equivalent ranks or employee ranks. The training periods of these programs are no more than eight weeks.

Secondly, there are training programs based on the criteria of leaders and managers. These training programs include training content for vice ministers and equal; directors of department of ministerial levels and equal; directors of department of provincial levels and equal; and heads of division level and equal. The training periods of these programs are no more than four weeks.

Thirdly, there are training programs to improve professional knowledge and skills for civil servants about two weeks or less.

Training for New Employees

Civil servants receive training when they enter the civil service. In brief, the time for training courses is as follows:

- For the political theory training programs (9 months): middle-level programs; Advanced programs.
- For the training program for CS grade standard (8 weeks): Senior Expert grade; Principal Expert grade, Expert grade, and Technician grade.
- For the training program for leader positions (4 weeks): Vice-minister level; ministerial department director level; provincial department director level; provincial district leader level; and division head level.
- For the training program on professional civil servants (2 weeks).

Senior Civil Service (Senior Management)

In Vietnam's civil service system, there is a defined group of staff in central and local government staff to be senior civil servant grades. Senior civil servants are civil servants who are appointed as a senior civil servant grade.

Senior civil servants are at the following levels: Central level – The Government, ministries, national Assembly, super court, and provincial levels – provincial committee members. Senior civil servants are identified, recruited, appointed, evaluated, and dismissed. To be senior civil servants, they should meet senior civil servant grade criteria. Senior civil servants are appointed by promotion civil servant grade exam with some tests such as a general subject, foreign languages, IT skill, and written proposals. Senior civil servants are evaluated by the performance assessment process as same as other civil servants. The same process dismisses senior civil servants as other civil servants go through if they poorly perform or abuse their power with violence. Senior civil servants contract annually with an agency or institute. Depending on the requirements of their organization, they could extend their contract more than one year.

Notes

1 Law on Cadre and Civil Servants, 2008, Article 5.
2 The Prime Minister Decision No. 1499/QD-TTg, 03/10/2020, on the number of civil servants for 2021.
3 Government Decree No. 34/2017/ND-CP, 03/4/2017, on functions, tasks, structure of Ministry of Home Affairs.
4 Government Decree No. 161/2018/NĐ-CP, on 29 November 2018 on correct, supplement regulations for recruitment, promotion of civil servants, and public servants.
5 Law on cadres, civil servants 2008, Article 11.

6 Law on cadre, civil servant, 2008, article 28 and 58.
7 Government Decree No. 56/2015/ND-CP, 09/6/2015, on evaluation of cadres, civil servants, and public servants.
8 Government Decree No. 101/2017/ND-CP, 01/9/2017 on training of cadres, civil servants, and public servants.

References

Government Decree No. 138/2020/NĐ-CP, on 27 November 2020 on recruitment, usage and management of civil servants.

Government Decree No. 115/2020/NĐ-CP, on 25 September 2020 on recruitment, usage and management of civil servants, public servants.

Kiet, A. (2020, January 9) 'Vietnam to raise salaries for civil servants from July 1', *Hanoi Times*, available at: http://hanoitimes.vn/vietnam-to-raise-salary-and-allowances-for-civil-servants-as-of-july-1-300748.html (accessed 1 October 2021).

Ngo, T. C. (2013) 'Public administration reform in Vietnam: Current situations and solutions', *Scholarly Journal of Business Administration*, 3(5): 110–16, available at: www.scholarly-journals.com/SJBA.

Ngo, T. C. (2014) *Training and Development in Public Sector*, Hanoi: Labor Publish House.

Ngo T. C. (2016) *The Public Administrative Organizations – Theory and Practice*, Hanoi: The Judicial Publishing House.

Ngo, T. C. (2018) *Civil Service and Performance Management*, Hanoi: National Politics Publish House.

PART II

Civil Service Systems With Non-Confucian Traditions

7

INDONESIA

Eko Prasojo, Defny Holidin,
and Fajar Wardani Wijayanti

Introduction

Civil service system in Indonesia and any other emerging democracies and econo-mies appear as a forefront outlet of how the state system works. Its administrative culture underpinning the system remains typical Asian societies which embrace a virtue of the predominantly crucial role of the state in handling public affairs (Touchton 2015). Therefore, the development dynamics of the Indonesian civil service system has fluctuated along with the progress of state reform, which stemmed from the prevalence of social structure and political regimes.

Within the dynamics, Indonesian civil service system had moved from previously being a political instrument of undertaking functions of the state during the Old and New Order Regimes (1959–1965 and 1966–1998, respectively) to recently being an agent of development and reform under democratization (Prasojo 2009). It was President Habibie who had insisted on an initial attempt in the making of neutral civil servants from politics by successfully promulgating the Public Person-nel Law 43/1999. This attempt marks a sharp differentiation from former President Suharto's New Order regime although Habibie had been part of Suharto's ruling party. This differentiation is not to say that the New Order regime had not to embrace neutrality or not made any effort to develop the professionalism of civil servants. The Suharto Administration also did but in different notions. The admin-istration assumed that the government is identical hence a representation of the state. This assumption implies every civil servant is the state apparatus and giving their loyalty solely to the governments is the ultimate manifestation of their dedi-cation to the country. According to this notion, the administration also puts civil servants into a bracket of professionals, namely Golongan Karya (Golkar) which stands for a professional association from the public and private sectors, including cooperative and nonprofit organizations supporting the government agenda. The

DOI: 10.4324/9781003326496-10

problem was the eligibility of Golkar as the only professional association to join political election along with competing merged-political parties. This situation had entrapped the civil service system into being merely a political machine serving the single-majority Golkar as the ruling party for three decades. The latter role of civil servants as the reform and development agent has an implication of civil service reorientation from merely keeping neutral from politics in the aftermath of the New Order dismantlement in 1998 – the so-called Reformasi (the reform) agenda that has not been succeeded though to date – to embracing professionalism toward meritocracy (Holidin 2017).

The State Civil Servant Apparatus (hereinafter referred to as *Aparatur Sipil Negara*/ASN), as the countershaft of the reform in Indonesia, has an important role in the bureaucratic sector. The Road Map of Civil Servant Development in Indonesia shows that the objective in the 1st Phase (2005–2009) is Good Governance; 2nd Phase (2010–2014) is Bureaucratic Reform; 3rd Phase (2015–2019) is Merit System; and 4th Phase (2020–2024) is World Class Government.[1] Indonesia has exerted numerous efforts with the purpose of accelerating civil service reform.

The philosophical basis underpinning the series of bureaucracy reform agenda is a desired effort of meritocracy development in the Indonesian administrative system, especially in terms of human resource management of ASN (Prasojo 2009). Acquiring learning takeaways from the experiences and policy practices of well-established traditions of both Anglo-American and Continental European public administrations, the Government of Indonesia seeks to apply the fittest model beyond the discourse of good governance. The spirit of meritocracy development of administrative system is entrenched in professionalism, which puts emphasis on performance-based management (UNDP 2015; Tanku and Shkelzen 2017). The open career system serves as an avenue toward this orientation. Since the institutionalization of bureaucracy reform agenda in 2010, the Government of Indonesia has been aware of recent and future challenges of various problems in the public sector. Meritocracy development provides modalities to manifest certain degree of adaptability and agility toward dynamic government institutions in the face of those problems. In terms of human resource management of ASN, the government has attempted an iterative process of reform from a mere personnel administration to merit-based human resource management, and it subsequently seeks to enhance this manifestation toward human capital development (Dwiyanto 2011).

Civil Service System

Central HRM Unit

There are several national level institutions in Indonesia bearing the responsibility for human resource management of ASN, as follows:

1. *Kementerian Pendayagunaan Aparatur Negara dan Reformasi Birokrasi* (Kemen-PANRB, literally meaning the Ministry for State Apparatus Empowerment

and Bureaucratic Reform, which might hereinafter be referred to as the Ministry of Administrative Reform for a general yet concise official name of Kemen-PANRB and they may be used interchangeably),

2. *Badan Kepegawaian Negara* (BKN, hereinafter referred to as the National Civil Service Agency),
3. *Komisi Aparatur Sipil Negara* (KASN, hereinafter referred to as the Civil Service Commission),
4. *Lembaga Administrasi Negara* (LAN, hereinafter referred to as the National Institute of Public Administration).

Out of these four institutions, the main institution in charge of the human resource management of civil servants is Kemen-PANRB. Kemen-PANRB is, thus, given a more extensive and deeper explanation in this section while others will be elaborated in the subsequent relevant section of this report.

Kemen-PANRB

As a policymaking ministry, Kemen-PANRB assists and is directly accountable to the President of Indonesia, generally, in guiding and supervising bureaucratic reforms encompassing all government institutions and, specifically, in civil servant empowerment. These tasks are a part of the third group of affairs, mentioned in Law of Government Ministries and Agencies 39/2008, that any government ministries and agencies are obliged to perform. This kind of affair holds the main task of supporting, in terms of coordination and synchronization spanning from visions to programs, within intersecting areas of tasks and functions across government ministries and agencies toward overarching desired policy goals at the national level.

The main tasks of Kemen-PANRB stand behind its main function, namely, policymaking of bureaucratic reform affairs comprising public accountability and oversight, organizational design and business process, public service manufacture and delivery, and human resource management. These main tasks and functions implicate that any policies made by Kemen-PANRB not only affect itself but all government institutions as well, including the very well-advanced bureaucratic reform undertaken by the Ministry of Finance/Kemenkeu, and no exception to secretary generals employing ASN reform in the legislative and judiciary branches of power. Nevertheless, the implication to state auxiliary bodies considerably vary due to their authorities that might allow them to have distinguished administrative mechanism in conducting human resource management affairs, especially those attributed with greater authorities in the 1945 Constitution following the 2002 fourth amendment, such as KASN and *Komisi Pemberantasan Korupsi* (KPK, Corruption Eradication Commission).

In terms of functions, Kemen-PANRB currently consists of four deputies and their supporting staff respectively. This structure is a result of the organization's rightsizing policy implemented by former Minister Azwar Abu Bakar and Vice Minister Eko Prasojo (2011–2014 period) under the Yudhoyono Administration that aimed at streamlining against overlapped functions across deputies, which consequently achieved structural efficiency.

The existence of Kemen-PANRB is historically rooted and can be traced back to the very beginning of the founding of the Republic of Indonesia in 1945. Since 1967 MENPAN – an acronym that has stood for today's Kemen-PAN (without RB), that is, Ministry of State Apparatus Empowerment – had obtained iterative stands of meaning which depended on policy emphasis throughout the period, ranging from mere ideological purification from political opposition force to arrangement of personnel empowerment, and it had become well-established since the 1990s leading up to the end of the New Order Regime. It was given the additional name of *Reformasi Birokrasi* (RB, Bureaucratic Reform) which completed the current Kemen-PANRB (hereinafter simply referred to as the Ministry of Administrative Reform interchangeably) since the second term of President Yudhoyono's administration in 2009. This period also marked a new policy emphasis and orientation toward merit-based human resource management of ASN.

BKN

BKN has an equal institutional position compared to Kemen-PANRB, it is hence subordinate and accountable to the President. It is mandated to handle the human resource management of ASN. Since BKN handles tasks specialized from bureaucratic reform policy in general, it ought to be accountable to the President through the ministry holding the general policy agenda, that is, Kemen-PANRB. This had consequently driven the organizational nomenclature positioning of BKN into a non-ministerial government agency (*Lembaga Pemerintah Non-Kementerian*/LPNK).

As derived from BKN's main task, it performs the following obligatory functions:

1) Formulating and enforcing technical personnel management policy;
2) Handling human resource management functions, including recruitment, mutation, termination, and pension, as well as redefining legal standing position of tenured civil servants (*pegawai negeri sipil*, PNS);
3) Administering pension, for current and retired government officials;
4) Administering human resource management information system;
5) Monitoring, supervising, controlling, and evaluating the implementation of personnel management;
6) Competence appraisal and assessment as well as competence potentials mapping of PNS;
7) Administering and developing recruitment of PNS;
8) Conducting research and development in the field of human resource management in the government sector;
9) Providing legal assistance deemed necessary to support its main tasks and functions, as well as problems hampering PNS;
10) Organizing education and training in the field of human resource management in the public sector;

11) Coaching for development of all organizational units under its responsibility and authoritative jurisdiction; and
12) Conducting oversight of the execution of its main task and functions.

To support its main tasks and functions, BKN has developed its organizational units into several deputies, inspectorate, and centers. The specialization of its deputies comprises fields of human resource management coaching, personnel transfer, human resource management information system, and oversight and control. Centers are devoted to conduct research and development for policy formulation as well as undertaking technical functions in various specialties: human resource management planning and ASN formation, coaching of functional positions, recruitment system development, competence mapping and assessment, human capital development of ASN, research and development in the field of human resource management in the public sector, legal assistance and consultation.

KASN

As any other civil service commissions in other countries experienced in establishing this kind of state auxiliary body – see Australian Civil Service Commission for instance – KASN holds similar obligatory tasks and functions. It is expected to be the independent guardian of meritocracy in the Indonesian administrative system. According to article 30 of Civil Service Law 5/2014, KASN is rightfully to conduct oversight of basic norms, code of conduct, and code of ethics any ASN should comply with. It seeks to guarantee implementation and further development of merit-system in the human resource management of ASN. This implicates that KASN is afforded a stronger institutional position than other state auxiliary bodies – or nonstructural state institutions (*Lembaga Non-Struktural*/LNS) since it holds both semi-legislation and semi-judiciary powers – equal to those held by the KPK.

Despite the authorities held by Kemen-PANRB and BKN, KASN has attributed the authority to formulate a merit-system for the human resource management of ASN and to conduct oversight to make certain that the policies are put into effect throughout all government ministries and agencies. KASN also holds the authority to make decisions deemed necessary to ensure the applicability of the merit-system, especially to give powerful verdicts over violations of the basic norms, code of conducts, and code of ethics, as well as over any acts that violate rules relating to the human resource management of ASN. The renown open and competitive selection of senior executive service has to deal with KASN for it is authorized to examine the processes and results. The decisions and verdicts made and given by KASN are stipulated to any government ministers, head of agencies, and any bureaucracy officials assigned as a personnel development officer (*Pejabat Pembina Kepegawaian*/PPK).

KASN consists of seven commissioners working in a collective-collegial manner. In conducting their tasks and functions, KASN commissioners are provided with substantial work supports from their assistances, and technical administrative supports from the Secretariat.

LAN

Out of the four institutions mentioned earlier, only LAN is not specifically in charge of policymaking and administering human resource management affairs. It serves the main function as a policy think tank advising the national administration in terms of broader issues relating to the institutional arrangement of public administration, which also comprises the human resource management aspect, while continuing to maintain partial roles in the training and education of ASN. These specialized technical functions have made LAN accountable to the President through Kemen-PANRB. Although LAN serves a supporting function to the President and Kemen-PANRB, it shares an important part along with BKN within a series of committees (1957–1967) in formulating personnel administration policy and nurturing the formation of the first generation of Kemen-PANRB under both Sukarno and Suharto Administrations. Please refer to Section 6: Training to acquire a broader elaboration of LAN's functions in recent practice.

Reform of civil servant as a human resource in the Indonesian administration is marked by the issuance of Civil Service Law 5/2014. The merit system in the law is defined based on qualifications, competencies, and performance fairly and reasonably regardless of political background, race, color, religion, origin, gender, marital status, age, or a condition of disability. Meritocracy has become the primary orientation of the bureaucracy reform as a whole. Based on comparative studies with many developed countries, improvement of civil service sustainability is the key to the success of administrative reforms as well as improving government support capacity for economic development in many developed countries (Berman 2011; Kim 2010). Meanwhile, during 1980–1990s Indonesia had imitated the efforts of industrialization in the style of developmentalism in Japan and Korea with a focus on increasing the competency of civil servants through formal education and skills training, as was the trend of the two reference countries (Hill 2014; Pepinsky 2012).

A number of key strategies were carried out in order to increase the meritocracy of the bureaucracy, especially in the aspect of the civil service system: (1) increasing selection for recruitment and placement of civil servants in an open

FIGURE 7.1 The civil servant recruitment process

Source: BKN. (2019, March 15). *Civil Servant Recruitment System.* Presented in Symposium 2019: State Capacity for Public Sector Reform and National Development in Southeast Asia and Korea.

and competitive manner; (2) developing professional competencies according to current and upcoming real bureaucratic needs; and (3) integration of civil servants human resources management across levels of government. These three things are explained further in another part of this chapter. In brief, the open recruitment of civil servants has been initiated since 2013 by the Ministry of Administrative Reform (*Kementerian Pendayagunaan Aparatur Negara dan Reformasi Birokrasi*, Kemen-PANRB) and the National Civil Service Agency (Badan Kepegawaian Negara, BKN) with changes initially implemented from a paper-based exam into the so-called computer-assisted test (CAT). This system is endeavored to eliminate the possibility of corruption, collusion, and nepotism by upholding objectivity in the process. Meanwhile, the selection of higher bureaucratic officials (Echelon I and II) was carried out through a panel team consisting of a combination of members from various backgrounds, ranging from bureaucrats, BKN, and academics. Competency developments include differentiation of managerial skills, technical competencies, and sociocultural competencies. This method uses a variety of modern competency development systems, including an assessment center used by the central government, which has been pioneered by the Ministry of Finance (*Kementerian Keuangan*, Kemenkeu) since 2007. Civil Service Law 5/2014 explicitly emphasizes integrated personnel systems in the management of civil servants in Indonesia by no longer distinguishing employment status between those belonging to central and local governments.

Recruitment

The National Civil Service Agency or *Badan Kepegawaian Negara* (BKN) – under the coordination of the Kemen-PANRB – has been mandated to manage human resources of National Civil Servant from planning, recruitment, promotion, until retirement. According to Armstrong and Baron (1998), human resource is the most important element that will determine the success of the organization. Planning and recruitment are the most crucial elements in human resource management because the first step would determine how the process works (Biles and Holmberg 1980; Ekwoaba et al. 2015). Since 2015, the Kemen-PANRB has enforced a Moratorium on the recruitment of civil servant in Indonesia. One of the aims of the moratorium is to balance the amounts of clerical officers who initially dominated the number of civil servants.

Before 2013, the recruitment and selection process was ineffective due to its manual process (paper-based), so the registration up to the selection stage was not transparent to the public, the process was very slow, and the organizer was not responsive to the problems that happened during the recruitment and selection process. Some cases show that someone could be recruited without a test through a nontransparent process, and not everyone knew that the position was made available. In 2013, the government began implementing a Computer Assisted Test (CAT) for the recruitment and selection of civil

126 Eko Prasojo, Defny Holidin, and Fajar Wardani Wijayanti

servants. The government ensured the execution of transparent, accountable, effective, and efficient recruitment through CAT (Buana and Wirakusuma 2015; World Bank 2018).

There are four steps in the Civil Servant Recruitment Process.

a. Registration

Once the planning/procurement of civil servant has been set, the registration will be opened. Every individual can register with a specific requirement. The government has considered the fairness of the civil servant recruitment in 2018 through a special formation. First, not only bachelor's degree holders or applicants who have master's degree can register, but vocational high school graduates can also register in some ministries or local government positions. Second, the government provides a disability formation comprising at least 2% of the total formation in the central government and 1% in local governments. Third, cum laude formation for those with a GPA over 3.5. The government allocates 10% in the central government and 5% in local governments. Fourth, the government allocates a Diaspora formation for performance athletes to be a civil servant. Last, young individuals from Papua and West Papua are welcome to occupy positions in both central and local governments. This provision is a form of equalization and fairness efforts in civil servant recruitment. The registration is executed using an online system, so everyone can access and monitor the entire process of the recruitment. The system was developed as transparent as possible, wherein only restricted data (e.g., personal data of the participant) could not be shown.

b. Document-Based Selection

In the document-based selection, each participant must fulfill all the required document files (e.g., bachelor's degree certificate, transcripts, identity card, family register). After the document files have been uploaded, the institution to which the participant applies will verify the document. Only participants who have passed the document-based selection will continue to the Computer Assisted Test (CAT) phase. In 2019, government has considered the transparency and fairness on document-based selection. The one who did not pass the document-based selection can re-confirm if they think they have followed all procedures in document-based selection. After that, the verification officer will do re-verification to make sure the document. This phase is an effort of the government to make the document-based selection more transparent and fairer for all people. Sometimes, there are some people who did not pass the document-based selection with no reason and no further explanation. On the other side, the registrants think that they already meet the document requirement. The government tries to solve this problem to make the document-based selection more transparent and fairer for all registrants.

c. Computer Assisted Test (CAT)

There are three stages in the Computer Assisted Test. First, the preparation process of the Material Test. Basic Competence Questions are prepared by the Ministry of Education and Culture (*Kementerian Pendidikan dan Kebudayaan*/Kemendikbud) while Technical Competence Questions are prepared by the respective Government Institutions. Second, once all government institutions have finished determining the questions, all questions would then be encrypted by the National Cyber and Crypto Agency (*Badan Siber dan Sandi Negara*/BSSN). Third, the encrypted test material will be transferred to the BKN Cloud Computing System. There are three institutions that contribute to prepare the materials and systems. The system is very secured and encrypted, so it could not be breached or stolen due to its use of high technologies. The testing material is divided into two competencies. First, Basic Competence (*Seleksi Kompetensi Dasar*/SKD), which consists of the Nationality Concept Test (*Tes Wawasan Kebangsaan*/TWK), General Intelligence Test (*Tes Intelegensia Umum*/TIU), and Personal Characteristic Test (*Tes Karakteristik Pribadi*/TKP), with a minimum passing grade to continue to the next competency. The Basic Competence is conducted via an online and real-time system using computers provided by BKN. Second, Technical Competence (*Seleksi Kompetensi Bidang*/SKB), which consists of an interview, a skill test, and a psychological test. The Technical Competence is aimed at exploring individual qualifications, abilities, capacities, competencies, and performance.

d. Result/Announcement

The result announcement is real time, so it can be monitored time by time. Registrants can observe what position they are in or how many scores they have accumulated. When the others have finished the test, the participant can also monitor whether their position or score goes up or down the ranks. The real-time result makes the test more competitive and transparent, so no one will suddenly appear without reasons (e.g., someone suddenly appearing with the highest score will not happen). From planning, recruitment, until the announcement, the civil servant recruitment system is based on a merit system. Civil servant policies and management are based on sound qualifications, competence and fairness without distinguishing any political factors, race, religion, gender, and disability conditions. World Bank on Global Report: Public Sector Performance (2019) stated that In Indonesia, the Civil Service Agency (BKN) succeeded in introducing a computer-assisted testing system (CAT) to disrupt the previously long-standing manual testing system that created rampant opportunities for corruption in civil service recruitment by line ministry officials. Now the database of questions is tightly controlled, and the results are posted in real time outside the testing center. Since its launch in 2013, CAT has become the de facto standard for more than 62 ministries and agencies.

The recruitment system for civil servants is an expensive bet that reciprocally determines and is determined by the organization's size, competency development strategy, distribution, and overall performance. In the context of the whole bureaucracy reform effort, reforming the civil service system in the aspect of recruitment shows its readiness and sustainability. As explained earlier, the ASN recruitment system is coordinated by the Kemen-PANRB and BKN through the proposed formation of various ministries/agencies and local governments at provincial and municipality levels. This computer-assisted test employs communication and information technology as a qualified way of eliminating the possibility of corruption, collusion, and nepotism by upholding objectivity in the process. Meanwhile, the selection of higher bureaucratic officials (Echelon I and II) is carried out through a panel team consisting of a combination of members from various backgrounds, ranging from bureaucrats, BKN, and academics.

The lack of number and qualification of current civil servants is still a challenge in achieving agency performance targets. Yet, unfortunately, this assumption is not accompanied by accurate strategic human resource mapping and necessary supporting data. The lack of adequate attention from leaders in ministries, institutions, and regional governments on the availability of data on the needs of human resource mapping, seeing individual staffing at the unit level the only source of reference in determining PNS recruitment policies (UI-CSGAR 2018). This condition will undoubtedly have a systemic impact, not only on the aspect of increasing employee expenditure ratios but also on the increasing potential for discrepancies between the quality competence of the required employees with the profile of recruits.

The aspect of the quantity of civil servants' human resources closely links to the issue of quality. Improving and increasing the competency of civil servants is carried out along with an increase in the number of civil servants at a ratio that adequately meets the national service needs of Indonesia's population of more than 260 million people. However, the parallel efforts between these two needs are not without problems. A temporary solution ever taken is the moratorium on recruitment for civil servants until the quality mapping and distribution of the real needs of civil servants in all lines of government are accomplished. In 2015, the Government of Indonesia re-implemented the policy of limiting the acceptance of prospective civil servants through the moratorium policy to provide opportunities for the central and local civil service officers to analyze positions and workloads at the agency level. Thus, the government aims to obtain a more accurate projection of the number of employee needs per post for the next five years. Based on the results of these calculations, Kemen-PANRB considers that there is still a shortage of employees in several positions because of the formation of new organizations and a large number of employees entering retirement (Kemen-PANRB 2017). In other words, the addition of new employees in 2017 is considered necessary to maintain the quality of public services while still paying attention to the ability of the country's finances.

Learned from its history, the moratorium policy is not a new thing. Previously, the policy on a temporary suspension of recruitment of civil servants had occurred for 16 months (from 1 September 2011 to 31 December 2012) based on a joint regulation of the Ministry of Interior (Kementerian Dalam Negeri, Kemendagri),

Kemen-PANRB, and Kemenkeu. The background is the same as the temporary moratorium conducted in 2015: to provide an opportunity for all central and regional agencies to perform the necessary analysis as a basis for knowing the needs of each civil servants. According to the State Secretary Office (Kementerian Sekretariat Negara, Kemensetneg), as of January 30, 2013, there were still many agencies at the central and local levels that have not compiled and various unsubmitted documents requested to organize employees and organizations as mandated. Ironically, at the same time, as many as 18 central agencies and 205 local agencies have submitted proposals for the formation of civil servants for 2013. Further search processes found that out of 18 central agencies, only four agencies (22.22%) have already had the projected need for civil servants for the upcoming five years. In contrast, only 71 of the 205 regional agencies (34.64%) had the required documents, including job descriptions, job maps, workload analysis, and employee redistribution (Kemensetneg 2013). The data shows a significant request from central and regional agencies (without an adequate database) to re-submit the proposal for civil servants' formation as soon as the moratorium completed. The same pattern also seems to be repeated in 2017. In the absence of accurate human resource needs of civil servants, consequently, two issues related to "proportion and distribution of skilled workers" and "alignment between study background and employee competences" do not become the focus of local officials, ministries and institutions.

Civil Service Classification and Status

According to Civil Service Law 5/2014, civil servants in Indonesia consist of Civil service (*Pegawai Negeri Sipil*/PNS) and Contract-Based Government Employees (*Pegawai Pemerintah dengan Perjanjian Kerja*/PPPK). PNS is an employee appointed as a permanent employee that possesses a nationwide registration number. PPPK is an ASN appointed via a labor agreement with the Personnel Development Officer (*Pejabat Pembina Kepegawaian*) in accordance with the Civil service Law. There are differences between PNS (permanent) and PPPK (contract), such as retirement benefits and work period, wherein PPPK is only employed for a period of one year, and extendable for further period. In general, the rights and obligations of PNS and PPPK are the same[2] and are only distinguished by the pension benefit received.

Positions among ASN are divided into Administratorial Position (*Jabatan Administrasi*), Functional Position (*Jabatan Fungsional*), and Senior Executive Service (*Jabatan Pimpinan Tinggi*).

1. Administratorial Position

    a. Administratorial Position, responsible for leading the implementation of the entire public service activities.
    b. Supervisory Position, responsible for controlling the implementation of the activities.

c. Executorial Position, responsible for implementing the activities of public service.

2. Functional Position

   a. Expertise (Main Expert, Associate Expert, Young Expert, and First Expert)
   b. Skill (Supervisory, Proficient, Skilled, Beginner)

3. Executive-Level Positions lead and motivate every civil servant. Executive-Level Positions are divided into Main Executive-Level Position, Senior Executive-Level Position, and Primary Executive-Level Position. Executive-Level Positions are not only made available to PNS, but non–PNS as well. There is an issue relating to the removal of Echelon III and IV and shift them to Functional Positions. This issue aims to downsize the organizational structure and save on routine government spending. The government has made the decision over the entire national and local government agencies and ensures that the shifting status upon the echelon III and IV removal would not deteriorate their usual income rate, as stipulated in the Presidential Regulation 50/2022.

The grading of civil servants in Indonesia is based on their last education status when they were appointed as PNS, and the promotion will subsequently be influenced by their work and performance. The salary and incentives accordingly follow the grade arranged by each institution. In Indonesia, civil servants are spread out in various positions. The total number of ASN in Indonesia is 3,995,634 with 23,4 (23,4%) of them in the central government and 3,058,775 (76,6%) in local governments. Figure 7.2 shows Indonesia's ASN composition.

Figure 7.2 shows that majority of civil servants in Indonesia still work in administrative issue (archives, files, mail, etc.). On the other hand, Managerial and Technical Positions still occupy 10% and 8%, respectively, out of all ASN. Managerial and Technical positions hold a strategic position in the bureaucracy. In the future, Indonesia will prioritize the managerial and technical positions in both central and local governments. The government will reduce the quantity of ASN holding general function, thereby consequently increasing the managerial and technical positions. The government had started to undertake such effort since the 2014 recruitment of ASN, which prioritized managerial and technical positions rather than general function position for the vacancy. This effort remains associated with the 2015 moratorium policy.

The existing condition of civil servant grade is determined by the tasks and functions of the institutions. The tasks and functions of government institutions in Indonesia encounter numerous issues, especially those relating to the overlapping tasks and functions among them. In the future, the civil servant grade will be arranged based on performance, load of job description, job risk, and several other considerations. Considerations relating to performance, job load, job risk, and several other matters will determine the grade level of the PNS, the structural

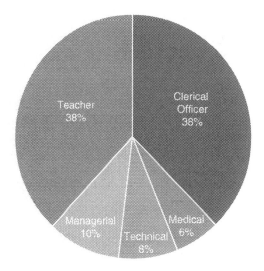

FIGURE 7.2 ASN composition

Source: Kemen-PANRB. (2019, March 14). *Human Resources Management Reform of Public Sector*. Presented in Symposium 2019: State Capacity for Public Sector Reform and National Development in Southeast Asia and Korea.

position of the grade, the requirement for promotion to accelerate to a higher grade, whether each institution has similar or different grades, and the various benefits that the civil servant grade entails.

Civil servants need to be protected or looked after to guarantee their work continuity while providing public services. Civil servants are entitled to have health insurance, occupational accident insurance, death insurance, and legal assistance. In Indonesia, the "protection" seems to be things like incentives, except legal assistance. However, legal assistance is not provided to ASN involved in legal issues or special crimes such as corruption, drugs, and terrorism. An ASN is not entitled to a legal assistance if he/she has obtained a decree proving that the ASN has been proven guilty by PPK with a disciplinary punishment in the form of respectful dismissal not at his/her own request as a civil servant and disrespectful dismissal as a civil servant.

Openness of Posts/Positions

The HRM process, from recruitment to retirement, carried out to fill the existing ASN positions (Administratorial Position, Functional Position, and Executive-Level Position) is implemented openly to enhance public transparency. The announcement of the various job positions including Executive-Level Position can be accessed via each of the government institution's official website, including a step-by-step guide of the recruitment process. Social media should become new tools for governments for broadening and enhancing their interaction with the public (Charalabidis and Loukis 2011; Tharmizi 2015). Anyone can contact the relevant government institution personally through social media. Technological development, especially social media, makes it possible to reach the participant even closer. Anyone can ask and share all activities involved in the process, so the public can also monitor the process. Government institutions would on occasion make time just to answer the questions participants have about everything related to the recruitment. Each participant can also talk to each other and share some information.

The administrators of the social media utilized by the government are highly responsive to any questions asked and they can provide answers to all the problems. The official website or social media administrators would at times put up the Frequently Asked Question as the menu on their social media or website. Thus, everyone can read it before asking the administrators about the recruitment. Social media administrators in one institution and others are integrated and help in answering each other's questions, so that when people ask about some cases in other institutions, when the relevant institution has yet to answer, other administrators from any of the other institutions will try to answer. For example, some people asked about the recruitment at the Ministry of Home Affairs and submitted a CC (Carbon Copy) to BKN. If the administrator from the Ministry of Home Affairs has not answered, the administrator from BKN will answer it as soon as possible. Furthermore, social media administrators establish interactive communication with the public, especially young people as prospective civil servants. It can be seen in Figure 7.3 how BKN's social media administrators provide advice related to public service selection on Twitter.

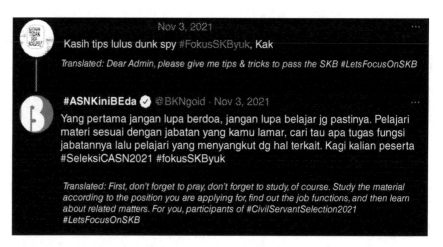

FIGURE 7.3 Communication between BKN and the public on social media (Twitter)

Source: BKN. (2021, November 3). BKN gives motivation, advice, and tips to prospective civil servants who will take the Computer Assisted Test (CAT). Accessed at https://twitter.com/BKNgoid/status/1455876904385335302

There are two shifting paradigms regarding openness of recruitment. First, the mindset of civil servants who are aware of the openness of the recruitment. Amidst increasing public expectation for a better governance, the government still attempts to determine what policies to choose and how to implement those policies to meet the public's expectation. Such condition makes BKN aware that they should be open to the public about the recruitment, and as a result they placed an administrator possessing appropriate characteristics to openly provide information. Second, the integration of openness information among public institutions both at the local and central levels of government. The public and local governments are starting to be aware that the relationship fostered between local-central and inter-central governments is most crucial to convey a publication of information to the public. They are also aware that they need to help each other in mutually informing shared data as quickly as possible.

The public is generally more familiar with recruitment of Administratorial and Functional Positions rather than the Executive-Level Position. Administratorial and functional positions are often made available on a large scale involving numerous government institutions of both central and local governments. Large-scale recruitment requires massive announcements through several platforms, such as official websites, social media, paper-based media, online media, and even advertisements on the street. Announcement of Executive-Level positions is commonly not as massive as Administratorial and Functional Positions. The news is often announced only through the official website and internal communication channels of the relevant government institutions. If the public does not intentionally look for the announcement, they will most likely not know about the job vacancy. In regard to Executive-Level positions, government institutions have not approached the public through familiar media, such as online media, television, and other internet sources.

According to BKN Regulation of the procedure for implementing civil servant transfer, mutation is the transfer of duties and/or location in several types. There are between central government, central-to-local government, local-to-central government, and between local government. There are several procedures to propose civil servant mutation. In general, the procedures are the same. The ministry/agency/local government should get permission from BKN/BKN (vertical institution in local government) and the institution one level above it.

In 2018, Government applied new rules for civil servants through the 2018 selection process. Civil servants will later be asked to devote themselves for the years and not permitted to transfer (mutation) from an area for a decade. These rules are made to guarantee sustainable public services in an area. If civil servants mutate in a short time, then public services in the area will not be optimal. Furthermore, the regulation is also made so that there is a balance of public services between regions. If this was not implemented, the civil servants would move to big cities. As a result, remote areas will lose the benefits of civil service from those who move to cities. In this aspect, the government considers the equality of civil servants in big cities and remote areas. The Government has tried to focus on remote areas so they can get better civil servants like big cities do.

134 Eko Prasojo, Defny Holidin, and Fajar Wardani Wijayanti

In Senior Executive Service policy, filling the Senior Executive Service (SES, hereinafter interchangeably refers also to the phrase *Jabatan Pimpinan Tinggi*/JPT) based on Civil service Law 5/2014 adheres to principles of competition, competency, and openness. Every Senior Executive's job vacancy must be announced in the mass media and/or submitted in writing to each ministry/agency/local government. In this way every civil servant can apply for the position as long as it meets the job requirements. At present the PNS Exchange occurs not only between the ministry and institution, but between the institution and local government, also the local government and other local governments. Specifically, for Senior Executive Service level 1 (Main and Intermediate) according to the Law can be applied for and filled out by the PNS, with the permission of the President. At present several level 1 SES positions have been filled by civil servants, such as the Director General of Culture, and the Deputy in the Ministry of State-Owned Enterprises (*Kementerian BUMN*). For positions under SES, filling positions is still a closed career and is carried out through internal assessments. For all levels of current positions Competency Assessment is carried out using a variety of methods. The law also provides the possibility of civil servant internship to private companies for some time vice versa for private parties who will be apprenticed in government.

Performance Assessment and Promotion

Since 1999 through Presidential Instruction of Government Institution Performance Accountability 7/1999, The President instructed all government institutions to report their performance accountability to achieve the vision, mission, and objectives of the organization. Indonesia has been concerned about performance as a vital element in achieving organizational objective. Presidential Instruction of Acceleration of Corruption Eradication 5/2004, on in the third dictum, the President had instructed to determine the performance indicators and targets in all line ministries which explain the achievements of performance either output or outcome. The reform was followed by several laws such as the State Finance Law Package until the Presidential Decree of Grand Design of Bureaucratic Reform 2010–2025. To ensure the success of achieving the objectives of bureaucratic reform and the success of achieving strategic planning, a performance management is deemed necessary to realize a more efficient and effective government.

Efforts in solving problems from upstream to downstream continue to be done, one of them by encouraging the government to optimize the planning process to be more effective, efficient, and results-oriented. Armstrong (2009) stated that performance management integrates better various management processes than Management by Objectives, managing for result, appraisal, and other similar concepts. This is manifested in the central government through the Kemen-PANRB which continues to improve in encouraging the government to improve good management through assistance to various institutions.

In Indonesia, performance assessment as an important part of performance management is conducted with Employee Work Objectives (*Sasaran Kerja Pegawai*/

SKP) and work behavior. Assessment of the Work Achievement of Civil service is regulated in Governmental Regulation of Work Achievement Assessment of Civil Servant Apparatus 46/2011. Every civil servant is annually assessed by using their SKP and Work Behavior to determine their performance. In practice, SKP does not represent the performance of civil servants. SKP only indicates the tasks or work that have been conducted daily and such conditions do not represent their performance. This indicates that the government is not yet concerned about performance assessment. This problem certainly does not stand alone. This is due to the fact that not all civil servants have measurable performance indicators. Thus, not all civil servants are performing their tasks and responsibilities accordingly. Some of them are still oriented toward routine work that does not produce any outcome and that is what they put on the SKP as performance.

Performance assessment in Indonesia is mostly conducted by the superior (a person holding an upper rank position) of subordinates or staffs. This assessment method tends to be ineffective for a number of reasons. First, the assessment tends to be more subjective coming from the superior, not objective. Second, the performance score is expected to improve year by year. The problem is when the score almost reaches its maximum point, then what should they do to prove what they have done. Third, other stakeholders (360-degree assessment) tend to be left unconsidered. Even if the 360-degree assessment were to be conducted, there is the possibility of an "awry" culture in the society. For example, if the other staff also assessed their friend, they would feel hesitant to give their score. If the scores are too low, maybe they would offend/hurt their friend, but if the scores are too high, possibly the person assessed does not deserve a high score on account of their poor performance. Another example is if the staff were to assess their superior, they would not give a bad score as they may think they will be transferred or given some sort of social punishment from the superior. Conducting a 360-degree assessment requires good method and preparation in place before putting it in practice.

SKP in some public institutions of both local and central governments is used to determine the performance incentive. This situation allows for the provision of performance incentives in Indonesia to be based not on one's performance. In many institutions, each level and grade of civil servants have their incentives, and they can receive them merely through the attendance requirement. The provision of incentives should take the worker's performance, workload, work risks, and other factors into consideration. Based on the current conditions employees who perform and those who do not could receive the same incentives. It is not surprising that many civil servants work only to fulfill their attendance record, instead of performance.

Another problem regarding performance incentives in Indonesia relates to the fact that performance incentive does not actually mean "incentives." There is a misinterpretation of the performance incentives because the performance of the civil servant has not been measured yet. Incentives are meant to motivate and improve the civil servants to work and produce good results in their performance. If the concept and the paradigm of real "incentives" were to be applied, the civil servants would obtain real "incentives" based on their performance, not on their tasks or what they have done without any actual outcomes. Kemen-PANRB is still trying to improve the performance assessment of civil service, so that performance could be set as the basis for providing incentives.

Indonesia also conducts promotion of civil servants in both local and central government organizations. Governmental Regulation Number 11 Year 2017 regulates promotions in the civil service. There are document-based selection and requirements that need to be fulfilled by civil servants in order to be promoted to a higher position. For example, to be promoted, a civil servant must pass the administrative requirement (grade of civil servant, SKP score, educational level, etc.). Public institutions have their respective Performance Assessment Team for assessing and evaluating candidates who are up for promotion. The considerations of the Performance Assessment Team are based on objective comparisons between competencies, qualifications, position requirements, assessment of work performance, leadership, cooperation, and creativity, regardless of gender, ethnicity, religion, race, and class. In practice, some promotion processes are often conducted based on relational intimacy, request of various parties, and many other cases. The decision is sometimes merely made by the leaders of the institution, hence indicating that the promotion does not utilize a merit system, although it cannot be generalized that all promotion processes are not based on a merit system.

Kemen-PANRB makes serious efforts in implementing a merit system in the promotion of civil servants at every level in the future. The assessment of civil servants will be collected through the National Talent Pool Management System. The civil servant who has competence and performs well will be promoted based on their qualifications, competencies, and institution's need. The civil servant with poor competence and performance will be trained and developed to improve their competence and performance, so once they have reached a better box (see Figure 7.4) they will be promoted. Figure 7.4 shows the promotion, rotation, and career path of civil servants in the future.

In the middle 2019, the President has ratified Governmental Regulation of Performance Appraisal for Civil Servant 30/2019. Governmental Regulation 30/2019 provides a mandate to all civil servants to perform and achieve individual targets and organizational objectives. Each civil servant must contribute from their performance to achieve the strategic objectives of both central and local government organizations. Civil servants should perform and generate outputs and outcomes that correlate with their organization's goals. Performance Appraisal will function as a reference in the identification of training, competency development, career development, provision of incentive, consideration of transfer and promotion, and other rewards. The transition of performance appraisal is the first step that will later refer to the effectiveness and efficiency of bureaucracy in Indonesia.

Performance management of individual civil servants continues to be improved and made one of the pillars of the change in the staffing system. Based on Civil service Law 5/2014, individual performance measures are used as a basis for promotion of positions, payroll, and employee development. Government Regulation

Indonesia **137**

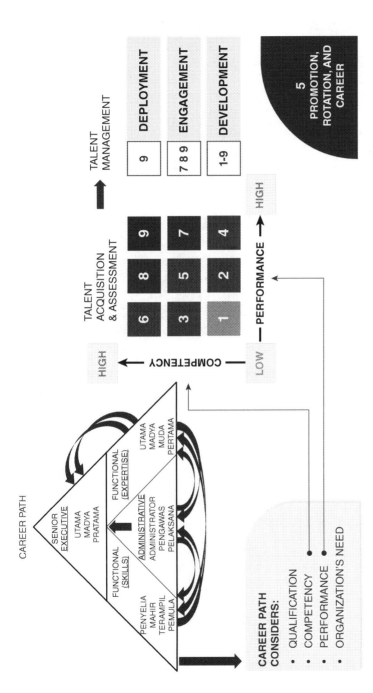

FIGURE 7.4 Promotion, rotation, and career of civil servants in Indonesia

Source: Kemen-PANRB. (2019, March 14). Human Resources Management Reform of Public Sector. Presented in Symposium 2019: State Capacity for Public Sector Reform and National Development in Southeast Asia and Korea.

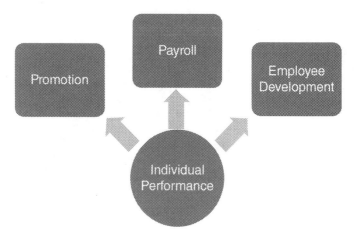

FIGURE 7.5 Improvement of performance management
Source: Kemen-PANRB, 2019.

of Performance Appraisal for Civil Servant Apparatus 30/2019 regulates the obligation for civil servants to sign performance contracts for one year. For civil servants who do not meet the contract performance for up to one year, they will be given a chance to fix it for 6 months and if not fulfilled, they will be given sanctions until termination. Especially for SES, officials can be moved or demoted because they do not achieve performance targets within 18 months. The current performance of civil servants is also used as a basis in the payroll system. Civil service Law 5/2014 makes performance the basis of the remuneration system currently being discussed by Government Regulation. Also, civil servants who did not achieve desired performance targets will get counseling and coaching in a couple of months, followed up by intensive monitoring and assessment of their subsequent performance. Not only does the counseling reach workforce aspect of an employee in their daily activities in the office, but it also covers the need for personal and family affairs since this might also determine their job performance. The coaching is usually undertaken by an ad hoc team supported by the agency's internal oversight taskforce (*aparat pengawas intern pemerintah*, APIP). The team held routine meetings with the employee(s) under examination as well as frequent monthly or quarterly assessment with their peers and superiors.

Training

A common means of increasing the bureaucracy's operational capacity is through training, and its nature in human resource management is, undoubtedly, an integral part of ASN development. Short-term trainings and internships have become a basic program in government ministries/agencies and local governments. Unlike local governments, human capital development in line ministries and government agencies have been spoiled with dispatching employees to study abroad, aside from common in-house trainings, along with bigger opportunities of scholarship portions allotted for civil servants provided by foreign scholarship schemes, such as Australian Awards, Chevening, NESO, etc., as well as domestic funding sourced from the national budget carried out by a number of ministries, such as the Kemenkeu, the Ministry of Communication and Information (*Kementerian Komunikasi dan Informatika/Kominfo*), and National Development Planning Agency (BAPPENAS).

Training of ASN, particularly in terms of tenured civil servants (PNS), comprises at least four main stages of ASN development: pre-recruitment, inducement, regular development, and capacity building for leadership hierarchies.

a) Pre-recruitment training is undertaken during formal education sessions given prior to the civil servant's acceptance as an employee with the status of a tenured PNS through a higher education institution run by a government ministry or agency. Some higher education institutions offer vocational training with a degree with compulsory commitment to work for the government upon graduation (*ikatan dinas*), some remain without such obligation. Both types of higher education institutions are funded by their own principal ministries/agencies. Although since 2017 there has been a plan, even a roadmap, to integrate the undertakings of all these higher education institutions into a holding run by LAN, institutional setting and merged budget arrangement seem to have a long way to go. Either way, the decision as to whether the candidates, or graduates with the compulsory commitment, shall enter the recruitment process and inducement to be a PNS by regulation depends on their merit.

b) Inducement (*prajabatan*) stage is a one-week regular introductory training. The training contains general administrative skills any pre-tenured employee needs to acquire.

c) Upon appointment as an ASN, there might be a series of regular developmental trainings depending on the necessary technical fields capacity building with a duration decided by the organizing ministries or agencies as these institutions usually have its own education and training centers (*pusat pendidikan dan pelatihan/*pusdiklat).

d) The ultimate training stage is the capacity building program conducted prior to taking up higher hierarchies of leadership position, renowned as *pendidikan dan pelatihan kepemimpinan* (diklatpim, leadership education and training).

Diklatpim has been developed from a mere routine conventional training to a rigorously applied policy training. LAN, the institution responsible for conducting studies for policy recommendation and educating civil servants, has continued to use the training to reconstruct their mind-set and attitude/culture-set. The conventional training models were neither effective to enhance civil servants' administrative skills nor significantly feasible in providing added value to bureaucratic reform, although high-caliber lecturers were put in charge.

140 Eko Prasojo, Defny Holidin, and Fajar Wardani Wijayanti

Based on a series of evaluations of the conventional *Diklatpim* training, a new model of training, which is the first of its kind, features a participant-centered learning, professionally tailored to their agency needs, and dealing with multiple-supervision by experts from various backgrounds. The curricula were therefore designed without strong relevance to the participants' home agency needs. Since 2013 LAN has developed new executive training curriculum and method replacing the conventional in-class lecture-heavy training that had been conducted so far for decades. This reform-oriented executive training does not merely conduct four-week in-class lectures in combination with case-based interactive discussion, but it also imposes tasks to be accomplished by participants in a group to actively design their own change management project by conducting research to generate practical solutions to real problems encountered in their home agencies. The task accomplishment, therefore, takes longer with an approximate period of one to six months as on-the-go training since the participants also have to resume their routine work. The output is in the form of policy recommendations that are linked to their problematic situations in the respective ministries/agencies/local governments. To assure that the learning process is guided using a high-quality standard, LAN charges multiple experts to work in collaboration to supervise each project. The supervisors come from various ministries/government agencies, employers of respective participant's home agency, and academics. Since 2015, the Head of LAN has issued a regulation regarding the new model of Diklatpim as an official benchmark for other government ministries and agencies as well as local governments to use.

Following the new mode of executive training, Kemen-PANRB has also launched a distinguished program, namely the Reform Leader Academy (RLA). Participants of RLA are mid-level (third echelon) and senior-mid level (second echelon) public officials coming from various ministries/government agencies and local governments that need prior approval from LAN. All participants are trained by using a similar method as the new mode of executive training to comprehend their understanding and sharpen their analyses on public issues/policy agendas. Since another important objective is reducing sectoral egotism in policy coordination among agencies, a training batch is composed of public officials from various home agencies to build up cross-agencies collaboration work. The first batch of RLA in early 2014 addressed the issue of ease in conducting business, and the public officials who attended this program were those coming from function-related agencies: Ministry of Industry, Ministry of Trade, Investment Coordination Agency, National Land Service Agencies, and provincial agencies of Jakarta. The result of the training came in the form of practical policy recommendations to be implemented further in each home ministries/government agencies and local governments. LAN conducts post-RLA monitoring and evaluation to assure effective progress in the implementation of the recommended policies.

Senior Civil Service

A group of high-ranking ASN in Indonesia has been formed since the very beginning of the country's establishment, and they are recognized as the holder of *Jabatan Pimpinan Tinggi* (JPT, Senior Executive Service; the name hereinafter referred to not only the position but also the subject holding the position). The nature of JPT differs from those who hold *Jabatan Administrasi* (JA, Administratorial Position) and *Jabatan Fungsional* (JF, Functional Technocrats or Functional Position). While the latter refers to pure exercise of administrative tasks and functions, the former undertakes exercise of not only administrative affairs but political ones as well. The JPTs are expected to deal with politically appointed or elected officials in the policymaking process, from agenda setting to policy formulation, hence undertaking the entire cycle of the policy process.

The hierarchical levels of JPT have their own triple-tier stage, from elementary to middle to principal levels. The hierarchical levels do not necessarily mean that JPT is an exclusive domain of central government. While having those at the top-tier organizational hierarchy, such as JPT, is a logical consequence of any organization, within the Indonesian nomenclature of ASN, JPTs are distributed across central government ministries and agencies as well as local governments. This is due to the decentralization policy implemented by the central government that allows local governments at the provincial and municipal levels a considerable degree of autonomous authority in running their local affairs. Consequently, top appointed officials at the local level are granted a proportional opportunity to hold a JPT position. This institutional architecture implicates that the hierarchical levels of JPT across government ministries and agencies as well as local governments determine which kind of positions belongs to it, as depicted in Table 7.1. This also means that any ASN holding the most superior positions at the institution consequently has the authority to act as the personnel development officer (*Pejabat Pembina Kepegawaian*, PPK) for their own subordinates.

Civil service Law 5/2014 on ASN with Kemen-PANRB as the main proponent contains a message to limit echeloning to the first and second tier (echelon I and II) to strengthen professionalization of ASN for the sake of meritocracy development. Nevertheless, this orientation is challenged by Law 23/2014 on Local Government with Kemendagri (*Kementerian Dalam Negeri*, Ministry of Home Affairs) as the main proponent. The law still affirms regulating complete echelon typology therein that might be the main reference of entire province and municipal governments in Indonesia. Subsequently, this conflicting regulatory framework is treated as a transitioning agenda with meritocracy as the main campaigning agenda.

As meritocracy development has been the new overarching policy orientation, processes of identification, recruitment, positioning of public officials to hold JPTs are undertaken through open and competitive selection mechanisms. This is expected to balance political tendencies inherently contained within the nature of JPT dealing with elected officials. Unless meritocracy development sufficiently

142 Eko Prasojo, Defny Holidin, and Fajar Wardani Wijayanti

TABLE 7.1 Civil servant positions

Administratorial Position	Functional Position	Senior Executive Service

1. Administratorial Position
  – – Echelon III
2. Supervisory Position
  – – Echelon IV
3. Executorial Position
  – – Echelon V
	1. Expertise
	a. Main Expert
	b. Associate Expert
	c. Young Expert
	d. First Expert
	2. Skill
	a. Supervisory
	b. Proficient
	c. Skilled
	d. Beginner
		1. Senior Executive Service (*Utama*)
		  – – Echelon Ia (head of non-ministerial government institution)
		2. Senior Executive Service (*Madya*)
		  – – Echelon Ia and Ib
		3. Senior Executive Service (*Pratama*)
		  – – Echelon II

Source: State Civil Apparatus Law 5/2014.

TABLE 7.2 Hierarchical level and typology of positions of JPT

Hierarchical Level of JPT	Typology of Positions Classified as JPT	Echelon
JPT Utama (Principal JPT)	Head of government implementing policy agency (*Lembaga Pemerintah Nonkementerian*/LPNK)	
JPT Madya (Middle JPT)	Secretary general/principal secretary,	I-a
	Director general/deputy,	
	Inspector general/principal inspector,	
	Chief of technical agency,	
	Assistance expert to the ministry,	
	Head of presidential office,	
	Head of vice-presidential office,	
	Military secretary to the President,	
	Head of office of advisory board to the president (*Dewan Pertimbangan Presiden*)	
	Secretary of provincial government	I-b
JPT Pratama (Elementary JPT)	Director/assistant deputy,	II-a, II-b
	Chief of bureau,	
	Secretary of directorate general,	
	Secretary of inspectorate general,	
	Secretary to chief of technical agency,	
	Head of centers/laboratory/technical units	
	Inspector,	II-a
	Assistant of provincial government secretariat,	
	Head of provincial government agency,	
	Secretary of provincial council,	
	Secretary of municipal government	

Source: Civil Service Law 5/2014.

matures, imposing open and competitive selection mechanisms to recruit the best candidates possessing necessary professional and personal traits to fill in the JPTs might be a temporary approach. The main idea of this new scheme is highlighting the role of merit-based selected JPTs to play a crucial role in inducing, driving, and securing change management process toward the overarching policy goals of the bureaucratic reform agenda, especially in terms of sustaining meritocracy development. Thus, the nature of JPTs is the agent of change, the coach–cum–trainer for the regeneration of reform-minded cadres, and the special task force guiding designated bureaucracy reform agenda.

As explained in the aforementioned section, openness here also refers to precandidature that anybody, coming from non-ASN – that is, those coming from private professionals – and contractual ASN position holder/PPPK – fulfilling enough the required expertise and skills – namely managerial, technical, and sociocultural ones – has equal opportunities and are encouraged to compete. Openness also implies having external parties, like academia or private professionals, to take membership in the selection committee, which is deemed necessary in the process. Nevertheless, there must be conditions and exemptions in any situation especially when it comes to certain positions of principle and middle JPTs. First of all, there must be a permission definitely mentioning the necessity to open certain JPT positions for non-ASN although the opportunity exists, as attributed in the Law in principle. Secondly, the term is exempted for JPTs related to fields of state security and secrecy, defense, human resource management of state civil and military apparatuses, natural resource management, and other fields that the President might consider its cruciality. Third, besides possessing expertise and skills required to perform the tasks and functions of a JPT, professional experience and minimum educational background are also of importance, as follows:

(a) for ASN:

- earned undergraduate education level at least bachelor or the highest vocational training licensed as "Diploma IV" equivalent to those of bachelor programs;
- has cumulative experience of handling a position with similar or adjacent fields of tasks and functions for a minimum of 10 years to apply for Principal JPT position, or a minimum of seven years for Middle JPT position, or a minimum of five years for Elementary JPT position;
- has experience of holding Middle JPT position or Principal JF position for a minimum of two years to apply for Principal JPT position, or holding Elementary JPT position or Principal JF position for a minimum of two years to apply for Middle JPT position, or holding JA position or Middle JF position for a minimum of two years to apply for Elementary JPT position;

(b) whereas for non-ASN:

- earned post-graduate education level at least a master's degree, professional degree, or certified professional education and training;
- has cumulative experience of handling position with similar or adjacent fields of tasks and functions for a minimum of 15 years to apply for Principal JPT position or for a minimum of 10 years for Middle JPT position;
- has no functionaries, memberships, or any ties to political parties in the last five years prior to application;
- has never been imprisoned or received equivalent punishment for committing crimes;
- has never been terminated from any ASN, police, or military positions.

Recruitment and selection of Principal and Middle JPTs are administered at the national level with BKN and BKN regional offices put in charge for such purposes. Elementary JPT is administered by the relevant government ministries and agencies and local governments through close coordination with Kemen-PANRB and BKN. All government ministries and agencies and local governments administering the recruitment and selection processes of JPT positions have to consult the results with KASN.

Institutional Deficiencies of Indonesian Civil Service Reforms

Bureaucracy reform in Indonesia has not yet escaped from a certain degree of discrepancies between formal and informal institutions. As any other emerging economies, greater emphasis on informalities has made the actual practice of the creation of competent bureaucracy different from those attributed as formal ones, which is typical East and Southeast Asian countries (Touchton 2015). Contrary to the initial efforts to institutionalize bureaucracy reform at the national level, there has been a counteracting trend right after the Jokowi Administration has taken office since 2014. The recent trend shows that civil servants have been entering ambiguous positions, that is, playing meritocratic role as a government reform catalysator vs. being brought back in instrumental apparatus under stricter surveillance and disciplinary order imposed by the political elites. The meritocratic role is designated in the 2010–2025 GDRBN, as mentioned earlier, and the Civil Service Law 5/2014 was taken into effect in 2014. Nevertheless, iterative changes of its role have currently occurred with more emphasis on stricter obedience to the government – the ruling parties – not only in terms of bureaucratic procedures but also ideological reasoning. These have very much deal with the recent political climate that the government has put its efforts against what it calls as radical sociopolitical right wings and opposition parties but subsequently seems to lead the regime to be less democratic (see Chacko and Jayasuriya 2018; Hadiz and Robinson 2017; Power 2018).

Given that ambiguous standing point, the Indonesian civil service system has at least five crucial areas of the institutionalized bureaucracy reform. Since the

Indonesia **145**

ambiguous positions have emerged due to conflicting orientations among parties, the five areas seem to become a battlefield between parties advocating the orientations. The areas include, but are not limited to, (1) recruitment and positioning, (2) integrated vertical and horizontal mobility, (3) neutrality from politics, (4) performance management and performance-based compensation, and (5) supervision and accountability. We describe a brief overview of these five areas and the dynamic of conflicting orientation therein, as follows:

1) Recruitment and Positioning

    The basic idea is to undertake bureaucracy reform from the very early doors an individual entering the organization. Recruitment and positioning of civil servants are two things that put the good and clean government at stake. When the processes feature bribery and abuse of power, an organization becomes prone to corruption. Since two decades ago, the Indonesian public sector has undertaken reform by borrowing ideas and norms from its private counterpart. Not only has this occurred in terms of privatization and deregulations of public services and agencies, but it has also implied greater openness yet competitive for private individuals to compete and take positions of public official without prior hierarchical mobility of tenure career within the bureaucracy. Kemen-PANRB has initiated this since 2011 and later the Province Government of Jakarta in 2012 even before the Civil service Law 5/2014 had not been issued. A general recruitment process has also employed information technology, that is, the computer-assisted test that allows automatic and real-time selection result for the recruitment since 2013. Since 2006 and 2007, respectively, Municipality Government of Sragen and the Ministry of Finance have even pioneered the use of assessment center before it had been imposed as national policy by BKN in 2013. While all these protocols become instrumentally more conducted, there is also a counteracting orientation or tendency to bring up external sources of workforce into the bureaucracy without getting through these protocols. The workforce is a group of people who can work with an elected official upon promised development programs and immediately implement his instructions over bureaucratic procedure and hierarchies. They can be a political companion who had supported the elected officials and/or technocrats in necessary competence areas. Although this is justified in terms of the allotted operational budget of the officials, the trend has become institutionalized through the formation of the presidential office and politically appointed vice-minister. This trend seems to make recruitment and positioning reform efforts have no use.

2) Integrated Vertical and Horizontal Mobilities

    The mainstream approach to enhance opportunities of getting the right people in the right place and the right time is integrated human resource

146 Eko Prasojo, Defny Holidin, and Fajar Wardani Wijayanti

management (HRM) system. This integration means integration of mobility pipelines for a civil servant to get promoted and mutation horizontally across the jurisdictional border of organizations and vertically escalating over different levels of government. For this purpose and approach, the government has attempted to consolidate personnel database across agencies and committed the open and competitive selection process for filling out available positions. In the near future, it also designates to have a national talent pool which is supported by the information and communication technology (ICT)-driven track record system. This leap is facilitated under the Civil service Law 5/2014 from formerly the separate system due to the old-style bureaucracy and strengthening patrimonialism in local governments at the beginning stage of liberal-devolutionary decentralization policy in early 2000s. Nevertheless, the remaining unestablished supporting instrument might open for rising opportunistic behavior of some civil servants to apply for the open-competitive selection processes. Another pitfall is, while this integrated HRM system is under the responsibility of the Ministry of Administrative Reform, predominantly areas of authority at province and municipality levels owned by the Ministry of Interior.

3) Neutrality from Politics

Although strong orientation toward professional civil servants has got emphasized in the Civil service Law 5/2014, all traits of neutral bureaucracy from politics, as regulated under the Public Personnel Law 43/1999, remain there. Therefore, the separation of bureaucracy from politics is the main norm. Nevertheless, this has recently experienced considerable change since the first term of Jokowi's presidency. Begun with imposing regulations prohibiting any individuals, especially the civil servants, to put the state's symbols, especially the head of the state and government institutions to shame – considered as part of hate speech toward the government, under his administration forbid any criticism against the government's policies. The situation has got back to the one Indonesia previously had experienced. Again, the Jokowi Administration assumes that the government is identical hence a representation of the state. This assumption implies every civil servant is the state apparatus and giving their loyalty solely to the governments is the ultimate manifestation of their dedication to the country. Very recently, the government has launched a portal aduanasn.id as an instrument to involve citizens and civil servants into government's political agenda of banning what considered as radicalism movement. This portal can be used by anybody, from civil servants to ordinary citizens and inhabitants throughout the online crowd mechanism.

4) Performance Management and Performance-based Compensation

When it comes to the manifestation of meritocracy, performance management is the key. While performance at individual civil servant recently gets greater attention along with the established one at an organizational level, it is also tricky and paradoxical among other human resource management functions. First, although the Government of Indonesia conducts multiple methods of performance measurement – from the quantitative sum of work results to 360° evaluation, the measurement unit gets less improved. The measurement unit emphasizes more at formalities than substantive quality of the work, for instance, number of reports and its volume in terms of number of pages are treated as the measurement unit of daily productivity, work hours spent daily, availability of proofs or evidence of a business than actual contribution to the goals of the business trips, etc. Second, there are emphases on organizational outputs such as data, reports, and indices. The emphases are more than how the organization conducts collaborative work in the process to produce those outputs leading to increasing silo among organizations, repetitive and redundant projects hence larger economic scale in total government spending. Third, there is general trending performance gaps between organizational outcomes and individual outputs. Fourth, even in a similar and agreed basis of performance measurements such as job description and workload analyses, different government ministries/agencies have launched various schemes or instruments. Therefore, civil service reform has contributed to the escalated essential problematic situation of the bureaucracy itself.

5) Oversight and Accountability

The Government of Indonesia has indeed developed its internal oversight and controlling over civil servants with a new orientation. Since 2008 the government has issued the regulation 60/2008 and commenced a new role of inspectors and auditors. Although their functions remain to prevent fraud in various forms, including maladministration and corruption, they are expected not to find out committed mistakes or faults of civil servants in conducting bureaucratic procedures. They should rather play their primary role as a partner with their colleagues to provide the best solution for productive work and minimize potentials of fraud. This attempt can be considered as a different route to prevent maladministration and corruption with a good-faith approach. This way, inspectors and auditors must assure quality works, manage risks, and give early warning. This attempt has stepped along with improvement of complaint-handling mechanism from stakeholders. Furthermore, since 2013 there are initiatives to launch a sort of whistle-blowing system that allows complaints, early warnings, and reports indicating fraud can be delivered anonymously to them by any individuals from inside and outside the organizations. It needs more improvement, especially given the way internal supervision and oversight from stakeholders have not linked together and not properly followed up, while a bill draft of national oversight system remains not accomplished throughout years since 2013. Nevertheless, current efforts preventing what the government considered as radicalism has shifted this orientation more than a problem of performance and fraud. Launched by the Ministry of Administrative Reform in cooperation with the Ministry of Communication and Information, the government provides an online crowd-sourced mechanism for any individuals – be they civil servants, ordinary citizen, or inhabitants – to report any civil servants exposed by radicalism. Nevertheless, there has been no pipeline mechanism for the incoming reports.

Notes

1 Kemen-PANRB. (2019, March 14). *Human Resources Management Reform of Public Sector.* Presented in Symposium 2019: State Capacity for Public Sector Reform and National Development in Southeast Asia and Korea.
2 Civil service Law 5/2014.

References

Books/Journals

Armstrong, M. (2009) *Armstrong's Handbook of Human Resource Management Practice*, 11th edn, London: Kogan Page.

Armstrong, M. and Baron, A. (1998) *Performance Management – The New Realities*, London: Institute of Personnel and Development.

Berman, E. M. (2011) *Public Administration in Southeast Asia: Thailand, Philippines, Malaysia, Hong Kong, and Macao*, Boca Raton, FL: CRC Press.

Biles, G. E. and Holmberg, S. R. (1980) *Strategic Human Resource Planning*, Glen Ridge, NJ: Thomas Horton and Daughters.

Buana, I. K. and Wirakusuma, M. G. (2015) 'Pengaruh penggunaan sistem computer assisted test pada efisiensi biaya dan akuntabilitas publikasian hasil', *E-Jurnal Ekonomi dan Bisnis Universitas Udayana*, 4(11): 797–822.

Chacko, P. and Jayasuriya, K. (2018) 'Asia's conservative moment: Understanding the rise of the right', *Journal of Contemporary Asia*, 48(4): 529–40.

Charalabidis, Y. and Loukis, E. (2011) 'Transforming government agencies' approach to e-participation through efficient exploitation of social media', *ECIS 2011 Proceeding*, Finland.

Dwiyanto, A. (2011) *Mengembalikan Kepercayaan Publik melalui Reformasi Birokrasi*, Jakarta: Gramedia Pustaka Utama.

Ekwoaba, J. O. et al. (2015) 'The impact of recruitment and selection criteria on organizational performance', *Global Journal of Human Resource Management*, 3(2): 22–33.

Hadiz, V. and Robinson, R. (2017) 'Competing populisms in post-authoritarian Indonesia', *International Political Science Review*, 38(4): 426–40.

Holidin, D. (2017) 'Perkembangan Aktual Reformasi Birokrasi di Indonesia', in D. Holidin, D. Hariyati and E. Sunarti (eds) *Reformasi Birokrasi dalam Transisi*, 2nd edn, Jakarta: Prenada Media Group.

Hill, H. (2014, January) 'Is there a Southeast Asian development model?' *Discussion Series Paper*, 26, Dept. International Economic Policy – University of Freiburg, Freiburg.

Kemen-PANRB (2017) *Organisasi Pemerintah yang Tepat Fungsi, Tepat Proses, dan Tepat Struktur serta Organisasi yang Berdasarkan Kinerja* [Government Organizations to Be Effective, Efficient, Structurally Fit, and Based on Performance], Jakarta: Kementerian Pendayagunaan Aparatur Negara dan Reformasi Birokrasi, Republik Indonesia (Kemen-PANRB).

Kemensetneg (2013) *Evaluasi Pelaksanaan Moratorium Penerimaan CPNS di Daerah* [Evaluation of Recruitment of Prospective Civil Servants at Local Level], Jakarta: Kementerian Sekretariat Negara, Republik Indonesia (Kemensetneg).

Kim, P. S. (2010) *Civil Service System and Civil Service Reform in ASEAN Member Countries and Korea*, Seoul: Daeyoung Moonhwasa Publication.

Pepinsky, T. B. (2012, March) 'The second East Asian miracle? Political economy of Asian responses to the 1997/1998 and 2008/09 crises (99 problems but a crisis ain't one political business and external vulnerability in island Southeast Asia)', *JICA-RI Working Paper*, 43, JICA Research Institute.

Power, T. P. (2018) 'Jokowi's authoritarian turn and Indonesia's democratic decline', *Bulletin of Indonesian Economic Studies*, 54(3): 307–38.

Prasojo, E. (2009) *Reformasi Kedua: Melanjutkan Estafet Reformasi* [Second Reform: Continuing the Relay of the Indonesian Reform], Jakarta: Penerbit Salemba.

Tanku, G. and Shkelzen, I. (2017) 'Meritocracy – the only criterion to have a professional public administration in the civil service', *Mediterranean Journal of Social Sciences*, 5(6): 165–70.

Tharmizi, H. (2015) 'E-government and social media: A case study from Indonesia's capital', *Journal of e-Government Studies and Best Practices*, 2016: 1–10.

Touchton, M. (2015) 'Trapping the tigers: Regulation of market entry and the rule of law in SE Asia', *The Social Science Journal*, 52: 8–21.

UI-CSGAR (2018) *Diagnostic Study: Grand Design Reformasi Birokrasi*, Jakarta/Depok: Universitas Indonesia Centre for the Study of Governance and Administrative Reform (UI-CSGAR) and Kementerian Pendayagunaan Aparatur Negara dan Reformasi Birokrasi, Republik Indonesia (Kemen-PANRB).

UNDP (2015) *Meritocracy for Public Service Excellence*, United Nations Development Programme (UNDP).

World Bank (2018) *Global Report: Public Sector Performance*, Washington, DC: The World Bank.

Law/Regulation

Republic of Indonesia, Civil Service Law 5/2014.

Republic of Indonesia, Examination and Accountability of State Finance Law 15/2004.

Republic of Indonesia, Government Ministries and Agencies Law 39/2008.

Republic of Indonesia, Government Regulation of Civil Servant Apparatus Management 11/2017.

Republic of Indonesia, Government Regulation of Internal Oversight and Controlling 60/2008.

Republic of Indonesia, Government Regulation of Performance Appraisal for Civil Servants 30/2019.

Republic of Indonesia, Government Regulation of Work Achievement Assessment of Civil Servants 46/2011.

Republic of Indonesia, Local Government Law 23/2014.

Republic of Indonesia, Presidential Instruction of Government Institution Performance Accountability 7/1999.

Republic of Indonesia, Presidential Regulation of Grand Design of Bureaucratic Reform 2010–2025 81/2010.

Republic of Indonesia, Presidential Instruction of Accelerating Corruption Eradication Number 5 Year 2004.

Republic of Indonesia, Public Personnel Law 43/1999.

Republic of Indonesia, Regulation of the Minister of Administrative Reform of Road Map of Bureaucratic Reform 2010–2014 20/2010.

Republic of Indonesia, Regulation of the Minister of Administrative Reform of Road Map of Bureaucratic Reform 2015–2019 11/2015.

Republic of Indonesia, State Finance Law 17/2003.

Republic of Indonesia, State Treasury Law 1/2004.

8

THAILAND

Amporn Tamronglak

Background

Prior to 1928, the public personnel management had no unified standard in personnel management policy, procedures, recruitment, etc. (Office of the Educational Affairs 2016). The individual agencies and ministries at that time had autonomy in handling their own personnel matters in their own ways, leading to injustice practices in every ministry. Then, King Rama VII took the opportunity to reform Thai bureaucracy as it had been the foundation of modern office today with four basic principles of (1) unification of personnel practices, (2) competence, (3) career civil services, and (4) discipline (Prasitsiriwong 2018). The first Civil Service Act was issued in 1928 and nine more have been promulgated. But the very first bedrock and the essence of human resources management in Thai public sector remain in the Act of 1928 that placed the central personnel commission as the appropriate role of advisors to the government (Prasitsiriwong 2018). The rest of the following laws have not cleared its role as a part of the government agency in managing and developing human resources in public sector and protecting the merit system.

In Modern Thai Bureaucracy, current statistics dated in April 2017 is about 2.16 million personnel from national to local level of administration. The dedicated agency in charge of all human resources management in Thai public sector is the Office of the Civil Service Commission (OCSC). It was first established in 1928 according to the Civil Service Act 1928 during the reign of King Rama VII to have main responsibilities in recruiting and training young public personnel. Based on current Civil Service Act 2008, the OCSC is the central personnel agency under the Prime Minister's Office, led by the Secretary-General, to provide the Prime Minister advice in Human Resources Management and protect the merit system practices of the civil service (OCSC 2014; Office of the Educational Affairs 2016).

DOI: 10.4324/9781003326496-11

152 Amporn Tamronglak

Thailand recently has a new elected government led by the former junta, General Prayuth Chan-ocha, ruling the military administration for the past five years. In an attempt to pull the country out of the low-income trap by leading the majority of the population from low-paying jobs, creating political stability, low corruption, and developing better education system and high capital index score, the new Prime Minister Prayuth Chan-ocha, unlike his predecessors, has designed a long-term plan for the country's national development extending over the next 20 years (The Nation 2018). The 2017 Constitution, ratified by the King on October 13, 2018, stipulates and requires the government to develop the national strategic plan for the first time and also enforce all public agencies to follow through (Constitution 2017).

The national strategic plan, which had been previously studied and proposed by two consecutive assemblies (the National Legislative Assembly (NLA) in 2015 and National Reform Steering Assembly in 2017), is now implemented and will be monitored by the newly instituted PM's Delivery Unit (PMDU), led by Prime Minister himself (Prime Minister's Delivery Unit 2018). Ten areas of strategic development were designed in an effort to set Thailand up for success in the next 20 years. Among 37 major reform agendas and 138 initiatives incorporated into all government ministries, departments, and agencies in coordination with the private sector is the administrative reform in Thai civil service management with the prime target to advance the country's capacity through innovation and digital technology, with new directions for developing the workforce and educating Thai citizens in science, technology, engineering, and mathematics (Prime Minister's Delivery Unit 2018).

As part of the administrative reform efforts, the OCSC will lead in transforming the government human resources management into the future, planning for recruiting the new cadre of personnel, redesign, revise, and develop the new performance management system, and revise all the administrative regulations in corresponding to the national strategic plan.

Civil Service System

The Office of Civil Servant Commission

The Structure of the OCSC

The Office of Civil Servant Commission (OCSC) is directly accountable the Prime Minister, led by the Secretary-General under the supervision of the Civil Service Commission (CSC). The CSC is comprising of the Prime Minister as Chairman or Deputy Prime Minister, Permanent Secretary of the Ministry of Finance, Director of the Budget Bureau, and Secretary-General of the Office of the National Economic and Social Development Board (NESDB) as ex officio commissioners, and about five to seven commissioners appointed by the King from qualified and renowned persons in the field and relevant fields of human resource management,

Thailand **153**

TABLE 8.1 Members of the Civil Service Commission

	Members	*Positions*
1.	Prime Minister or Deputy Prime Minister authorized by the Prime Minister	Chairperson
2.	Permanent Secretary of Ministry of Finance	Commissioner
3.	Director of Bureau of the Budget	
4.	Secretary-General of the Office of the Social and Economic Development Commission	Commissioner
5.	Specialist in the area of Human Resource management	Commissioner
6.	Specialist in the area of Management	Commissioner
7.	Specialist in the area of Law	Commissioner
8.	Secretary-General of the Office of the Civil Service Commission	Commissioner and Secretary

Source: OCSC (2014, p. 12).

administration and management and law, recruited under the rules, procedures, and conditions prescribed by CSC Regulation (OCSC n.d. a). The Secretary-General of the Civil Service Commission, by the Civil Service Act, shall be a commissioner and secretary of the CSC. It is also required that all commissioners shall not be a holder of a political position, executive committee member, or holder of a position responsible for the administration of a political party or an official of a political party, and not already being an ex officio commissioner (OCSC 2014, p. 8).

In carrying all its duties and responsibilities, Section 12 of the 2008 Act authorizes the Civil Service Commission to appoint the following Civil Service Sub-Commissions and a committee to act on its behalf on different matters as follows (OCSC 2014, pp. 8–11):

1) Civil Service Law and Regulations;
2) Discipline and Termination of Government Service;
3) Position Classification and Remuneration;
4) Enhancing Efficiency of Human Resource Management (HRM);
5) Development of Human Resource Management (HRM);
6) Preparation of the Public Sector Workforce;
7) Development of Public Sector Workforce Quality;
8) The Establishment of an HR Recruitment System and Standards;
9) Personnel Assessment for Appointment to Knowledge-Worker Positions;

154 Amporn Tamronglak

10) Ethics Promotion for a Clean and Transparent Bureaucracy;
11) Certification of Legal Officer Standards in the Public Sector;
12) The Civil Service Commission Medical Board.

Responsibilities of the OCSC

According to the Civil Service Act of 2008, the OCSC's duties are to carry out the overall human resources management of all public personnel from recruitment till retirement from the services, including workforce and manpower planning, recruitment policy and procedures, human resources and career development, discipline, certification, evaluation of personnel performance, protecting the merit system and good governance for the benefit of the people and the sustainable development of the nation. Though there are other specialized public personnel agencies, OCSC is the main and primary agency that will provide guidance and foundation of human resources management principles and practices in promoting professionalism for all types of public personnel to follow and apply in any different contexts, including position classification, recruitment and selection, disciplines, compensation and welfare, and training development (OCSC 2014, pp. 14–18).

The OCSC's major roles are to carry duties as assigned by the Civil Service Commission, give advice and consultation to ministries and departments regarding public sector human resource management rules, regulations, and procedures, and all responsibilities regarding developing, reinforcing, analyzing, and researching public sector human resource's policy, strategy, system, procedure, standards, etc. (Civil Service Act 2008, Section 8).

The CSC, on the other hand, will provide the Council of the Ministers on human resources regulations, rules, procedures, remunerations, policies, and strategies on public sector human resource management with respect to compensation standards, human resource management and development, including workforce management that government agencies can use as operational guidelines, monitoring and evaluating the implementation of human resources management in ministries and departments, etc. (OCSC 2014).

Recruitment of Civil Service Personnel

Since the major administrative reform in 2008, a number of Thai laws have established the legal basis for the general merit-based practices in recruiting and selecting personnel into the government departments. The 2008 Constitution guarantees equality to all Thai people. Section 30 particularly spells out equal rights to be enjoyed by all male and female. Any discrimination against a person based on origin, race, sex, age, physical conditions or health, economic or social status, religion belief, education, or different political view shall not be constitutionally permitted. In corresponding law, section 3/1 of the State Administrative Act of 2002 elicits that state administration must be for the benefits of Thais by providing essential public services with efficient and worthy results, minimized red

Thailand **155**

tape, accountability, responsiveness, participatory decision-making, etc. In all, the government administration has to comply with the Good Governance principles influenced by World Bank and International Monetary Fund (IMF) during the economic crisis since 1997. The information Act of 1997 also has given the public rights to know the information about public service tasks and able to monitor recruitment procedures (OCSC 2014).

At present, the Civil Service Act 2008 defines four categories of civil servant positions, comprising executive positions, managerial positions, knowledge worker positions, and general positions (Civil Service Act 2008).

(1) **Executives** are heads of government agencies and deputy heads of government agencies at ministerial and departmental levels and other positions prescribed by the CSC as executive positions. There are two levels of executives: primary level and higher level.

TABLE 8.2 Duties and responsibilities of CSC in brief

1. Giving advice and suggestions to the Council of Ministers concerning policies, strategies on public sector human resource management with respect to compensation standards, human resource management and development, including workforce management that government agencies can use as operational guidelines;
2. Making proposals to the Council of Ministers for consideration concerning adjustment of civil service remunerations, position allowances, welfare and fringe benefits; and development as guidelines for execution of government agencies;
3. Approving appropriation of workforce for government agencies;
4. Issuing CSC rules and regulations concerning human resource management in accordance with the Civil Service Act;
6. Interpreting and resolving problems arising from the execution according to this Act which needs approval of the Council of Ministers to become effective;
7. Supervising, overseeing, monitoring, and evaluating the implementation of civil service human resource management in ministries and departments to maintain justice and standardization of human resource management, including inspecting and monitoring performance pertaining to this Act;
8. Formulating policies and issuing rules concerning King's scholarships and government scholarships that correspond with public human resource management policies;
9. Issuing directives or rules concerning the provision of education, supervision, and assistance to public personnel, King's scholars, government scholars, and private students under supervision of the CSC;
10. Prescribing rules and procedures for accrediting the credentials of the holders of degrees, vocational certificates, or other credentials for the purpose of instatement and appointment as civil servants, and determination of salary rates or remuneration as well as position levels and categories for such credentials;
11. Determining rates of fees in performing duties on human resource management under this Act;
12. Managing, monitoring, and updating a personnel record system;
13. Carrying out other duties as allowed by the Act.

Source: OCSC (2014) *Guide to OCSC*. Nonthaburi: OCSC.

156 Amporn Tamronglak

(2) **Managerial positions** are heads of government agencies at levels lower than departments and other positions prescribed by the CSC as managerial positions. There are two levels of managers: primary level and higher level.

(3) **Knowledge worker positions** are those who hold bachelor degrees as prescribed by the CSC for performing duties in such positions. Five levels have been classified, including practitioner level, professional level, senior professional level, expert level, and advisory level.

(4) **General positions** are those who are not executive positions, managerial positions, and knowledge worker positions, as prescribed by the CSC. Four levels of classification are operational level, experienced level, senior level, and highly skilled level.

Qualifications

To become a civil servant at the entry level, a minimum level of education is laid down for each level. Certificate/Diploma holders are eligible for the general positions at operational level. A person with Bachelor's Degree or Master's Degree and Doctoral degree is eligible to apply for knowledge worker positions at practitioner level (Civil Service Act 2008).

Certain general qualifications and prohibition are considered a must for all applicants. In general, it includes being Thai nationality with at least 18 years of age and pure faith in the democratic form of government with the King as Head of State. There is also a list of prohibitions for a person not to have, for instance, holding a political position, mentally insane/disabled person, morally defective of being socially objectionable, adjudged bankrupt, a committee member of the political party, a criminal offender, punishments by discharge, dismissal or expulsion from a state enterprise or other state agencies, any laws, and the Civil Service Act of 2008, or cheating in an entrance examination for the government service or for entry to work in other state agencies, etc. (Civil Service Act 2008).

To the extent a person prohibited above intends to join the service, the CSC may consider a waiver and allow entry into the government service if such a person has already retired from work or retired from government service for more than two years for prohibitions of being discharge, dismissal, or expulsion from a state enterprise or other state agencies, any laws, and the Civil Service Act of 2008. And a minimum of three years of retirement from government for the punishment by expulsion for a breach of discipline under this Act or other laws. In all cases, four-fifths of the number of the CSC commissioners present at the meeting must give the consent for the decision by secret ballot (Civil Service Act 2008).

Recruitment and Selection Process

In principle, the recruitment and selection in Thai Civil Service is based on the merit system of neutrality, equality, fairness, and competence. It is the main responsibility of OCSC representatives to advice ministries and departments to ensure their compliance to OCSC regulations as well as to promote fairness,[1] equity,[2] transparency,[3] and standardization[4] in recruitment (Simananta and Aramkul 2002; OCSC 2012).

To ensure the recruitment of qualified persons for the needed positions in compliance with the aforementioned principle of merit system, the Act of 2008 has provided at least three processes to be taken by the candidates to possess (1) knowledge, law and regulations concerned, (2) necessary skills (Computer, English Proficiency, Mathematics, Data Management), and (3) identified competencies through competitive examination, selection, and appointment for expert and specialist (OCSC n.d. b).

a) *Competitive examination:* Recruitment of a new personnel can be done from the list of those who pass the competitive examination for such position. In this case, the agency or department in need of new recruit shall call the person who passes the general examination and on the top of the list for further special subject or specific examination for particular position or further interview as they see fit. Details on examinations shall be in accordance with rules, procedures, and conditions prescribed by the CSC (Section 53 of the Civil Service Act 2008). The purpose of having the holistic examination is to ascertain that the person possesses the knowledge and skills for that job, the ability to learn, developed, or trained to do a job, and the suitable behaviors, attitudes, and personalities required for a job. Explicitly, the examination will undertake in three phases: General Examination, Specific Examination, and Position Suitability Assessment.

The general examination is designed to measure general abilities, acquired information, and analytical skills, covering mathematics, verbal, and reasoning skills in the first part. The second part assesses the comprehension and expression of the Thai language. The general knowledge examination is administered and responsible by OCSC for most social science degrees in economics, law, computer, accounting, and political science (Civil Service Act 2008).

The Specific examination is the responsibility of departments to measure specific skills or knowledge required to perform in a certain position in those departments (Civil Service Act 2008).

The last test, particularly the interview, is applied for a particular position, through the review of personal history and records, work experience, educational background, as well as observation of behaviors. During the interview, the candidate will be judged by his or her suitability in communication skills, emotional stability, ethical principles, values as well as sociability and capacity to adapt to the social environment, creativity, and personality. This is also implemented by departments (Civil Service Act 2008).

The candidate shall pass the examination of all three phases if the score of at least 60 percent is attained for each. Those who pass all three examinations will be ranked on the basis of their scores and placed on the eligible list for appointment

158 Amporn Tamronglak

when the positions are open to be filled. The eligible list will be valid for future appointment for two years (Civil Service Act 2008).

b) *Selection:* In the case where competitive examination deems inessential, agencies can select graduates from universities operated by that agency and approved by the CSC, or graduates with an educational background in needed fields or degrees. The CSC will determine and review the list of necessary and priority fields, facing a personnel shortage every two years. The interview or other suitable methods will be applied. The candidate, if selected, must remain in the position for at least one year and may not be transferred to other departments.

On the other hand, the person can be appointed to the agencies if he or she can get a scholarship to study abroad from the government scholarship programs, for instance, the King's Scholarship and the Royal Thai Government Scholarship, which will be announced annually (Section 55 of the Civil Service Act 2008). The OCSC will administer the process in cooperation with the departments and state universities requesting the candidates. The scholarship recipients after their graduation and training abroad are, by contract, to fill the positions in response to the manpower needs of civilian ministries, public agencies, state universities, and departments.

c) *Appointment:* Lateral entry for a person with special knowledge, ability, expertise, and experiences as experts or specialists is also allowed by Section 56 of the Civil Service Act 2008 when reasons have been justified. Details of methods, procedures, criteria for selection, and the transfer of listed person from one list to another shall be made by the OCSC.

In sum, though the selection process is designed and administered by OCSC, agencies and departments enjoy certain autonomy in recruiting and selecting the most suitable candidates through specific and desirable examination and own assessment as they see fit.

Civil Service Classification and Status

The milestone of classification system reform was first set during the reign of King Rama VII in 1975 when the ranking system of public personnel was transformed into position classification (PC) of 11 grade levels (Class 1-Class 11 or C1-C11), depending on the complexity of job. Then, it was classified into three categories: general positions, professional or expert positions, and executive administrative positions. The PC was found to be an obstacle of the development and career advancement of capable civil servants and not able to keep up with the dynamic administrative reform of state administration.

In 2002 with highlight of New Public Management (NPM) and Good Governance concepts, the State Administrative Act of 2002 section 3/1 aimed to improve

Thailand   **159**

the government administration to become more efficient, results-oriented, red-tape and waste reduction, flexible, accountable, responsive, etc. The PC was replaced with the new classification system, comprising four kinds of civil servant positions as mentioned earlier: Senior Executive Service (Head of Ministry, Permanent-Secretary, Head of Department, Secretary-General, Director-General from primary to higher level), Middle Management (Head of Bureau or Head of Division from primary to higher level), Knowledge Workers (performing line functions from practitioner, professional, senior professional, expert, and advisory), and Operation and Support (performing supporting tasks from operational, experienced, senior, highly skilled) (Section 45 of the Civil Service Act 2008). The new system requires a new "role profile," the revision of responsibilities and qualifications descriptions, role, and corresponding competency for each position. The new position classification system is a basis for more flexible recruitment and selection of new personnel of lateral entry for each category, career advancement, training and development, and performance-based compensation system (Simananta and Aramkul 2002; Osatit n.d.).

Employment Status and Retirement

Being a civil servant in the Thai public sector, which has historically been the most prestigious employment, is viewed as an honor in Thai society due to the extremely arduous recruitment and selection process. Employment status or employment condition of civil servants in Thailand is a long-term and permanent hiring once a person passes all the requirements and probation period, if not legally discharged for any wrongdoings. The retirement age is set at 60 years. However, due to the current demographic change of aging society, low birthrate happening in Thailand, and particularly the burden of the government budget on the retirement pensions in the future, the government has recently reviewed its retirement policy for government officials. New retirement plan, announced in the Royal Gazette in April 2018, extends the retirement age from 60 to 63, which will begin the implementation by the end of 2019 and will have full impact in 2024. It is planned that civil servants who turn 60 in 2019 or 2020 will continue to work for one more year, while those who will turn 60 in 2021 or 2022 will stay until they are 61 years of age, and those who will turn 60 in 2023 or 2024 will stay until they are 63 years of age. The plan would cover 11 areas of politics, public administration, laws, justice procedures, the economy, natural resources and environment, public health, mass media and IT, social issues, energy, and anticorruption (*Bangkok Post*, April 10, 2018; Fernquest 2016).

Mobility Opportunity

Thai personnel system is open for lateral entry if the person has fulfilled all requirements as specified in general civil service regulations mentioned earlier and if the positions are open for transfer. Internal and external mobility are all possible and competitive required by laws (Civil Service Act 2008).

Performance Assessment and Promotion

The very first systematic performance management was introduced in 2009 as stated in the OCSC Order 1012/20. The performance management was defined as a systematic process of connecting and linking organization performance objectives with team and individual performance in pursuing the final goals of public organizations through the process of smart objective setting, appropriate personnel development, continuous performance monitoring, coherent appraisal with objectives, and reasonable rewarding in response to the performance (OCSC 2009b).

The performance management process is designed into five stages of planning, monitoring, developing, appraising, and rewarding (Figure 8.1).

The very first step in the performance management process is to plan for what to be done, set the targets to be achieved (performance indicators and achievements) and design flexible and adjustable individual development plan (IDP) depending on the targets and planned performance achievements (OCSC 2009b, pp. 3–4).

Then, the planned in the first step will be used to monitor progress in individual performance if it is advancing and implemented according to the visualized targets. If it does not reach the desired results, adjustments in plans will be done as appropriate. Results will be measured regularly and discrepancy will be closely supervised (OCSC 2009b, p. 3).

In the third stage, the results from the second stage will reveal important information about (1) individual performance and achievements and (2) observable behavior, happening as expected or not. Considering all information combined will help design the practical development plan for the achievable goals. Details of performance measurement and indicators will be discussed later (OCSC 2009b, p. 3).

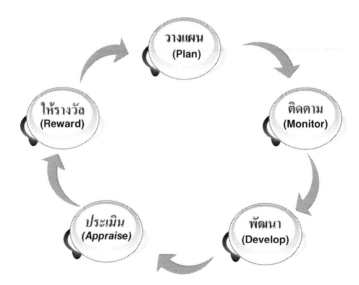

FIGURE 8.1 Performance management process in Thai public sector

Source: OCSC (2009b, p. 3). Manual.

The fourth stage is the performance assessment of what has been done in a year. The actual results will be compared with the targets, set earlier together, and agreed by both supervisors and subordinates (OCSC 2009b, p. 4).

The final stage of performance management is to reward those who have achieved the targets. It is the means to motivate and provide morale to the person to stay motivated, feel self-esteem, and self-actualization. The rewards can be in the form of money (salary increase or promotion) or in-kinds due to limited government budget, like compliment, public recognition, etc. Those who fail to reach target will not be rewarded with salary increase, but only rare and serious cases. Mostly minimum salary increase is given to everyone to provide financial support and motivation to all civil servants so as to earn their living that catch up with the high cost of living each year (OCSC 2009b, p. 4).

Performance Appraisal System

The OCSC has set a general framework for performance appraisal system for all Thai public servants in 2009 composed of at least two major elements: (1) job performance or achievement and (2) behavior of a person or competency or abilities to fulfill job. Each agency may also add the third component as they see fit and appropriate. The assessment will be done biannually in March (October of previous year, based on budget year, till the end of March of the following year) and September of the same year (OCSC 2009b, p. 4).

Performance Criteria

In doing the assessment, the supervisor and subordinate will have to consult and discuss what is to be expected in his or her performance. Basically, the performance assessment criteria can be judged in three categories, such as activities appeared in the agency four-year strategic plan and action plan, job or activities assigned to the person, and special assignments like urgent or emergency tasks/activities (OCSC 2009b, p. 7).

Four categories of indicators are used in the assessment to measure the quantity of work (the number of activities/tasks completed), quality (correctness, neatness as compared to standards), timeliness (in time, time used in performing and completing the task as compared to standards), and value for money of the performance (pay less for more) (OCSC 2009b, pp. 8–9).

To all civil servants, all elements are not equally given weight. The job performance is counted for at least 70% while the behavior or trait component is counted for 30% or less. Therefore, the possible ratios of two major factors are 70:30, 80:20, or 90:10. However, for those who are in their probation period, the ratio of two elements is 50:50 in assessing their overall performance (OCSC 2009b, p. 9).

In the measurement, a normal five level-scale of excellent, great, good, fair, and need improvement is applied to everyone, civil servants, and those working during probation. The person who fails the appraisal will not get rewarded for salary

162 Amporn Tamronglak

TABLE 8.3 Levels of measurement

Measurement Levels	Scores	Remarks
Excellent	Defined by agencies	The agency has to publicly post an
Great	as appropriate	announcement for those who get
Good		"excellent" and "great" performance
Fair	At least 60%	results, if a five scale is utilized.
Need improvement	Below 60%	Will not get salary increase

Source: OCSC (2009b, p. 10) Table 2.1.

increase. In this case, a written agreement to make improvement and perform better in the following year will be made and signed by both supervisor and a failed individual. The document is the contract as a promise made by the individual to keep improving in any specific areas. If he or she fails to fulfill his/her promise, he or she will have to leave the services. Those who pass the assessment will be promoted with higher salary. Not everyone gets the same amount of monetary increase, the "pay for performance principle" will be applied to everyone as stipulated by Civil Service Act 2008. The summary of the measurement and performance results application is in Table 8.3.

To ensure transparency and integrity of the appraisal process, screening committees at division and provincial levels are set up, composing of Chief Human Resource Officer (CHRO) acting as Chairperson, at least four civil servants appointed by Governors (at the provincial level) or Head of HR function. More committees are allowed to be appointed to do the initial consideration and provide policy advice to the screening committees (OCSC 2009b).

Performance Appraisal Tools

The OCSC has designed three assessment forms to be used by every public agency.

Form I is a compulsory form, providing a summary of performance evaluation results. The three-pages long form includes the notification of the evaluation results, the summary of the performance scores, and the individual performance development plan. A slight adjustment in the content of the form is allowed, but major substance has to be remained (OCSC 2009b, p. 14).

Form II is the individual job performance assessment, including key performance indicators (KPI) (OCSC 2009b),[5] targets level for the tasks,[6] and the weight for each indicator, agreed by two parties (supervisor and subordinate). This form contains details of performance activities to be assessed as specified in Form I. Therefore, it can be modified to fit the job and individual assignments (OCSC 2009b, p. 15).

What will happen if a person has been transferred or assigned new task and activities which are not acknowledged in the assessment form from the beginning? In this case, changes and adjustments in the KPIs and Targets can be done on the conditions agreed by both parties. In all circumstances, KPIs and targets can be changed, replaced, added, deleted, or set higher. The only condition that KPI and target are not allowed to be modified is when a person is not capable of performing that task or activities. That is to say, an exception cannot be made for the reason of failing to perform the task.

Form III is to assess individual behavior, traits, or competencies. Details of each aspects need consultation, discussion, and agreed by both supervisor and subordinate. Like Form II, this form can be changed and modified to fit the individual assignments identified in Form I (OCSC 2009b, p. 16).

Competency Assessment

It is required by all to use five core competency as part of the performance assessment, including achievement motivation, service mind, expertise, integrity, and teamwork. In doing the assessment, there are two ways that can be done: only immediate supervisor (single-rater appraisal) or multi-rater appraisal (self, co-worker, supervisor, subordinate, and customer) (OCSC 2009b, pp. 48–49).

As the appraiser, there are scores of 1–5 to be given when doing the assessment on each competency. The OCSC has given detailed guideline for single rater and multi-rater. For instance, 1 point is for "strongly need development" or "unable to perform" or below expectation (less than 60%), 2 points for "developing" or "inferior" compared to others in the same level (60–70%), 3 points for "fair" or "average" (71–80%), 4 points for "good" (81–90%), and 5 for "excellent" (91–100%) (OCSC 2009b, p. 52). Agencies are allowed to apply the systematic competency-based performance assessment differently as they see fit and applicable to each position which can be learned from the competency dictionary book or the OCSC assessment manual. In practice, when doing the assessment of each competent, we can compare the same position of one agency with the equivalent agency or compare with what have been specified and described in the competency dictionary. Another way of assessment using competency is to see if a person has performed their task as expected. In other words, that person will receive the highest score if he or she can perform his/her task beyond expectations (OCSC 2009b, pp. 56–57).

The other different method of assessment is to combine various measures as aforementioned using two dimensions of the completeness or perfection of the performance and the frequency performing the tasks, resulting in four types of performance: entry, developing, proficient, and very proficient (OCSC 2009b, pp. 58–59). Details are shown in Table 8.4.

Employing the hybrid scale model for the assessment is not that simple. There are at least two steps in this practicum. First a person will be assessed which level of competence for his or her performance, applying the competency dictionary. For this particular purpose, let's say that he or she deserves the competency level 3. Next is to look into the other two dimensions of the completion of work and the frequency of the performance. In doing this, another thing will be taken into

164 Amporn Tamronglak

TABLE 8.4 Competency-based assessment using hybrid scale

	Less Than 40% Completion	*40–80% Completion*	*More Than 80% Completion*
Occasional	Entry	Entry	Developing
Moderate	Entry	Developing	Proficient
Moderate	Developing	Proficient	Very Proficient

Source: OCSC (2009b, p. 59).

TABLE 8.5 Deduction points criteria

	Entry	*Developing*	*Proficient*	*Very Proficient*
Deduction	0.75	0.5	0.25	0

Source: OCSC (2009b, p. 59).

account and deducted (Table 8.5) from the original score. In this case, for instance, he or she is not very consistent in doing the assignment, sometimes 80% complete and some other times 60% done. Therefore, from Table 8.3, the person is given a Proficient for not very consistent in performance result and, from Table 8.4, will be deducted for 0.25 from the original score of 3 (OCSC 2009b, p. 59). The final score would be 2.75 (3–0.25).

The application of the competency framework explained above is rather comprehensive and systematic. However, it is very to be apprehended by the agencies. As a result, the competency-based performance assessment has never been put in use. From my previous research for the Reform Commission in 2017–2018, the agencies found it quite complicated to do and time-consuming. The system is now under the review of the new administration. In the end, a simple evaluation form has been implemented, leaving more rooms for personal judgments of the evaluators (OCSC 2009b).

What if the evaluation results are not satisfied? In the case of dispute over the performance evaluation results, the person can make an appeal to the complaint and discipline unit within the agency. Both will have the chance to explain to the complaint and discipline unit. If it is still not settled, the appeal can be raised and sent to the Administrative Court. The decisions from the Administrative Court will be final.

Probation

According to Section 59 of the Civil Service Act 2008, it requires all first entry personnel to be assessed for their performance within the first six months in order to review if they should be proceeded for hiring to continue their public services. The probation period of at least six months to one year is a mandate for all newcomers (Civil Service Act 2008; OCSC 2010). During the probation, they would go through a series of learning processes designed by OCSC to get them ready to serve the public, including attending orientation, joining legal foundations seminar for practices in civil services and e-learning self-study (OCSC regulations 2010, p. 38).

The orientation gives the introduction and foundations of general environments of public organizations, public service vision, mission, organizational structure, and organigrams, and gets acquainted with supervisors and colleagues. In a way, it is the first encounter of the newcomers to the new environments, culture, and people in the public services, providing and building moral support (OCSC regulations 2010, p. 38).

The self-learning study is through e-learning, logging into the courses designed by the OCSC on www.ocsc.go.th, covering basic knowledge for all newcomers. For instance, there are modules on foundation knowledge of laws and regulations for civil services, ASEAN skills, languages (Laos, Vietnamese, Myanmar, Bahasa Malays, and Yawi or Kelantan-Pattani Malay), Information Technology skill (Microsoft Excel, Data visualization, Project Management), Human Resources Management, Gender role, public ethics, public official letter writing, and general knowledge of management. To determine if they pass the courses, they need to do the pre-test and then post-test after the self-study (OCSC 2019).

A one to two weeks joint seminar is prepared by the units the newcomers are placed for hiring or they can join the seminar program organized by other units, but paid by own units. The main purpose of the two-week-long seminar is to cultivate new mindset and culture of working in the public service, build teamwork and networking, develop new skills and competencies necessary for the implementation of their task, and learn public service virtues (OCSC 2019).

To determine if the newcomers would be allowed to become civil servants, at least two assessments will be performed: the first three months and six months of probation. After the completion of all three processes, their performance will be evaluated based on the OCSC's framework as previously explained, composing of their achievement and their behavior at work. A minimum score of 60% for each component is considered and certified a "pass." Then, they can continue their public service career. The evaluation process is done by three assessment committees assigned by their related supervisors who know their assignments. In case they fail the assessment due to uncontrollable circumstances, such as pregnancy leave or serious sickness, etc., the probation period can be extended for another three months, but all the probation period cannot exceed 12 months (OCSC Regulations 2010, pp. 38–39).

Training

People are now considered human capital and the most valuable resources in public service management, in creating high potential persons and added intellectual value to public agencies, leading to effective, efficient, and sustainable services. Given new, dynamic, and changing context of government sector today, requiring more flexible, efficient, and responsive policies, the civil servant development system

166 Amporn Tamronglak

needs to be the driving force and ready to provide sufficient highly qualified personnel for any circumstances (Bossaert 2005). For this reason, the OCSC initiated a civil servant development policy, approved by the Minister in 1989 and later revised in 1996 (OCSC, Civil Service Training and Development 2009a).

The bureaucratic reform in 2002 has set the new direction and perspective in developing and strengthening the civil servants' ability to perform and public organizational culture, resulting in the development of a civil servant development strategy and approved by the Cabinet on July 27, 2004, as a guideline for civil servant development. The paradigm shift in development civil servant resource in Thailand was transformed in 2008 when the administrative reform act (Civil Service Act 2008) refocused the mindset and practices of public personnel development from specialist and expert to generalist and result-based oriented.

The Civil Service Training Institute (CSTI) was established in the OCSC and is currently responsible for the study, analyze, research, and develop human resource training and development policy and guidelines in the public sector, including the development of training courses, monitoring and evaluating civil servant government scholarship students, and producing training media and technology (Ministerial Regulations 2009). The CSDI also continuously provides different in-house training and development courses for new recruits, high potential civil servants, middle managers, senior executives, personnel management officers, and human resource development officers through various channels of in-class, distance learning, and other electronic forms. Examples of training and development programs regularly offered every year include:

- Good Civil Servants for new civil servants,
- New Wave Leader (starting the first batch in 2009 till the 24 batch this year),
- The Civil Service Executive Development Program (SED1): Visionary and Moral Leadership,
- The Senior Executive Development Program (or SED2), focusing on global issue to become global leader,
- HR Profession Program for HR practitioners or officers,
- Blended Learning Course for HR practitioners or officers,
- Efficiency Building, focusing on quality of work life of civil servants in politically sensitive areas of three Southern Provinces, targeting 2,500 personnel per year,
- Post-career training program to prepare for retirement,
- E-Learning for all personnel such as basic knowledge and skills in writing government official letters, MS Excel for management, financial management for civil servants, project management, strategic planning and management, and so on,
- Other programs, collaborations between Thailand and Singapore and ASEAN countries, Singapore-Thailand Senior Officials Development Programme (SG-TH SODP), Singapore-Thailand Leadership Development Program,

Thailand **167**

- Digital Literacy Project, to prepare all civil servants for digital Thailand policy,
- Leadership for Change, for local government leaders in driving and carrying government strategic reform policies initiated by current reform,
- Civil Servants 4.0, preparing all civil servants for 4Cs (Change, Collaboration, Creative, and Corruption Free) in the new Thailand 4.0 policy,
- Etc.

All training and development courses and program will announce each year and can be accessed and applied online via OCSC website. Other courses that Thai public personnel can take and get financial support or scholarship from the government for New Wave, talented personnel, High Performance and Potential persons (from High Performance and Potential System/HiPPS), middle managers, and executives are Leadership, Strategist, Project management, Digital Transformation, Talent Management, etc. (OCSC 2019).

Besides, the CSTI, there are other training institutes or units for special profession, for instance, Public Prosecution Official Training Institute, Judicial Training Institute, Police College, Prison Academy, Local Personnel Development Institute, Bangkok Metropolitan Administration Development Institute for Teachers and Education Personnel, etc. (OCSC 2019).

It is a must that all new civil servants attend the Orientation Training and Development Programs offered online. For middle managers, in order to be promoted to higher positions or levels, they are required to take HRD e-learning courses, pass the leadership development programs I and II, and the last workshop training. Promotion to higher rank is not many and very competitive, only few can be selected to fill vacant executive positions.

Senior Civil Service Development

One of the remarkable changes in the bureaucratic reform in 2002 was the elimination of Position Classification (PC system) or the grade level and replaced with more flexible career advancement of civil servant positions. Senior Executive Service, such as Head of Ministry, Permanent-Secretary, Head of Department, Secretary-General, Director-General from primary to higher level, was created and their training and development are specially designed to be global leader, especially to pursue, monitor, and collaborate with the new 20-years national strategic plan recently developed by Prayut Chan-o-cha government effective in 2018 (OCSC 2019).

Senior Executive Service (SES) are encouraged to participate in leadership development programs offered by CSTI under the supervision of OCSC or equivalent executive training and development programs organized by other agencies and certified by OCSC, for example, Executive Training by the Institute of Administration Development, Ministry of Interior and Thailand National Defence College. The OCSC also recognizes those SES who have attended both, one of the equivalent executive training programs and the Extra Training Courses for Senior Executive, including

- Foreign Affairs Executive Programme by Devawongse Varopakaan Institute of Foreign Affairs, Ministry of Foreign Affairs,
- Ministry of Finance,
- Ministry of Justice,
- Ministry of Agriculture and Cooperative, and
- King Prajadhipok's Institute (OCSC 2019).

There are two main training courses for SES leadership development in Thailand: (1) Civil Service Executive Development Program (CSED1): Visionary and Moral Leadership and (2) The Senior Executive Development Program (or CSED2). Each has different focus.

The first Civil Service Executive Development Program is a four-month-long development covering a six-day boarding for management mindset building and three months of in-class development on various subject matters of effective management, global and internal contexts, quality of work life, etc., and field trip visits in Thailand and abroad. To qualify for the completion of the program, each is required to do an individual research and group assignments on national competitiveness. A combination of various methods of learning from in-class discussion to executive forum, brainstorming, site visit to neighboring ASEAN countries' border, and action learning has been employed throughout. Two groups of training courses are offered annually (OCSC 2019).

The Senior Executive Development Program is a six-month-long development, regularly once a week basis, targeting Head of Department, Secretary-General, and Director-General at the primary level (previously C11 level). In this course, the SES are expected to learn from experienced SES who will be their role model and develop skills in strategic management of their interests. Five methods of training and development are applied in the process, for instance, in-class learning, senior consultant, executive networking, academic forum, and field trip. The details of topics for learning and discussion can be proposed and self-designed by participants.

The last course for executive learning is call "Extra Training Courses." This takes 18 days or 115 hours of completion. Two groups are offered annually. The eligible person to apply for this program is the same as the above two programs. All training content would be the same or similar to the executive program but is a supplement to those who have participated and passed the executive training programs offered by other public agencies certified by OCSC. Basically, the curriculum is five days or 40 hours stay-in, 59 hours on managing professionally, and 16 hours of group project on any interested national strategies, plus field trips. Training and development methods are quite similar to other programs (OCSC 2019).

Notes

1 Fairness of assessment at any stage of selection process and decisions being made are deemed justified. Each candidate must be assessed on the basis of the individual merit and his/her suitability with a given job and relevant criteria applied consistently to all the candidates.
2 Equity refers to the equality of opportunities, openness in employment, and equal treatment to all applicants.
3 Transparency means open communication and public announcement of job information about recruitment process, its practices, and decisions.
4 Standardization of selection procedures and techniques are used at each stage of selection and valid in accordance with needs and requirement of a given job. A fair and equal competition is guaranteed while selection procedures are administered with flexibility, efficiency, and value for money.
5 OCSC has recommended three different methods to define key performance indicators such as Goal-Cascading Method, Customer-Focused Method, and Workflow Charting Method. The goal-cascading method is the hierarchical way of setting overall KPIs and target and then cascade down the organizational scalar chain from the top to individual person at the bottom of the pyramid. KPIs and targets are logically aligned from top-down. The customer-focused method is suitable for service function. The KPIs and target are set from the results of customer's survey in given feedback on their perceptions of the quality of services received from the service provider. The last method is used when there are many people involved in the process of doing the work. In the workflow, one person may take part in only certain activity, performing certain role. A role-result matrix is created to set KPIs and target for each person in the workflow charts. Details on how to define and apply each method can be found in the OCSC manual on performance appraisal (OCSC 2009b).
6 Targets are given in five levels from the lowest of 1 with 1 point to the highest level with score of 5 points. Level 1 means the least acceptable achievement, getting 1 point. Level 2 means target below acceptable standard, getting 2 points. Level 3 means target at acceptable standard, getting 3 points. Level 4 is target moderately difficult to achieve, getting 4 points. Level 5 is target highly difficult and challenging to achieve, getting the highest 5 points.

References

Bossaert, D. (2005, June) 'The flexibilisation of the employment status of civil servants: From life tenure to more flexible employment relations?' Survey for the 44th meeting of the Directors general responsible for Public Administration of the EU member states, European Institute of Public Administration, Luxembourg.

Civil Service Act, B.E. 2551 (2008).

Constitution of the Kingdom of Thailand (2017).

Fernquest, J. (2016, March 28) 'Civil servants to retire at 65', *Bangkok Post*, available at: www.bangkokpost.com/learning/work/912924/civil-servants-to-retire-at-65%20 28/03/2016.

Ministerial Regulations (2009) 'Ministerial regulations on the division of the office of civil service commission, prime minister office', available at: www.ocsc.go.th/sites/default/files/attachment/law/ministry_rule_of_div_2552.pdf

The Nation (2018, October 15) 'Weak education holds back Thailand in worldwide human-capital index', *The Nation*, available at: www.nationmultimedia.com/detail/asean-plus/30356417.

170 Amporn Tamronglak

OCSC (2009a) 'Civil service development', available at: www.ocsc.go.th/csti.

OCSC (2009b) *Public Sector Performance Appraisal Manual: Performance Management System and Performance Appraisal System*, Nonthaburi: OCSC, available at: www.ocsc.go.th/sites/default/files/attachment/circular/w20-2552-rules.pdf.

OCSC (2010) 'Regulations on probations', available at: www.ocsc.go.th/sites/default/files/attachment/law/law_civil_service_rules2553_02_0.pdf.

OCSC (2012) 'Compensation', available at: www.ocsc.go.th/compensation.

OCSC (2014) *Guide to the Civil Service Commission*, Nonthaburi: OCSC.

OCSC (2019) 'HRD: E-learning 2019', available at: www.ocsc.go.th/sites/default/files/attachment/circular/w20-2552-rules.pdf.

OCSC (n.d. a) *Bureaucratic System in the Kingdom of Thailand*, Nonthaburi: OCSC: Kornkanok Publishing.

OCSC (n.d. b) 'Recruitment in Thai civil service', available at: www.jobdst.com/content/ocsc/jobdst-ocsc3.pdf (accessed 11 April 2019).

Office of the Educational Affairs (2016) *'History of OCSC', Royal Thai Embassy*, Washington DC, available at: http://oeadc.org/english/history-of-ocsc.

Osatit, C. (n.d.) 'Historical development of the management side of employment relations in Thailand', available at: www.academia.edu/19865021/A_Brief_on_Thailand_Employment_System?auto=download.

Post Reporter (2018, April 10) 'Govt officials to retire at 63 not 60,' *Bangkok Post*, available at: www.bangkokpost.com/news/general/1443683/govt-officials-to-retire-at-63-not-60.

Prasitsiriwong, V. (2018 May 25) 'Why there are only "Commission" in the central personnel agencies in Thai public sector?' *Prachatai*, available at: https://prachatai.com/journal/2018/11/79572

Prime Minister's Delivery Unit (PMDU) (2018, March 20) 'National strategy', available at: https://pmdu.soc.go.th

Simananta, S. and Aramkul, A. (2002) 'Decentralization of recruitment in Thai civil service', available at: http://unpan1.un.org/intradoc/groups/public/documents/UN/UNPAN021828.pdf.

9

MALAYSIA[1]

Khadijah Md Khalid and Nur Hairani Abd Rahman

The Malaysian Civil Service: An Overview

Malaysia is a federation consisting of 13 states and three federal territories (Kuala Lumpur, Labuan, and Putrajaya). Present-day Johor, Kelantan, Kedah, Perlis, and Terengganu (known as the Unfederated Malay states), which were under indirect British rule, have distinct administrative norms and practices compared with that of the four states of Selangor, Perak, Negeri Sembilan, and Pahang which were directly ruled (referred to as the Federated Malay states) by the British. Two of the 13 states – Sabah and Sarawak – which are located on the Borneo Island had also experienced British colonial rule, but each was governed separately, thus making them unique in many aspects and having different implications on their present-day public service. For example, the Sarawak state government appears to have more autonomy than that of the other states in the Malaysian Federation. Two states – Penang and Melaka – together with Singapore, were part of the Straits Settlement. Under the Straits Settlement, Penang, Melaka, and Singapore were governed directly by the British. (Singapore later became part of the Malaysian Federation in September 1963 but left in 1965.)

Upon gaining independence from Britain on August 31, 1957, Malaya (later merged with Sabah, Sarawak, and Singapore in September 1963 to form the Federation of Malaysia) began to embark on many socioeconomic programs and initiatives for the betterment of its citizenry. Since the majority of the population still lived in rural areas in the 1950s and 1960, rural development was given prominence by the postcolonial leadership of the country. Since the first two prime ministers (Tunku Abdul Rahman, 1957–1969 and Tun Abdul Razak, 1970–1976) had earlier served in the colonial civil service, the administrative machinery was quite responsive to the needs and demands of the newly independent Malay(a)sian citizens. The country was able to focus on a series of economic and social development programs, beginning with the First Malaysian Development Plan, 1965–1970.

DOI: 10.4324/9781003326496-12

172 Khadijah Md Khalid and Nur Hairani Abd Rahman

During its formative years, the nature of public administration in Malay(a)sia was mainly centered on the maintenance of law and order (as security was critical then because the country was under the Emergency)[2] and collection of revenue to support an economy that was trade-oriented in nature. Exports were made up of natural rubber and tin produced by large foreign-owned plantations (Mahbob and Md. Khalid 2018).

The political leadership of the newly independent country was committed to work hand-in-hand with the professionally trained senior public administrators or civil servants in building the nation (Md. Khalid 2020). Malaysia was fortunate to have inherited a relatively professional and efficient civil service from the British.

It was unfortunate that development efforts were abruptly interrupted by the May 1969 ethnic riots in Kuala Lumpur. The May 1969 incident led to the formulation of the New Economic Policy (NEP), covering the period of 1971–1990, which had the target of national unity by implementing the distributive economic policy of poverty eradication and restructuring of society to ensure that ethnic identification along economic function would be finally eliminated (Md. Khalid and Abidin 2014).

The public service took a significant turn when Tun Razak became Prime Minister in 1970 after the suspension of Parliament following the 1969 riots. The more interventionist role of the state in the economy led to the expansion of the country's public service. The growth of the public bureaucracy was very much related to the more robust socioeconomic programs of the Razak government.

The implementation of the NEP throughout the 1971–1990 period aimed at eradicating poverty and addressing inter-ethnic economic imbalances. The role of the public service in development was very important then especially in planning of policies and programs, in implementation of projects, in enhancing human resource development, and in promoting trade and investments.[3]

In effect, since independence, the evolution and development of the Malaysian public service have always been in tandem and influenced by the changing needs and demands of the Malaysian society, politics, and economy. Tun Hussein Onn (1976 to 1981), who succeeded Tun Razak as the country's third Prime Minister, continued many of the policies of his predecessor, with a stronger emphasis on promoting national unity and integration as well as combatting corruption.

When Mahathir took over the premiership (1981–2003), he introduced several major policy changes including those pertaining to administrative reforms which aspired to make the civil service more efficient and productive. Mahathir introduced a two-prong approach to make the civil service more efficient and productive. One was developing policies for civil servants by using various administrative circulars provided by MAMPU starting in 1991. Among the administrative circulars meant to improve public efficiency were the use of the punch card system, the use of productivity tools to measure performance, and the use of documented standard operating procedure (SOP) documents.[4]

The other strategy for improving the public delivery system was the more pro-Big Business (local and foreign investors) of the Mahathir administration also had an impact on the civil service. Mahathir, who was critical of the large public bureaucracy, wanted "to roll back the state" via his controversial privatization policy. In his effort to reduce the size of the public bureaucracy, several major government agencies such as those in charge of public utilities, namely electricity (National Electricity Board) and communication (*Telekom Malaysia*) were privatized. It was during Mahathir's tenure that the Executive became more dominant at the expense of the civil service and other institutions.

At the same time, the visionary Mahathir, who was known to be fascinated by things Japanese (Md. Khalid and Lee 2003). and East Asian values, began to introduce several new initiatives and programs. Inspired by the success of Japan Incorporated (Japan Inc), Mahathir launched "Malaysia Incorporated" in 1983 which emphasized closer ties between the public sector and the private sector.[5] In effect, the first Mahathir's government began to introduce many administrative policies to help boost the public bureaucracy in fulfilling the vision of Malaysia as an industrialized economy.

The robustness and excessiveness of the Mahathir rule (1981–2003) in terms of his bold economic policies and administrative reforms had left the public bureaucracy "exhausted."[6] It is, thus, not surprising that many quarters including the civil service welcomed the appointment Ahmad Badawi (2003–2009) as the country's fifth Prime Minister in October 2003.

The leadership style of Abdullah Ahmad Badawi was characterized as open and consultative where it encouraged participation from various and diverse groups within the Malaysian society. These components have allowed various quarters including the public to have significant degree of participation in government policies and programs. In addition, the premiership of Abdullah Badawi had also emphasized on spiritual and integrity elements among public servants (Husin et al. 2007; Welsh 2013; Md. Khalid 2013).

The Institute of Integrity Malaysia (IIM) was founded by the Abdullah administration to create more awareness among the public on the principles of good governance in Malaysia post-Mahathir. Many programs were organized to promote integrity and ethical conduct particularly among the civil servants. Greater emphasis was given to the need to improve the public delivery system via PEMUDAH (*Pasukan Petugas Khas Pemudahcara Perniagaan*), which is the Special Task Force to Facilitate Business. PEMUDAH was set up to improve the overall of Malaysia's business environment, particularly to address the bureaucratic red-tapes and to enhance public service delivery. The main objective of this agency is "to achieve globally benchmarked, customer-centric, innovative, entrepreneurial and proactive public and private sector delivery service in support of a vibrant, resilient and competitive economy and society" (mpv.gov.my).

Malaysia under Najib (2009–2018) was beset with many critical issues and challenges which were closely related to poor public governance and mismanagement of the economy. Prior to Najib's financial scandal cases, and upon helming the premiership, Najib attempted to be a technocrat in leading Malaysia. One of his first attempts at transforming Malaysia was the New Economic Model (NEM) in 2010, which was supposed to replace the 1970 New Economic Policy. The NEM was short-lived as Najib faced major pressure from members of his ruling elite due to one of its objectives of having a competitive market by reducing some of the implemented affirmative actions. Najib's attempt at transforming the civil service through the Public Service New Remuneration or the Saraan Baru Perkhidmatan Awam (SBPA) in 2011 also met with a quick demise due to pressures from within the bureaucracy.[7]

Since the beginning of the financial scandal which rocked the Najib administration in 2015 (Channel News Asia 2018),[8] Malaysians have been seriously affected by the maladministration of the economy by the Executive where many senior civil servants were implicated (together with the Prime Minister) in several major financial scandals that eventually led to the defeat of UMNO-led Barisan Nasional which had governed the country for more than 60 years.

The issues of rampant corruption, greater racial polarization, higher costs of living, youth unemployment, poor quality of education and lackluster civil service had angered many Malaysians and eventually led to the victory of *Pakatan Harapan*

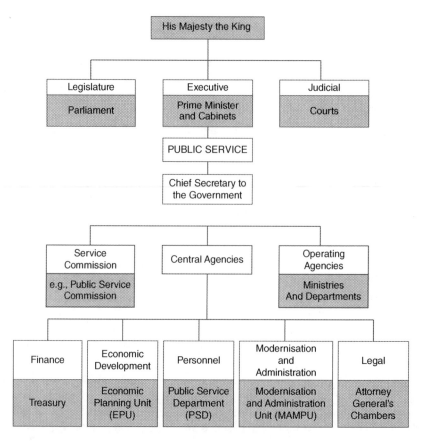

FIGURE 9.1 Malaysian government structure (Mokhtar 2011).

(PH), an Opposition coalition led by former Prime Minister, Mahathir Mohamad (1981–2003, 2018–2020) in the 14th General Election in May 2018. The civil service which was briefly under the PH government and succeeded by the current *Perikatan Nasional (PN)* ruling coalition in February 2022 is facing serious challenges in managing the multifarious issues and problems associated with the COVID-19 pandemic amid the major uncertainties in global economy and politics.

The Malaysian Public Service System

In the Malaysian parliamentary system, the Executive which is headed by the Prime Minister remains the most powerful branch of government. The present-day Malaysian public service, which is part of the Executive, has been significantly influenced by its unique historical (namely British colonial rule), sociocultural and political processes.

The history of the modern-day Malaysian public service began with the founding of the Malayan Establishment Office (MEO) in colonial Singapore in 1934. In the first decade of independence (1957 to 1967), the Federal Establishment Office (FEO) which was the precursor of the present-day Public Service Department (PSD) acted as the main central agency of the country's civil service.

The MEO was later renamed the Federation Establishment Office (FEO) when it was relocated to the Federal House in Kuala Lumpur. FEO was briefly renamed Establishment Office of Malaysia (EOM) in 1967 and the name was soon changed to Public Service Department (PSD) in 1968 (refer www.jpa.gov.my). The Department was again relocated to the PSD Complex in Kuala Lumpur in the same year and remained there until 2001. The PSD finally moved to its current location in Putrajaya when the new administrative capital was officially opened by the country's fourth Prime Minister, Mahathir Mohamad (1981–2003, 2018–2020).

The Malaysian public service which is part of the Executive branch of the government is helmed by the Chief Secretary to the Government who also acts as the Secretary to the Cabinet. The Malaysian public sector comprises three main components of public service, which are federal, state, and local government.

There are four sources of administrative authority *(punca kuasa)* of the PSD, namely:

(a) The Federal Constitution (Part 10, Articles 132–148)

For example:
Article 132 (Definition of Public Service)
Article 147(1): Pension

Article 132(1)
For the purposes of this Constitution, the public services are -
(a) The armed forces;
(b) The judicial and legal service;

(c)   The general public service of the Federation;
(d)   The police force;
(e)   The railway service;
(f)   The joint public services mentioned in Article 133;
(g)   The public service of each State; and
(h)   The education services.

Article 132(2)

(2)   Except as otherwise expressly provided by this Constitution, the qualifications for appointment and conditions of service of persons in the public services other than those mentioned in paragraph (g) of Clause (1) maybe regulated by the federal law and subject to the provisions of any such law by Yang di-Pertuan Agong or the King;

(b)   Acts

For example: Act of Ministerial Functions (1969) and Act of Statutory Bodies (Discipline and Surcharge) (2000)

(c)   General Orders

For example: Chapter B (Allowance), Chapter C (Leave), Chapter E (Housing and Government Office Building), Chapter F (Medical), Chapter G (Working/Office Hours and Overtime)

(d)   Rules

For example: Service Circulars, Service Circular Letters (*Surat Pekeliling Perkhidmatan*)

According to Article 132 of the Federal Constitution, the Malaysian public service also includes teachers, the police force, and members of the Armed Forces. At present, about 100,000 positions in the civil service remain vacant. However,

TABLE 9.1 Breakdown of the number of public servants (as of 2018)

Commission	No. of Public Servants
Malaysian Armed Forces Council	124,539
Judicial and Legal Service Commission	6,126
General Federal Service	630,234
Royal Malaysian Police	117,548
State Commission	79,623
Education Service Commission	446,172
Others:	
Federal Statutory Bodies	123,398
States Statutory Bodies	14,404
Local Authorities	48,902

Source: Informant's data.

without these vacancies being filled in, Malaysia still employs one of the highest numbers of public servants in the region. However, the high number of civil servants in the Malaysian public bureaucracy is due to the fact that three major sectors – Education, the Army, and the Police – are considered as part of the civil service. As such, the high number of public servants does not reflect the "true" representation of the country's civil service. The three sectors combined employ close to 700,000 "civil servants" (see Table 9.1).

Central Agency

The Public Service Department (PSD), known as *Jabatan Perkhidmatan Awam* (JPA) in Malay, is the central agency that manages the human resources of the public sector in Malaysia. PSD states its mission as "Leading the Development of Public Service Human Resource." In the Malaysian context, the public (civil) service is part of the Executive. The Chief Secretary to the Government is the most senior civil servant in the Malaysian public service. The Public Service Department (PSD) can be considered the central agency in charge of human resource management at the federal level.

Tasks and Functions

The PSD plays a leading role in the country's human resource management. Its two main agendas are to develop the institutional capacities of the public sector and to ensure its smooth and efficient management and operation. In the context of present-day Malaysia where politics have become increasingly complex and competitive, it is thus imperative that the Malaysian public service continues to promote transparency, accountability, good governance, and excellent public service delivery.

The new ruling coalition, Pakatan Harapan (PH), under Prime Minister Mahathir Mohamad has reiterated the importance for the public service to remain politically neutral and accountable in serving the *rakyat* (citizens). In addition, public servants have been constantly reminded to serve the political master or government of the day without fear or favor and avoid waste, mismanagement, and abuse of power.

The PSD consists of 10 divisions including one training institute (known as INTAN or National Institute of Public Administration) and four supporting yet critical units. Each division or unit has its own specific tasks or functions, and they are as follows (adapted from PSD website) (Public Service Department n.d. b):

a) Human Capital Development Division: This division is mainly responsible for identifying and providing scholarships for promising young scholars who would later join the public service upon the completion of their studies. The division is also tasked with organizing a series of training programs

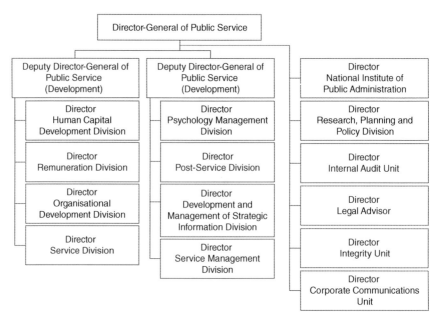

FIGURE 9.2 Organizational chart (refer to www.jpa.gov.my/).

for current serving officers and staff to equip themselves with new or latest knowledge and skills throughout the year. All civil servants are encouraged to embrace lifelong learning concepts or principles in order to remain relevant and efficient.

b) Remuneration Division: The main responsibility of this division is to ensure that the remuneration system or scheme is fair and acceptable to all staff irrespective of their grades or ranks.

c) Organizational Development Division: One major function of this division is to ensure that all public sector agencies or departments have relevant schemes of service. The division is also tasked to provide its officers/staff with efficient and effective organizational structures which are conducive in meeting their work or professional objectives.

d) Service Division: The division's main task is to formulate and implement effective and strategic public service policies which include the career development of the management and staff of the public sector.

e) Psychology Management Division: The main task of this division is to ensure the effectiveness of policies and programs, particularly those pertaining to promoting the psychological wellbeing of public servants at all levels.

f) Post-Service Division: The division is responsible for the provision and timely disbursement of appropriate/relevant retirement benefits to recipients (pensioners) based on their entitlements.

g) Development and Management of Strategic Information Division: The main function of this division is to implement strategic ICT policies and programs which will help to enhance the overall competency and performance of the civil service.

h) Service Management Division: The division is primarily tasked with managing human resources and services efficiently and effectively.

i) Research Planning and Policy Division: The core function of this department is to conduct research where the (research) findings and outputs will, in turn, provide important input for sound and effective policy formulation on human resource management. Ideas and suggestions from this Division can be used to institute reforms in order to help improve the overall quality and effectiveness of the human resource management.

j) National Institute of Public Administration: INTAN is the most important training institute for civil servants from all levels, schemes, and grades. It was first founded in 1959 under the name of the Staff Training Centre (STC) in Port Dickson. The Centre was later expanded and transformed and officially renamed INTAN in June 1972. In addition to organizing training programs which emphasize on character building, knowledge and skill development and leadership of public officials, INTAN is also tasked with conducting research, consultancy, and publication.

k) Internal Audit Unit: This unit acts as the custodian in promoting as well as safeguarding ethical values and practices in the civil service. The unit's main responsibility is to assist the public service in achieving its objective of managing its resources, namely finance, prudently, efficiently, and effectively. The unit is also responsible for introducing a strict and systematic approach to assess the effectiveness of controls and good governance in the Malaysian public service. It has the duty and responsibility to ensure that the financial management of the public service is in accordance with the laws, rules, and procedures set by the government.

l) Legal Adviser: The main task of the Legal Adviser in PSD is to provide quality and professional legal advice and counsel in accordance with the Federal Constitution and the laws of the land.

m) Integrity Unit: This unit plays an important role in consolidating and coordinating all managerial matters pertaining to the inculcation of ethical values and conduct, integrity, and other positive traits among the public servants under one specialized unit. Its main function also includes instituting integrity and compliance as well as introducing preventive measures and mechanisms which could help detect and deter the abuse of power, corruption, and mismanagement among the civil servants.

n) Corporate Communication Unit: The unit is entrusted with the role of enhancing the corporate image of the PSD and also acts as the conduit between members of the public alongside other stakeholders with the PSD, namely the office of the Director-General.

In the Public Service Department (PSD), the Service Division can be regarded as the most important division. This division consists of:

a) Common Service Management Branch (*Cawangan Pengurusan Perkhidmatan Guna Sama*)
b) Special Unit for High Potential and Subject Matter Expert (SME)
c) Operational Service Branch (*Cawangan Operasi Perkhidmatan*)
d) Policy and Consultancy Branch *(Cawangan Dasar dan Perundingan)*

Recruitment

Political Appointment

The Malaysian government allows the recruitment or appointments of officers holding certain positions based on political considerations. There are several types of political appointments.[9] The first one refers to the appointment for the positions of a private secretary, senior private secretary, special officer, press officer, and others who are assigned to ministers and deputy ministers. Selected individuals who are assigned to serve a particular minister or deputy minister, come from the pool of PTD officers. Suitable candidates for these positions are first identified and shortlisted by their respective departments or ministries. Nominations of the shortlisted candidates/officers will be conveyed to the Head of Service (*Ketua Perkhidmatan*). The minister or deputy minister then decides whether to accept or decline the nomination made by the Head of Service. In most cases, the nominees will accept the appointments and will serve the minister or deputy minister throughout the whole duration of service. The second type of political appointment is when a minister and deputy minister request the appointment of officers from other departments, agencies, or ministries. The human resource department of a particular ministry will submit names/nominations to the secretary general of the respective ministry. A federal minister can also request the service of an officer from a state agency which has to be consented by the respective state governments. The third type/category of political appointment involves the recruitment of private secretaries, senior private secretaries, special officers, press officers, and others from outside the civil service. Since these appointees do not come from the conventional pool of government officers, their nominations must be approved by the prime minister. The political appointees may be also sourced out from various organizations, including from the private sector.

A good example of a political appointment was the recruitment of Johan Mahmood Merican as the Chief Executive Officer of TalentCorp, a federal agency which was established in 2011 during the Najib administration (2009–2018). TalentCorp was set up to help the government to identify and encourage Malaysian talents in various sectors and professions who are working abroad to return and serve the country. Johan Merican was the Principal Private Secretary to the Minister in the Ministry of Finance when he was appointed to helm TalentCorp. Johan served TalentCorp from 2011 to 2016, and from 2016 to 2018 he was reassigned to the Economic Planning Unit (EPU) as Deputy Director General (Human Capital). He is currently the National Budget Director at the Ministry of Finance.

Two notable political appointments included a well-known political activist, Latheefa Koya of *Pakatan Keadilan Rakyat* (PKR). Latheefa was named Chief Commissioner of the Malaysian Anti-Corruption Commission (MACC) (The Star 2019, June 5) and Azhar "Art" Harun as Chairman of the Electoral Commission (EC) (Bedi 2018). It is interesting to note that the past Chief Commissioners of the MACC and Chairman of the EC were appointed from among the senior civil servants. The appointments of these two personalities to their respective positions were deemed controversial as both were closely associated with the ruling PH coalition. A lawyer by training, Latheefa Koya was a member of the Central Executive Committee of *Parti Keadilan Rakyat* (PKR – People Justice Party), a major partner in the ruling coalition and had also served as the director and founder of an NGO, Lawyers for Liberty. Prior to their appointments, only senior civil servants were appointed as the Chief Commissioner of MACC and Chairman of EC respectively.[10]

What is ironic is that the current government is "guilty" of appointing public officers who are clearly politically aligned with them. The PH administration used to criticize the *Barisan Naisonal* leadership for hiring many politically inclined individuals to key positions in the government which added to the financial burden of the country because many were paid quite exorbitantly as consultants.

It was reported that 3,250 political appointees who had served under the previous Barisan Nasional government had their services terminated by the new ruling (*Pakatan Harapan* or PH in short) party. Soon after PH assumed power after the May 2018 GE, vice chancellors from five public universities were replaced. The reason for their termination (of service) was to allow the Ministry of Education to appoint those with new ideas and leadership to swiftly drive the reform agenda for Malaysian tertiary institutions (*The Star Online* 2018, September 21).[11]

Soon after assuming his cabinet position as the new Minister of Youth and Sports, Syed Saddiq decided to end the service of five prominent individuals, including a chairman, board members and directors, of *Perbadanan Golf Subang*, Institute for Youth Research Malaysia IYRES), *Perbadanan Stadium Malaysia*, and the National Sport Institute, respectively, as part of the ministry's effort to promote greater accountability and transparency. The decision to discontinue the services of these individuals was perhaps due to the negative public perception of the Ministry of Youth and Sports which was ranked as one of the most corrupted ministries in Malaysia (Malay Mail 2018, 2 August).

Civil Servant Recruitment

There are two types of employment status or conditions for the Malaysian civil servants, permanent and contractual. Permanent staff generally enjoy a lifetime employment together with several other benefits including housing, health services,

182 Khadijah Md Khalid and Nur Hairani Abd Rahman

and pensions upon retirement. At present, about 98% out of the 1.6 million civil servants are working on a permanent basis. Besides that, civil servants are also employed on a contractual basis, either for a short duration or a long term. At present, less than 2% of those employed in the Malaysian civil service are on contract basis.[12] However, more and more staff are now hired on a contractual basis to lessen the financial burden of the government.

Recruitment Process

Malaysians who are interested to join the civil service are advised to check with the Public Service Commission (known as *Suruhanjaya Perkhidmatan Awam* or SPA in short). SPA is responsible for the recruitment and confirmation of service, while the PSD is responsible for placement of officers or staff and policy matters. Interested candidates must apply online via the SPA portal. Since the application is valid for only one year, the applicant has to apply again after one year. Applicants are advised to apply for relevant positions based on their academic qualifications and work experience. There are instances whereby "overqualified" applicants do not disclose their highest academic qualifications or credentials to compete with "less qualified" applicants for certain positions/grades.

TABLE 9.2 List of service classification

No.	Service Classifications	Salary Code
1.	Transport	A
2.	Arts and Talent	B
3.	Sciences	C
4.	Education	D
5.	Economy	E
6.	Information System	F
7.	Agriculture	G
8.	Skills	H
9.	Engineering	J
10.	Security and Civil Defense	K
11.	Legal and Judicial	L
12.	Administrative and Diplomatic	M
13.	Administrative and Support	N
14.	Prevention	P
15.	Research and Development	Q
16.	Social	S
17.	Maritime Enforcement	T
18.	Medical and Health	U
19.	Finance	W
20.	Police	Y
21.	Armed Forces	Z

Source: Public Service Department (n.d. c), www.interactive.jpa.gov.my/

Malaysia **183**

TABLE 9.3 Appointment grade

Grade	Open/Common Service
Grades 41 to 54	• The appointment grade is opened to all applicants/potential employees • It is common (open) and closed service • It depends on the academic qualification for the positions or respective grades of services applied

Source: www.jpa.gov.my/en/permanent-temporary-appointment

TABLE 9.4 Service structure

No	Structure of Service	Entry Qualifications	Role & Responsibilities
1	Top Management	(Premier) Grade (First Degree & Higher) (Special) Grade (First Degree & Higher)	Strategic role in leading, advising, planning, and formulating policies and being role model • Recognition of special expertise • Spearheading research and findings and its application in their respective fields of specialization
2	Management and Professional	First Degree & Higher	Planning and assisting in policy formulation, management, implementation, and evaluation and its enforcement in their respective role functions
3	Support	Diploma/STPM	Management of work related to the operations, supervision, and enforcement relevant to their role functions
4		SPM	Carrying out duties that are physical and routine in nature
5		PMR/PT3	

Source: www.jpa.gov.my/skim-perkhidmatan

TABLE 9.5 Numeric grading according to entry qualification

Service Group	Entry Qualifications	Numeric Grade Range	Example
Top Management	Promotion from Management & Professional	VU1 – VU7/ VK5 – VK7	• Chief Secretary to the Government (VU1) • Director General of Public Service (VU2) • Medical Officer Grade VK
Management and Professional	Tertiary Qualification (First Degree & Higher)	41–54	• Administrative & Diplomatic Officer Grade M41, M44, M48, M52, M54 • Lecturer Grade DS45, DS51/52, DS53/54, VK7

(Continued)

184 Khadijah Md Khalid and Nur Hairani Abd Rahman

TABLE 9.5 (Continued)

Service Group	Entry Qualifications	Numeric Grade Range	Example
Support	Diploma/Malaysia Higher School Certificate of Education	29–40	• Asst. Wildlife Officer Grade G29, G32, G36, G40 • Asst. Curator Grade S29, S32, S38, S40
	Malaysia Certificate of Education (SPM)	19–28	• Forest Ranger Grade G19, G22, G26, G2
	Lower Secondary Assessment/ Lower Certificate of Education	11–18	• Driver Grade H11, H14, H16, H18

Source: www.spa.gov.my/spa/laman-utama/gaji-syarat-lantikan-deskripsi-tugas

The academic degrees of the applicants must have been conferred by colleges/ universities which are recognized by the government and accredited by the Malaysian Qualifications Agency (MQA). Apart from college/university degrees, diplomas, high school certificates (STPM/STAM), Certification of Education Malaysia (SPM), Certificate of Skills Malaysia (SKM), Certificate of Polytechnic and other certificates must also be recognized by the government. Different qualifications and requirements are needed for certain jobs under different schemes. All applicants regardless of the types and schemes must obtain at least a Credit in Bahasa Malaysia (National Language), Mathematics and History for Malaysian Education Certificate (in Malaysia known as *Sijil Pelajaran Malaysia* (SPM)).

The recruitment process of civil servants differs from one department/ministry. Although there is a common recruitment process for almost all government agencies and ministries, some of the agencies and ministries have their own set of rules, procedures, and requirements. An example is recruitment of teachers for public schools. Since teachers are regarded as public servants, they are recruited by the Education Service Commission. Teachers have to go through different selection and recruitment processes. The basic academic qualifications for teachers have also changed over time. At present, public school teachers, either in primary or secondary school, are expected to have a basic degree and possess a diploma in education. Over the years, the academic qualifications and requirements of the principals (high schools), headmasters/headmistress (primary or elementary schools) have also changed in order to ensure the quality and performance of these educators in the public-school system. This is also to ensure that their competencies are in line with the changing needs and demands emanating from the domestic and international environments.

The recruitment process also differs from one profession or ranks to another. For instance, recruitment of Diplomatic Administrative Officers. For the "elite"

Diplomatic Administrative Officers (also known as *Pegawai Tadbir Diplomatik –* PTD), the recruitment is administered quite differently from those in other services/ professions. Potential candidates, known as cadets, must first attend a three-day assessment program where they are evaluated on the aspects of leadership, public speaking, and teamwork. Special tests will be administered for all candidates. The next level is the interview where the final selection will be made. Potential cadets will enroll later in a ten-month training at the Institute of Public Administration (INTAN), a training institute within the PSD. The programs include the Diploma of Public Administration (DPA), which was accredited by the Ministry of Higher Education in 2016. PTD cadets (as they are popularly known) who fail to perform or for some other reasons (e.g., due to a disciplinary issue) will be expelled. The DPA programs contain four academic modules. The cadets must pass all the modules and must maintain a minimum of grade B. In addition, PTD cadets are also required to be placed in the rural areas (*kampung*) and also assigned as an intern at selected departments or ministries. The cadets will be evaluated by an assigned mentor under the mentor-mentee programs, which has been introduced under the DPA. Under the PTD scheme, there is a three-year probationary period for all new cadets who have successfully fulfilled all the requirements to be part of the "elite" civil service.

Merit-Based Recruitment at Entry Level

All recruitments for government officers in all categories are based on merit. All applicants must fulfill the minimum qualifications and other requirements at the entry level for every position in the respective category. For certain professions or services such as doctors serving at public hospitals, recruitment is administered by the Ministry of Health. Doctors under the government scheme are recruited after going through stringent procedures to ensure that only qualified doctors are allowed to work in government hospitals and clinics.

Examination

Applicants are generally required to go through certain stages before they can be offered certain positions in the Malaysian civil service. After applying for the positions through the Public Service Commission's (PSC's) website, all applications will be screened through. Applications which meet the requirements will be forwarded to the next stage that is the examination.

Examinations in the civil service are designed to gauge the level of knowledge, understanding, and skills of the candidates before or after joining the civil service. There are four objectives of examinations in the Malaysian civil service (Public Service Department n.d. a):

(a) Intake to service: Examination is conducted for the purpose of recruitment in the public service to meet specific service scheme requirement such as the Administrative and Diplomatic Services, Prison, Fire, and Education.

(b) In-service Verification: Newly appointed members of the civil service are required to pass the examination for in-service verification.
(c) Promotion by appointment: This exam is intended to "substitute" the academic qualifications required to assume higher grade positions
(d) Rewards and allowances: The examination is conducted to gauge the level of competency of civil servants and used as a justification for payment of certain allowances.

Under the PSC, there are five scopes of examination to cater for different types of positions, which are (a) talent test/audition; (b) aptitude test; (c) dicta typing test; (d) physical and fitness test; (e) psychological test. Applicants are required to first apply to sit for an examination which is relevant to his position that he is applying for. Given the growing competitiveness of the Malaysian civil service in recent years, the examinations have become more stringent, yet more convenient ("hassle-free") for the candidates/applicants. For example, candidates who are interested to join the PTD scheme used to sit for the examination at the designated center. However, since 2014, the PSD has introduced online examination, which can be taken by applicants from all over the country simultaneously. Regardless of their locations, applicants can sit for the examination as long as they have internet access to the PSC's website. In 2018, thousands of candidates had sat for the PTD examination to fill in 750 vacancies only. Out of the 750 vacancies, 200 were reserved for excellent students who were sponsored by the PSD (Public Service Department 2018).[13] This clearly illustrates that it has become increasingly difficult and competitive for Malaysian graduates to join the public service. The PSD has introduced and imposed more stringent criteria and requirements to ensure only the best are recruited join the Malaysian public service.

Civil Service Classification and Status

Civil Service Classification

At present (as of April 2022), there are 231 schemes of services under 21 service classifications in the Malaysian civil service which do not include police, army, and teachers (Public Service Department 2018.).[14] The 21 classifications are as follows:

Job Security for Civil Servants

The Malaysian Civil Service provides a relatively attractive job security for all its permanent employees. In fact, many Malaysians particular from predominantly Malay ethnic group, prefer to serve in the civil service for various reasons. Although it generally argued that the salaries for civil servants are less attractive than that of their counterparts in the private sector, yet many would like to join the service because of its benefits particularly the heavily subsidized healthcare and housing loan. One of the most attractive benefits working in the civil service is the lifetime employment. Once employed as government servants, it is not easy for the PSD to terminate their services, even though the employees could be found "problematic" and have disciplinary issues later while in service. Thus, the termination of "problematic" employees must be done according to the rule of law to protect the livelihood and welfare of the employees and also the government as the employer.

Openness of Posts/Positions

External and Internal Mobility

External mobility: The recruitment and mobility of the Malaysian civil servants depend largely on whether or not they are employees under a common (open) service or a closed service system. Generally, civil servants who serve in the common or open service are prepared to be transferred out from one department or a ministry to another. For example, an administrative assistant or clerk who works in a particular department in the Ministry of Works can be assigned to serve at another department in the same ministry or another ministry, for example, the Ministry of Transport. A senior federal (PTD) officer can be appointed as the State Secretary or the State Development Planning Officer in six out of the 13 states in the Malaysian federation (former Federated Malay States and Straits Settlements). The salary of this federal officer is paid by the respective state government (Public Service Department 2012).[15]

Another important category of employees in the civil service is the support staff, which includes clerks and technicians. This group (comprising of support

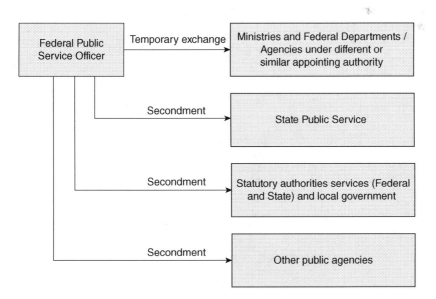

FIGURE 9.3 Secondment, temporary transfer, and permanent exchange (refer to Service Circular No. 12 Year 2008).

188 Khadijah Md Khalid and Nur Hairani Abd Rahman

staff) differs from the Management and Professional (also known as *Pengurusan dan Profesional* – P&P) group because they provide service at the lower level at almost all government departments or ministries. Civil servants who occupy lower rank positions such as clerk can be assigned or transferred from one department or a ministry to another. In this context, these groups are similar to the officers in the PTD scheme who are in the higher rank. Support staff who includes administrative assistants, clerks, technicians, and many other categories, provide an important service to the group of employees.

Internal Mobility: The closed service system refers to employment which can only be filled in or occupied by personnel/staff from within the same scheme of service. Public universities in Malaysia are a good example of a closed public service whereby all its staff from the support group (clerical/administrative staff) until the senior academics cannot be re-assigned or transferred to another federal government agency or even another university. However, a federal government officer from the PTD (another scheme) can be seconded to fill in a position in a university as the Registrar or Bursar of the university. Likewise, a senior academic can also be seconded to assume a senior management position at a federal department or ministry, for example, the Ministry of Education or Ministry of Foreign Affairs.

TABLE 9.6 Common (open) and closed service

Types	Scheme	Recruitment Agency	Service Management (primary)	Supporting	Evaluation
Common or Open Service	M, Q, J, F, L, N, S, DV	Public Service Commission (PSC)	Public Service Department (PSD)		SPA & website
Closed Service	DS, DG	Education Service Commission	Ministry of Education Ministry of Higher Education	Public Service Department: – Salary – Scope of work	
	Y	Police Force Commission (*Suruhanjaya Perkhidmatan Polis*)	Royal Malaysian Police	– Need approval from Public Service Department	
	Z	Malaysian Armed Forces Council (*Majlis Angkatan Tentera*)	Malaysia Armed Forces	(PSD) if wish to increase or decrease scope and salary.	

Source: www.interactive.jpa.gov.my

Under the PH government, several appointments of Vice Chancellors in public universities have been sourced from the University of Malaya, a leading public university in Malaysia.[16],[17] Other examples such as the Ministry of Defence, Ministry of Foreign Affairs, and Ministry of Works have different recruitment and selection processes despite being part of the Malaysian civil service. These differences are mainly due to the fact that the highly "specialized" talent or profession of the employees (officers) are not relevant to the needs or requirements of other federal or state government agencies. These officers are working in a close service system and as such remain at the same ministry or department until they retire (mandatory age of retirement is 58–60). Another example of a closed service are doctors and other healthcare workers in the Ministry of Health. Diplomats who serve at the Ministry of Foreign Affairs are likely to remain working in the same ministry because it is considered as a closed service ministry.

Under External mobility, civil service in Malaysia offers two types of mobility program which are secondment and cross-assignment/cross fertilization programs. These two programs can be applied directly by those who are qualified, and it can be considered as professional position since these two involve high-ranking positions at particular organizations, in either public or private sector (Public Service Department 2012).

Concept of Secondment: An officer with certain expertise or specialization can be assigned on a temporary basis to other federal ministries and even state agencies outside his or her organization upon request by the "host" agencies. In fact, a federal employee can be seconded to a state agency upon request by the state government. An academician or a university lecturer from a public university can be seconded (or on loan) as a Consultant to the Ministry of Foreign Affairs (MOFA) or the Ministry of Education (MOE) to assist the Ministry in a highly specialized task or assignment. In recent years, there have been cases whereby senior academicians who were initially attached temporarily or on secondment but later moved permanently to other federal government department or agency. The Malaysian cabinet/Ministry of Foreign Affairs (MOFA) has recently introduced a new ruling which states that only career diplomats (from the PTD scheme) can be appointed as Ambassadors or High Commissioners (to Commonwealth countries or former British colonies). In previous years, retired or former senior politicians, army generals, and other professions could be appointed to assume the role of envoys. In fact, at one time, a senior Member of Parliament (MP) was appointed as Ambassador to the United States and was accorded a Minister's salary and benefits/perks.

Cross Assignment/Cross Fertilisation Programme: In its effort to build a more competent and robust public service, the Malaysian government has introduced another initiative called "Cross Assignment/Cross Fertilisation" programme (refer to JPA.BK (S) 230/19 Jld.3 (26) which specially focuses on the leadership aspect of the civil servants. When the program was first introduced ten years ago (2009), it only involved the exchanges between and among civil servants at the federal level.

The Cross Assignment/Cross Fertilisation Programme can also be regarded as another type of recruitment at the management level which mostly involve senior personnel from both the government sector and selected personalities from the private or corporate sector. The program was initially introduced in 2008 as a short (one to two years only) exchange program between Government-Linked Companies (GLCs) and the civil service. The current Secretariat for the program is Talent Corporation Malaysia Berhad (TalentCorp) which took over the role from Khazanah Nasional, a key investment arm of the Malaysian government in early 2012 (www.talentcorp.my). The main objective of this specially designed talent program is to help build a new group of high caliber leaders in both the public and private sectors. The exchange of talents particularly from the public service to the GLCs and other corporate sectors is part of the continuous effort to enhance the leadership qualities of the civil servants which were initiated by the previous Najib administration.

Performance Assessment and Promotion

Performance Assessment

The performance of each civil servant irrespective of his or her employment scheme and grade is assessed every year. The actual performance of each civil servant is assessed based on the Key Performance Indicators (KPI) for those senior officers serving in top management while the performance of civil servants in other categories is evaluated through the Annual Performance Assessment Report (*Laporan Nilaian Prestasi Tahunan* or known as LNPT). The annual work target is set earlier in the year and must be agreed by both the respective civil servant and his immediate assessor who is the Head of Department. Assessment of every staff is based on the following aspects (refer *Panduan Pelaksanaan Sistem Penilaian Prestasi Pegawai Perkhidmatan Awam Malaysia*) (Public Service Department n.d. d):

a) Work output (50%)
b) Skills and knowledge (25%)
c) Personal quality (20%)
d) Peer relationship and cooperation (20%)
e) Activities and contributions (5%)

Public servants who have provided outstanding service could be presented with special awards such as *Pingat Perkhidmatan Cemerlang* (PPC) or *Anugerah Perkhidmatan Cemerlang* (APC). Every year, a maximum of 8% of the total number of 1.6 million civil servants are selected for the APC category out of which about 2% deserve to be awarded with the PPC.[18] Outstanding public servants are presented with Certificate of Excellence and some monetary incentives. Annual increment is given to public servants who have met the requirements of the LNPT assessments. Nonperformers refer to those who receive marks below 60% in their total annual performance assessment. Those who are evaluated and identified as nonperformers will be called for counseling and will be put under a probationary period if they continuously receive poor assessment by their respective superiors. Civil servants who do not perform well or nonperformers also include those who are always late coming to work and absent from work (absenteeism). Normally they will be called by the department's Disciplinary Action committee. Nonperformers are monitored by their immediate superiors or supervisors who are appointed by a council. If a staff continues to slacken or does not perform well, he/she can be dismissed under the "Exit Policy."[19] They are not entitled to receive any pension and gratuity even if they have served the government for many years.

Exit Policy

The Malaysian public bureaucracy has often been criticized by the general public (tax payers) for being too big and costly, and also slow in responding to the changing needs, demands, and expectations of the citizenry. The public service is generally perceived as being inefficient despite numerous efforts to improve its delivery system. One of the major issues in the civil service concerns the performance of the personnel or staff at all levels, particularly those serving in certain ministries, departments, and agencies who have to deal directly with the general public.

The government has introduced the **Exit Policy** which is designed to address underperforming staff with "disciplinary" issue and other problems which affect the quality of services to the public. The **Exit Policy** was introduced by the government in 2015 (Public Service Department 2015) to ensure that civil servants remain committed, effective, and productive in executing their duties and responsibilities.

The **Exit Policy** is in line with the aspiration of the government to achieve the developed/high-income status by the year 2020. Understandably, the civil servants were initially apprehensive about the introduction of the **Exit Policy** because they fear it would be used indiscriminately against them. However, the policy has been put on hold by the new government which has decided to revert to the old Malaysia Remuneration System.

Career Advancement

PSD has introduced two schemes to allow for a better growth trajectory for civil servants with exceptional performance which are High Potential Leadership program and Subject Matter Expert (SME). A special unit under the Service Division known as Special Unit for High Potential and Subject Matter Expert (SME) (SUPREME) was introduced by PSD in 2016 to manage these two schemes. For High Potential Leadership program, the main objective of this program is to identify and further enhance the competency of excellent public servants for future leadership and senior management roles. Public servants who possess excellent leadership qualities can either apply directly or by nomination by their superiors. Qualified public servants are expected to undergo a series of assessment based on a competency model setup by PSD. The public servants are expected to Think, Lead, Speak, and Act (TLSA) and are continuously challenged in various aspects in this program. Public servants are also assessed by a team of panellists who are not known to them to ensure a fair, transparent and just assessment.[20]

Meanwhile for Subject Matter Expert (SME), its aim is to identify excellent public servants with vast knowledge and expertise in their respective fields or areas of specialization. This program is more suitable for civil servants who serve in technical fields, such as health, meteorology, maritime, science, engineering, and so on. In order to ensure transparency and equality of opportunity, the public servants/offices can apply directly to this SME program. Similar to High Potential Leadership Program, SME applicants are required to undergo a series of assessment. However, the assessment is highly technical and is related to the field expertise or specialization of the public servants. The assessment also includes tests and interviews. To date, there are 111 public servants under the SME program. This merit-based program is fair and open to all public officials who have succeeded in building their niche and areas or expertise (irrespective of race, ethnicity, grade, age, etc.).

The SME unit is expanding to include other fields of the public service which would allow more highly competent officers to join the "elite" program. The SME initiative also provides equal opportunity for public servants to rise well above the rank by recognizing their expertise. Public servants who are currently enrolled in this program are monitored and entrusted with managing at least three projects in a year. These 39 excellent public servants have to maintain a certain minimum score to remain in the SME program.[21]

Promotion Criteria

Promotion in the Malaysian civil service refers to the gradual increment of lower grade to a higher grade within the same service scheme with the approval of the Promotion Board. Considerations/criteria for civil servants to be promoted are based on merit which include the following:

(a) Efficiency and work performance
(b) Qualifications, knowledge, skills and experience
(c) Personal attributes including suitability to the new position, integrity, possess good leadership potentials and skills
(d) Participation in external activities and contributions towards the community and the country

(see Pekeliling Perkhidmatan Bilangan 7 Tahun 2010)

Any potential civil servant who has fulfilled the above criteria will be assessed through interviews and examinations or has to undergo the Assessment Centre procedure of promotion. If there is more than one candidate who fulfills the requirement, the Promotion Board must consider other criteria. In addition, a civil servant who wishes to apply for promotion has to fulfill the general conditions, which are as follows:

(a) Must already been confirmed in service
(b) Has achieved impressive level of performance
(c) Application must be endorsed by the Head of Department/Head of Service
(d) Is free from any disciplinary action
(e) Has declared property ownership
(f) Has been cleared from (passed) the Malaysian Anti-Corruption Commission (MACC) filtration
(g) Name is not listed as defaulter in any educational loan institution
(h) Other conditions/criteria prescribed by the Promotion Board
(see Pekeliling Perkhidmatan Bilangan 7 Tahun 2010)

Additional criteria have been included in the performance assessment leading to promotion for the civil servants from different professions or scheme of service. Promotion criteria are also based on the type of government agencies or departments they are working with. For example, the basic criteria for promotion for lecturers in research universities are their quality research and publications, teaching and supervision, academic leadership and recognition, consultation, and service to the university. Nevertheless, the promotion criteria can change over time. For example, age or seniority is no longer seen an important criterion as compared to before, particularly during the early days of the Malaysian public service. In recent years, younger public officials who perform extremely well can be promoted within a short span of time. The government realizes that there should be some flexibility in the promotion exercise, so as to help retain talents and experts within the civil service (Public Service Department 2010).

In recent years, promotion exercises for civil servants, particularly those in senior positions have been questioned by certain quarters of the Malaysian society (Public Service Department 2013). While the promotion process is clear, what is not so clear is the merits of promotion for senior civil servants. There were quite a number of examples of "fast-track" promotions involving senior civil servants who were seen to be closely aligned to the previous ruling party particularly during the last few years of the Najib administration. In effect, the ambiguities surrounding the criteria or merits for promotion for senior civil servants have affected morale of the public service.[22]

Training

The Civil Servants Training

Civil servants in Malaysia do not undergo or receive the same initial training at the entry level of their service. Their orientation and induction process into the public service differ from one grade/scheme to another. Training in the Malaysian civil service refers to the process of transferring knowledge and skills in a systematic manner. All training programs are aimed at increasing of knowledge, understanding, and skills or competency of the public servants in managing the current needs and demands of their organizations. Training for the civil servants includes attending courses, on job training and mentoring or coaching which contribute toward the professional development and organizational excellence. All civil servants are expected to equip themselves with relevant attitudes, knowledge, and skills/expertise via the human resource development programs which are based on lifelong learning and competency development (see *Pekeliling Perkhidmatan Bilangan 6 Tahun 2005*). The main objectives of the human resource training policy in the public sector are as follows:

(a) To achieve high quality of work
(b) To increase competency and productivity
(c) To develop positive values and attitudes
(d) To create value-creation and value-added in public sector
(e) To provide more opportunities or avenues for career progression

The training structures involve all service of schemes and classifications which have five phases (refer *Pekeliling Perkhidmatan Bilangan 6 Tahun 2005*):

(a) Pre-placement training is carried out for newly appointed staff of the public service who have not been assigned to any ministry or department. Pre-placement training is exempted for those who have taken the Pre-Service course in certain public service scheme before being offered the new position.
(b) Basic training is conducted for all civil servants who have been appointed to a particular scheme, starting from the day of appointment until three years tenure.
(c) Intermediate training involves developing competencies as well as increasing competencies for civil servants who have been in the service between three to ten years.
(d) Advanced training is conducted for civil servants who have served for more than ten years with the objectives of strengthening their competencies.
(e) Transition training is conducted for members who are due to leave the service two years before retirement.

INTAN is the leading training institute for civil servants in Malaysia which was first established in 1959 (renamed in 1972). In addition, there are numerous training institutes operating within government ministries and agencies. For example, the Chartered Tax Institute of Malaysia (CTIM) is registered under the Ministry of Finance and has been conducting specialized training programs for its own staff and also courses for international public officers. The Institute of Diplomacy and Foreign Relations (IDFR) is another example of a training institute within Ministry of Foreign Affairs (MOFA) which conducts tailor-made courses for officials from MOFA and also public officials from foreign countries across the globe.

Malaysia **195**

TABLE 9.7 Lists of training institutes/providers

No	Institutes (in Malay)	Institutes (in English)
1	Institut Latihan Islam (ILIM)	Islamic Training Institute (ILIM)
2	Institut Latihan Kehakiman dan Perundangan (ILKAP)	Judicial and Legal Training Institute (ILKAP)
3	Akademi Audit Negara (NAA)	National Audit Academy (NAA)
4	Akademi Kepimpinan Pendidikan Tinggi (AKEPT)	Higher Education Leadership Academy
5	Pusat Kecemerlangan Kejuruteraan dan Teknologi (CREaTE)	Center of Engineering Excellence and Technology (CREaTE)
6	Akademi Pengangkutan Jalan, Malaysia	Road Transport Academy, Malaysia
7	Akademi Kastam DiRaja Malaysia (AKMAL)	Royal Malaysian Customs Academy (AKMAL)
8	Maktab Penjara Malaysia	Malaysian Prison College
9	Pusat Latihan Pengajar & Kemahiran Lanjutan (CIAST)	Centre for Instructor and Advanced Skill Training (CIAST)
10	Institut Kemajuan Desa (INFRA)	Institute for Rural Development (INFRA)
11	Akademi Imigresen Malaysia (AIMM)	Malaysian Immigration Academy (AIMM)
12	Institut Latihan Perumahan dan Kerajaan Tempatan (i-KPKT)	Institute of Housing and Local Government Training (i-KPKT)
13	Institut Latihan Pentadbiran dan Pengurusan Pengangkutan Laut (MATRAIN)	Maritime Transport Administration and Management Training Institute (MATRAIN)
14	Institutes (in Malay)	Institutes (in English)
15	Institut Latihan Islam (Ilim)	Islamic Training Institute (ILIM)
16	Institut Latihan Kehakiman dan Perundangan (ILKAP)	Judicial and Legal Training Institute (ILKAP)
17	Akademi Audit Negara (NAA)	National Audit Academy (NAA)
18	Akademi Kepimpinan Pendidikan Tinggi (AKEPT)	Higher Education Leadership Academy
19	Pusat Kecermelangan Kejuruteraan dan Teknolohi (CREaTE)	Center of Engineering Excellence and Technology (CREaTE)

For the year 2018, PSD had conducted a total of 132 courses which include competency and mentoring, internal audit, safety protection, accounting management, and personal well-being. Meanwhile, INTAN has conducted 224 courses throughout the year which include leadership, self-professionalism, discipline management, project management, and data science for big data analytics (INTAN 2019).[23] Suitable or relevant civil servants can either apply to participate in any of the courses after being assigned or recommended by their respective departments. In most instances, the expenses of participating in the courses are borne by their respective departments or agencies. However, while many training courses are designed and targeted for general workers and junior civil servants, very few are meant for senior management officers. It has been argued that senior civil servants are also not keen on attending the courses organized by the local training institutes or centers mainly due to their relevance and suitability.

Training is very important to help improve the public service delivery. The Malaysian public sector has undergone several stages of transformation, starting with the most significant one in 1980 when the government adopted the New Public Management techniques to improve its efficiency. The advent technology has also impacted the public service delivery. Civil servants must now equip themselves with new knowledge and latest technology to ensure that they are ahead or at least, on the same par with their clients – the public. In short, civil servants are strongly encouraged to behave like their counterparts in the private sector and provide excellent services so that the public sector is perceived to be as efficient as the private sector practices (Khalid 2008).[24]

Senior Civil Service

A senior civil servant refers to an office who assumes the highest position in a particular agency or ministry such as the Chief Secretary to the Government (also known as *Ketua Setiausaha Negara* (KSN)), Secretary-General (example: Secretary-General in Ministry of Agriculture and Agro-Based Industry), or Director-General (example: Director-General of Public Service). Except for the most senior members of the top management (who are assessed based on KPI), other civil servants in this category are appraised through the Annual Performance Appraisal/Evaluation Report (LNPT). The frequency of assessment is once a year. There are three dimensions of assessment namely core, functional, and contribution. The assessment system for senior civil servants is based on Key Performance Indicator (KPI). Senior civil servants also must be assessed either by only one Assessor (First Assessor (*Pegawai Penilai Pertama*)) or both assessors (First Assessor and Second Assessor (*Pegawai Penilai Kedua*)). For example, a Secretary-General of a particular ministry is evaluated by both assessors (the Director-General of Public Service Department (first Assessor) and the Chief Secretary to the Government (as the second Assessor). As for the Director-General of a Department, he or she is assessed by one assessor only (the Secretary-General of the respective ministry).

Special Acknowledgments

The authors wish to record our heartfelt appreciation to Tan Sri Dr. Sulaiman Mahbob, former Director-General of the Economic Planning Unit, the Prime Minister's Department, and the many individuals from the various divisions and units of the Public Service Department (PSD), Malaysia, particularly Datuk Dr. Kamarudin Min, Director of INTAN (former Director, Research Planning and Policy Division); Mr Yusrizal Ahmad, Deputy Director, Service Division; Mr. Zaimy bin Shaari, Deputy Director, Special Unit for High Potential and SME (SUPREME), Public Service Department; and Dr. Ridzuan Kushairi Mohd Ramli of the Economic Planning Unit and Dr. Abd Wahab Che Mat from the Ministry of

Education and several officers from the various ministries/departments who wish to remain anonymous for their invaluable assistance and support in preparing this report.

Notes

1 The chapter mainly focuses on the latest changes and development in the Malaysian civil service which had taken place in the aftermath of the 14th General Election on May 9, 2018, until the collapse of the PH government in February 2020, following the "shocking" resignation of Mahathir Mohamad as the country's 7th Prime Minister (2018–2020). Mahathir had earlier served as the 4th Prime Minister of Malaysia from 1981 to 2003 under the Barisan Nasional (BN) government. Since February 2020, Malaysia has had two prime ministers, and they are both from Perikatan Nasional (PN), another "fragile" coalition consisting of a few political parties including UMNO.
2 The Emergency was declared by the British colonial authority in 1948 and officially ended in 1960. However, the country was still under grave security threats by the Communist Insurgents in most of the 1960s and well into the 1970s
3 Ibid.
4 Personal communication with Dr. Ridzuan Kushairi Mohd Ramli, Principal Assistant Secretary, Human Resource Policy Division, Ministry of Human Resource, 4 December 2019.
5 Khalid, K. and Lee, P. P. (2003). *Whither the Look East Policy*, Bangi: Penerbit Universiti Kebangsaan Malaysia.
6 For more analysis on the first Mahathir administration (1981–2003), see, for example, the works of Barry Wain (2010). Malaysian Maverick: Mahathir Mohamad in Turbulent Times. Basingstoke: Palgrave Macmillan and In-Won Hwang (2003). Personalized politics: the Malaysian state under Mahathir. Singapore: ISEAS/Silkworm.
7 Personal communication with a mid-level civil servant who wishes to remain anonymous.
8 Channel News Asia (2018, May 22) '1MDB scandal: A timeline', available at: www.channelnewsasia.com/news/asia/1mdb-scandal-a-timeline-10254406 (accessed 8 December 2019)
9 Jabatan Perkhidmatan Awam (2018) 'Pekeliling Perkhidmatan Bilangan 2 Tahun 2018: Perjawatan dan Urusan Perkhidmatan di Pejabat Menteri dan Timbalan Menteri. (JPA. BPO(S)253/2/8–128 Jld.2 (80)', available at: https://docs.jpa.gov.my/docs/pp/2018/pp022018.pdf.
10 The Star Online (2018, September 21) 'Nation – Art Harun is new EC chairman', *The Star Online*, available at: www.thestar.com.my/news/nation/2018/09/21/art-harun-is-new-ec-chairman.
11 Shagar, L. K. (2018, July 31) 'Maszlee: Removed varsity heads were political appointees', *The Star Online*, available at: www.thestar.com.my/news/nation/2018/07/31/maszlee-removed-varsity-heads-were-political-appointees (accessed on 30 November 2019).
12 Personal communication with Mr. Yusrizal bin Ahmad, Deputy Director of Service Division, Public Service Department, 29 April 2019.
13 Public Service Department (2018) 'Annual report 2018', available at: https://docs.jpa.gov.my/docs/pnerbitan/ltahunan/lp2018.pdf (accessed 8 December 2019).
14 Public Service Department (2022) 'Klasifikasi Perkhidmatan', available at: www.interactive.jpa.gov.my/ezskim/klasifikasi/klasifikasi.asp (accessed 28 April 2022).
15 Public Service Department. *Pekeliling Perkhidmatan Bilangan 14 Tahun 2011: Sistem Penilaian Prestasi Pegawai Perkhidmatan Awam di bawah Saraan Baru Perkhidmatan Awam*, Kuala Lumpur: Government of Malaysia.
16 The New Straits Times (2018, December 6) 'UKM appoints new vice-chancellor', *The New Straits Times*, available at: www.nst.com.my/education/2018/12/437795/ukm-appoints-new-vice-chancellor (accessed 7 December 2019).

17 The Star Online. (2019, October 2) 'Prof Faisal Rafiq appointed new USM VC effective Oct 4', *The Star Online*, available at: www.thestar.com.my/news/nation/2019/10/02/prof-faisal-rafiq-appointed-new-usm-vc-effective-oct-4#pgmRSEcOTVm8iRPj.99. (accessed 7 December 2019).

18 Personal communication with Mr. Yusrizal bin Ahmad, Deputy Director of Service Division, Public Service Department, 29 April 2019.

19 Malaysia kini. (n.d.). (2016, December 2) 'Underperforming civil servants may face exit policy', *Malaysia kini*, available at: www. www.malaysiakini.com/news/321955 (accessed 7 December 2019)

20 Interview with Mr. Zaimy bin Shaari, Deputy Director, Special Unit for High Potential and SME (SUPREME), Public Service Department, 29 April 2019.

21 Interview with Mr. Zaimy bin Shaari, Deputy Director, Special Unit for High Potential and SME (SUPREME), Public Service Department, 29 April 2019.

22 Personal communication with a mid-level civil servant who wishes to remain anonymous.

23 Institut Tadbiran Negara (2019) 'Kalendar Latihan INTAN 2019', available at: http://fac-apps.intan.my/calintan/ (accessed 8 December 2019)

24 Khalid, S. N. A. (2008) 'New public management in Malaysia: In search of an efficient and effective service delivery', *International Journal of Management Studies*, 15(Bumper Issue): 60–90.

References

Bedi, R. (2018, September 21) 'Art Harun is new EC chairman', *The Star Online*, available at: www.thestar.com.my/news/nation/2018/09/21/art-harun-is-new-ec-chairman.

Channel News Asia (2018, May 22) '1MDB scandal: A timeline', available at: www.channelnewsasia.com/news/asia/1mdb-scandal-a-timeline-10254406.

Husin, A. et al. (2007) 'Abdullah Ahmad Badawi Tiga Tahun di Putrajaya: Menjejaki Pencapaian dan Strategi Masa Depan Negara', *Akademika Journal of Southeast Asia Social Sciences and Humanities*, 71(1): 131–40.

Hwang, I. W. (2003) *Personalized Politics: The Malaysian State Under Mahathir*, Singapore: ISEAS/Silkworm.

INTAN (2019) 'Jumlah kursus', available at: https://www.dtims.intan.my/list_course/all?page=25 (accessed 22 April 2022).

Khalid, S. N. A. (2008) 'New public management in Malaysia: In search of an efficient and effective service delivery', *International Journal of Management Studies*, 15: 60–90.

Mahbob, S. and Md. Khalid, K. (2018) 'Public bureaucracy in Malaysia', Paper presented at the SSK Conference on The State of Public Bureaucracy in East Asia, Seoul, South Korea, 6–7 July 2018.

Malay Mail (2018, August 2) 'After sending thank you notes, Syed Saddiq sacks nine political appointees in his ministry', available at: https://www.malaymail.com/news/malaysia/2018/08/02/after-sending-thank-you-notes-syed-saddiq-sacks-nine-political-appointees-i/1658563 (accessed 25 August 2022).

The Malaysian Insight (2018, September 23) 'Investigate "unusual" promotions of 30 civil servants, Putrajaya urged', available at: www.themalaysianinsight.com/s/97935 Accessed 20 April 2022.

Md. Khalid, K. (2020) *The Power of Deeds (The Untold Story of Abdul Kadir Shamsuddin)*, Kuala Lumpur: MPH Group Publication.

Md. Khalid, K. and Abidin, M. Z. (2014) 'Technocracy in economic policy-making in Malaysia', *Southeast Asian Studies*, 3(2): 383–413.

Md. Khalid, K. (2013) 'Malaysian foreign relations and diplomacy under Abdullah Ahmad Badawi', in Bridget Welsh and James U. H. Chin (eds) *Awakening: The Abdullah Badawi*

Years in Malaysia (pp. 527–50), Petaling Jaya: Strategic Information and Research Development Centre (SIRD).

Md. Khalid, K. and Lee, P. P. (2003) *Whither the Look East policy*, Bangi: Penerbit Universiti Kebangsaan Malaysia.

Mokhtar, R. A. (2011) *Quality of Work Life Orientation: Antecedents and Effects on Organizational Commitment in the Malaysian Public Service/Rosslina Binti Ahmad Mokhtar*, PhD thesis, University Malaya.

The New Straits Times (2018, December 6) 'UKM appoints new vice-chancellor', available at: www.nst.com.my/education/2018/12/437795/ukm-appoints-new-vice-chancellor.

Public Service Department (2018) 'Annual report 2018', available at: https://docs.jpa.gov.my/docs/pnerbitan/ltahunan/lp2018.pdf.

Public Service Department (n.d. a) 'Panduan Pelaksanaan Sistem Penilaian Prestasi Pegawai Perkhidmatan Awam Malaysia', available at: https://docs.jpa.gov.my/docs/pekeliling/pp02/bil04/Lampiran-A2.pdf.

Public Service Department (n.d. b) 'Program & Bahagian', available at: www.jpa.gov.my/info-korporat-sm/program-dan-bahagian.

Public Service Department (n.d. c) *Panduan Menduduki Peperiksaan Perkhidmatan Awam*, Kuala Lumpur: Government of Malaysia.

Public Service Department (n.d. d) *Panduan Pelaksanaan Sistem Penilaian Prestasi Pegawai Perkhidmatan Awam Malaysia*, Kuala Lumpur: Government of Malaysia.

Public Service Department. *Pekeliling Perkhidmatan Bilangan 2 Tahun 2012: Dasar Baru Pelantikan Secara Peminjaman, Pertukaran Sementara dan Pertukaran Tetap*, Kuala Lumpur: Government of Malaysia.

Public Service Department. *Pekeliling Perkhidmatan Bilangan 2 Tahun 2018: Perjawatan dan Urusan Perkhidmatan di Pejabat Menteri dan Timbalan Menteri*, Kuala Lumpur: Government of Malaysia.

Public Service Department. *Pekeliling Perkhidmatan Bilangan 5 Tahun 2011: Dasar dan Prosedur Penempatan Pegawai Di Bawah Program Penempatan Silang (Cross Fertilization Program)*, Kuala Lumpur: Government of Malaysia.

Public Service Department. *Pekeliling Perkhidmatan Bilangan 6 Tahun 2005: Dasar Latihan Sumber Manusia Sektor Awam*, Kuala Lumpur: Government of Malaysia.

Public Service Department. *Pekeliling Perkhidmatan Bilangan 7 Tahun 2010: Panduan Pengurusan Pemangkuan dan Kenaikan Pangkat dalam Perkhidmatan Awam*, Kuala Lumpur: Government of Malaysia.

Public Service Department. *Pekeliling Perkhidmatan Bilangan 7 Tahun 2015. Pelaksanaan Dasar Pemisah (Exit Policy) Bagi Pegawai yang Berprestasi Rendah Dalam Perkhidmatan Awam*, Kuala Lumpur: Government of Malaysia.

Public Service Department. *Pekeliling Perkhidmatan Bilangan 8 Tahun 2013: Kenaikan Pangkat secara Time-Based Berasaskan Kecermelangan bagi Pegawai Kumpulan Pelaksana Yang Berada di Gred Lantikan*, Kuala Lumpur: Government of Malaysia.

Public Service Department. *Pekeliling Perkhidmatan Bilangan 14 Tahun 2011: Sistem Penilaian Prestasi Pegawai Perkhidmatan Awam di bawah Saraan Baru Perkhidmatan Awam*, Kuala Lumpur: Government of Malaysia.

Shagar, L. K. (2018, July 31) 'Maszlee: Removed varsity heads were political appointees', *The Star Online*, available at: www.thestar.com.my/news/nation/2018/07/31/maszlee-removed-varsity-heads-were-political-appointees/.

The Star (2019, June 5) 'Manner of appointment quizzed', *The Star Online*, available at: www.thestar.com.my/news/nation/2019/06/05/manner-of-appointment-quizzed.

The Star Online (2018, September 21) 'Nation – Art Harun is new EC chairman', available at: www.thestar.com.my/news/nation/2018/09/21/art-harun-is-new-ec-chairman.

Wain, B. (2010) Malaysian Maverick: Mahathir Mohamad in Turbulent Times, Basingstoke: Palgrave Macmillan.

Welsh, B. (2013) The Awakening: The Abdullah Badawi Years in Malaysia, Petaling Jaya: Strategic Information and Research Development.

APPENDIX

Interviews and Personal Communication

Tan Sri Dr. Sulaiman Mahbob
Former Director-General, Economic Planning Unit (EPU), Prime Minister's
Department
(He is currently Chief Executive Officer of National Recovery Council
(NRC) and Chairman of Board of Trustee, Malaysian Institute of Economic
Research (MIER)

Datuk Dr. Kamarudin Min
Director of National Institute of Public Administration (*Institut Tadbiran Awam
Negara* (INTAN))
(Former Director, Research, Planning and Policy Division, Public Service
Department)
(Retired from Public Service in July 2021)

Mr. Yusrizal Ahmad
Deputy Director
Service Division
Organisational Development Division
(Effective September 2021, Yusrizal has been reassigned to Scheme of Services
Policy Sector)
Public Service Department

Mr. Zaimy bin Shaari
Deputy Director
Special Unit for High Potential and SME (SUPREME), Public Service
Department

(He is now Director of Petroleum Regulatory Division, Ministry of Domestic Trade and Consumer Affairs)

(Effective May 2022, Zaimy is the Director of Petroleum Regulatory Division, Ministry of Domestic Trade and Consumer Affairs)

Dr. Ridzuan Kushairi Mohd Ramli
Principal Assistant Director
Economic Planning Unit (EPU)
Prime Minister's Department

Dr. Abd Wahab Che Mat
Senior Deputy Under-Secretary
Division of Policy Planning and Coordination
Ministry of Education
(Retired from Public Service in January 2020)

10

THE PHILIPPINES

*Maria Fe Villamejor-Mendoza and
Minerva Sanvictores Baylon*[1]

Brief Historical Background on the Philippines Civil Service

The Philippine public bureaucracy is a product of its colonial past and present. It adopted the systems of its colonial masters, for example, mainly Spain and the United States. And over time, after independence, it has been shaped by the frameworks of governing and governance of its national leaders.

Before the Spaniards came, the country consisted of scattered but politically and economically self-contained communities called *barangays*. There was no central government or any formal administrative organization to speak of, as it was deemed not necessary (Cariño 1987; Veneracion 1988). The life, structure, and values of the pre-Spanish communities had not yet laid down the foundation of an actually emergent or established public bureaucracy (Corpuz 1957).

When the Spaniards colonized the country in 1521–1898, they established a theocratic rule, where the church wields immense power over the state (Reyes 2011) and where the colonial government and bureaucracy was highly centralized. The bureaucracy served as the Spanish government's machinery to achieve the objectives of colonization and protect and promote the colonizers' interests. The system of appointment and recruitment in government was not professional. Positions in government offices were for sale to the highest bidders while other appointments were gained through royal *merced* or favor, encouraging political patronage, instead of merit and fitness. These led to, among others, incompetence, inefficiency, and corruption in government (Corpuz 1957; Cariño 1987; Veneracion 1988).

The outstanding characteristic of the Spanish colonial regime . . . was the wide discrepancy between the letter of the law, which upheld idealistic and noble standards, and actual practice, which was repressive and oppressive (Endriga 1985). Three centuries of capricious, corrupt and exclusive colonial administration bequeathed

DOI: 10.4324/9781003326496-13

204 Maria Fe Villamejor-Mendoza and Minerva Sanvictores Baylon

four things: (1) the idea that everything should be rigidly run from Manila; (2) a suite of go-slow bureaucratic techniques best summed up by the Spanish expression "obedezco pero no cumplo" or "I obey but don't comply" and "no novedad" or "do not commit or introduce innovations on royal prescriptions"; (3) a profound distrust of government on the part of the indigenous people; and (4) the notion that it is somehow patriotic to subvert the bureaucracy (Endriga 1985; Veneracion 1988).

When the Americans came after the end of the Spanish-American War in 1898 and the Philippines was ceded to America by virtue of the Treaty of Paris, the formal introduction of the civil service system occurred with the establishment of the Philippine Civil Service in 1900, as reflected in *Act No. 5 (Civil Service Act)*, "An Act for the Establishment and Maintenance of an Efficient and Honest Civil Service in the Philippine Islands." It established the framework for a merit-based civil service system, mandating the appointment and promotion to government positions according to merit and fitness, characterized by professionalism and careerism, ensured security of tenure, and with appointments determined by open competitive examinations as far as practicable (Endriga 1985; Tjiptoherijanto 2008; Brillantes and Fernandez 2011; Reyes 2011).

This led to the establishment of the Bureau of Civil Service (BCS), with a mandate that the "greatest care should be taken in the selection of officials for civil administration." To head the various executive and line agencies, the Philippine Commission preferred American civilians or military men who had been honorably discharged. All recruits, both American and Filipino, were to be "men of the highest character and fitness "who could conduct their duties unaffected by "partisan politics" (Tjiptoherijanto 2008).

In addition to the above, several highly significant pieces of legislation regarding the civil service in the Philippines have been enacted. Among many are the following:

R.A. 2260 or the Civil Service Law of 1959, which introduced personnel policies like promotion based on a system of ranking positions, a performance appraisal system to improve employee performance, and a more participative approach to management and interaction with employees;

RA 6040 of 1969, which decentralized some civil service functions, particularly examinations, appointments and administrative discipline;

PD 1 of 1972, after the declaration of Martial Law, which reorganized the entire bureaucracy. Among others, it reiterated the decentralization of personnel functions, and restructured the Civil Service Commission (CSC) to make it more amenable to its quasi-legislative and quasi-judicial functions. In 1975, PD 807 or the Civil Service Decree of the Philippines redefined the role of the CSC as the central personnel agency of the government.

The Administrative Code of 1987, issued by President Corazon Aquino through Executive Order 292, essentially reiterated existing principles and policies in the administration of the bureaucracy and for the first time recognized the right of government employees to self-organization and to conduct collective negotiations under the framework of the 1987 Constitution. Efforts continue until the present to further reform and strengthen the civil service, through proposed legislative bills and other measures.

In sum, the civil service in the Philippines today is very much a creation of the U.S. occupation and administration of the country (Endriga 1985). The system broadly follows the American as opposed to Commonwealth or European traditions of public administration. The main tenets of the modern civil service are enshrined in the 1987 Constitution, Article XI, Section 1 of which declares that "Public office is a public trust. Public officers and employees must, at all times, be accountable to the people, serve them with utmost responsibility, integrity, loyalty, and efficiency; act with patriotism and justice, and lead modest lives."

Civil Service System

The Central Human Resource Management (HRM) Unit

There is a plethora of laws, Executive Orders, Administrative Orders and Codes, Presidential Decrees, and other mandates governing the Philippine civil service. The result is a high level of complexity as the rules are scattered in numerous locations. However, there is a Civil Service Commission (CSC), the principal constitutional body responsible for HRM in the Philippine civil service. The administration (as opposed to "management") of the modern civil service is anchored on Article IX (B) of the Constitution, which vests overall responsibility for the civil service in the CSC.

Under Article IX, the CSC, "as the central personnel agency of the government shall establish a career service and adopt measures to promote morale, efficiency, integrity, responsiveness, progressiveness, and courtesy in the civil service." It also has responsibility for strengthening the merit and rewards system, integrating all human resources development (HRD) programs for all levels and ranks, and institutionalizing a management climate conducive to public accountability.

The CSC as the central personnel agency of the government is a Constitutional Commission. As such, it enjoys independence from the three branches of government – the Executive, Legislative, and Judiciary. It is a policymaking body that performs quasi-legislative and quasi-judicial functions. It formulates personnel policies and guidelines for the whole bureaucracy and under a decentralized setup, and the CSC delegates the implementation of these policies to individual agencies.

The organizational structure of the CSC is shown in Figure 10.1.

The CSC has the following features, functions, and relationships:

- The Commission is a collegial body composed of the Chairman and two Commissioners. They have a fixed tenure of seven years without reappointment. Of the first appointed, the Chair shall hold office for seven years, one Commissioner for five years and the other for three years.

206 Maria Fe Villamejor-Mendoza and Minerva Sanvictores Baylon

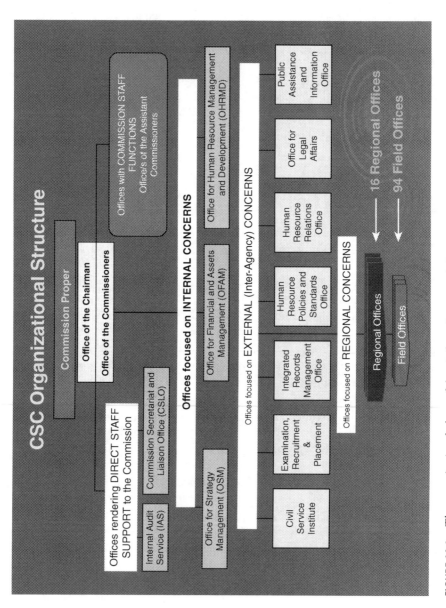

FIGURE 10.1 The organizational chart of the civil service commission

- Providing technical advice and assistance to the collegial Commission are the four Assistant Commissioners.
- Each central or regional office is headed by a Director except for some offices, which are under the direct supervision of an Assistant Commissioner.
- The central office of the CSC houses the executive offices and 12 staff and line offices.
- The CSC has 16 Regional Offices and 103 Field Offices in the 16 administrative regions of the country.
- The heads of the central and regional offices administer the functions, programs, and operations of their respective offices (www.csc.gov.ph).

All officials in government, including that of the CSC, who are occupying the Third Level positions (which in the CSC include Assistant Directors, Directors, Assistant Commissioners, and the Commissioners) are appointed by the President of the Philippines.

Moreover, the appointment of Heads of offices including Constitutional Commissions like the CSC needs the consent or approval of the Commission on Appointments (CA). The CA is a Constitutional body composed of the Senate President as ex-officio Chair, 12 Senators, and 12 Congressmen. Although its membership is confined to the members of Congress, it is considered an independent body separate and distinct from the Legislature (comappt.gov.ph).

The creation of the CA was not intended to curtail the President's appointing authority but primarily to serve as a check against its abuse. It ensures that the President has exercised the power to appoint wisely, by appointing only those who are fit and qualified. To this end, the CA's Statement of Policy provides "that the powers vested in the CA by the Constitution shall be discharged with only one impelling motive, which is the efficient and harmonious functioning of the government" (comappt.gov.ph).

Despite this official declaration, the CA has been primarily perceived as politicizing and therefore undermining the appointment process and its very objective. It can become the rubber stamp of the President if the members and the President belong to the same political party, or a stumbling block if the CA and the President belong to opposing political parties. There were allegations, even from the nominees for the positions, that the confirmation of the appointment could also be determined by the willingness of the candidates to accommodate the favors being asked by the CA members for their own agenda or projects.

It called to mind the case of one Presidential nominee to the position of Chair of the CSC who was not confirmed by the CA. He was a lawyer by profession and was formerly a Secretary of a technical office under the Office of the President. For some unexplained reasons, he was not confirmed by the CA. This led to the President submitting another nominee, also a former Secretary and a medical doctor by profession, whom the CA subsequently confirmed (Legaspi 2009). In such instances, the independence, competence, and fitness of the appointees could be put aside.

It may be noted that there are powers granted to Constitutional bodies like the CSC to protect their independence and political neutrality. One is fiscal autonomy, which mandates the automatic and regular release of the approved annual appropriations or budget. Members of the Constitutional Commissions are among the government officials who can be removed from office only by impeachment. In addition, decisions by the CSC on administrative cases are appealable to the Court of Appeals while any decision, order, or ruling by the Commission may be brought to the Supreme Court (Philippine Constitution 1987).

As may be inferred, the Philippine civil service is broadly based on the U.S. model, and the main tenets of civil service are contained in the 1987 Constitution. The Civil Service Commission is the main constitutional body responsible for human resource management (HRM), and it has broad responsibilities including promoting and maintaining morale, efficiency, integrity, responsiveness, and courtesy in the civil service. However, it also shares some responsibilities with other agencies, including among others, the Commission on Appointments, the Career Executive Service Board (appointment and management of executive-level civil servants), and the Department of Budget and Management (establishment controls, payroll management, and some elements of agency-level performance management).

The CSC has a total of 1,204 employees as of December 2018. Table 10.1 shows that more than 68% of its employees are in its Regional Offices.

To reiterate, as the central human resource agency of the government, it is mandated to (a) establish a career service and adopt measures to promote morale, efficiency, integrity, responsiveness, progressiveness, and courtesy in the civil service; (b) strengthen the merit and rewards system; (c) integrate all human resource development programs for all levels and ranks; and (d) institutionalize a management climate conducive to public accountability (1987 Philippine Constitution, Article IX-B, Section 3).

The more specific functions of the CSC to operationalize its mandate are defined in Executive Order No. 292, otherwise known as the Revised Administrative Code of 1987. EO 292 embodies the principles and policies in the administration of the bureaucracy. The specific functions of the CSC include among others,

TABLE 10.1 Number of CSC personnel by office, 2018

Office	Warm Bodies
Central Office	381
	(31.6%)
Regional Office	823
	(68.3%)
Total	1,204

Source: www.csc.gov.ph

The administration and enforcement of the merit system for all levels and ranks in the civil service and the promulgation of policies, standards, and guidelines for the civil service to promote economical, efficient, and effective personnel administration in the government. A more comprehensive list can be found in Annex A.

The Philippine Civil Service: Definition, Size, Classification, and Status

Definition

The Philippine public bureaucracy, otherwise known as the civil service or the administrative system of the government is generally defined as "the sum total of all administrative agencies of government" (De Guzman et al. 1988). It also refers to a "network of public organizations constituted to implement, help formulate, monitor, and assess public policies" (Alfiler 2008). It covers all branches – executive, legislative, and judiciary – instrumentalities, and agencies of government, including government-owned and -controlled corporations (GOCCs), and other constitutional bodies and their interrelationships (Philippine Constitution 1987). With the aim to sum up the role of bureaucracy, De Guzman et al. (1988) explain, "through this institution the resources of the country are best rationalized and transformed into concrete programs and projects towards attaining the goals of development."

Size of the Philippine Civil Service

In a span of 53 years, the size of the bureaucracy has been growing at a fast rate of 787%, from only around 0.273 million in 1964 to 2.4 million in 2017. The increase in the size of government personnel can be primarily attributed to the expanding role of the government that saw the creation of more government agencies. From the recent decade (2004–2017), however, its growth has been arrested and stabilized to 64% which may be attributed to the reform efforts before and during this period, for example, 5-year effectivity of RA 7041 or the Attrition Law; agency-specific streamlining programs; changes in budgetary allotments which funded only the filled positions; and to some extent, the exit of positions in the disposed or privatized units of government (Mendoza and Baylon 2018).

In terms of the size and cost bureaucracy, the Philippine civil service is not considered large relative to others. There are approximately 1.7 million career civil servants including at the subnational level in Local Government Units. Based on an estimated population of 106.5 million, this provides a ratio of 1.6% (or approximately 16 civil servants per 1,000 of population). The level of spending on wages and salaries is approximately 28.6% of total public expenditure in 2017. Real wages in the public sector are competitive and generally higher than in other sectors of the Philippine economy including the private sector. Civil service pay is both arguably satisfactory and sufficient to attract and retain quality employees (World Bank 2018).

210 Maria Fe Villamejor-Mendoza and Minerva Sanvictores Baylon

Table 10.2 shows the distribution of the employees by major subdivisions – national government agencies (NGAs), government-owned and -controlled corporations (GOCCs), state universities and colleges (SUCs), local water districts, and local government units (LGUs) from 1964 to 2017. Despite the enactment of the 1987 Local Government Code, which decentralized government services to the local government units, civil servants at the national level still comprise a substantial number to the level of 54%.

Civil Service Classification and Status

Positions in the Philippine civil service are classified into career service and non-career service. *Career service* is characterized by (1) entrance based on merit and fitness to be determined as far as practicable by competitive examination, or based on highly technical qualifications; (2) opportunity for advancement to higher career positions; and (3) security of tenure (Executive Order No. 292, Revised Administrative Code of 1987, Section 7).

In terms of the number of government employees according to position classification (Table 10.3), almost 65% belong to career service. From 2004 to August 31, 2017, the size of the bureaucracy grew by 64%. About 27% of the inventory of government human resource works on job-order basis for the government. Seventy percent of job-order workers can be found in local governments.

Career positions are permanent positions with security of tenure. Promotion to higher level of appointment must meet certain qualification standards and performance. Career officers are further categorized into first, second, and third levels. Table 10.4 lists the career appointments by these levels:

1. The First Level covers clerical, trades, crafts, and custodial service positions. Included here are nonprofessional or sub-professional work in a nonsupervisory or supervisory capacity requiring less than four years of collegiate studies;
2. The Second Level includes professional, technical and scientific positions which involve professional, technical or scientific work in a nonsupervisory or supervisory capacity requiring at least four years of college work up to Division Chief level; and
3. The Third Level covers positions in the Career Executive Service (CES).

Non-career service refers to appointments that have a fixed term or temporary status in government. Their appointments are not based on the usual tests of merit and fitness, and tenure is otherwise limited. They include "elective" officials (national, sub-national); appointment of officers holding positions at the pleasure of the president; chairpersons and members of the commissions and boards with fixed term of office, including their personnel and confidential staff; contractual personnel; and the emergency and seasonal personnel (EO 292, Section 9).

The number of government employees occupying non-career and Jos/COS were segregated only in the 2000s, with the number greatest in 2016 and 2017.

TABLE 10.2 Number of government personnel, by year and major subdivision, 1964–2017

Year/Subdivision	1964	1974	1984	1994	2004	2008	2010	2016 (July)	2017 (Aug)
National Government Agencies (NGAs)	201,401	194,735	667,114	796,795	1,001,495	798,584	913,087	1,255,188	1,316,068
Government -Owned & -Controlled Corps (GOCCs)	n.d.	n.d.	134,453	112,858	103,977	82,457	66,222	100,658	113,409
Local Government Units (LGUs)	71,444	85,432	189,876	316,023	370,277	272,610	365,725	827,615	869,988
State Universities & Colleges (SUCs)	n.d.	n.d.	n.d.	n.d.	n.d.	n.d.	51,051	92,136	95,213
Local Water Districts (LWDs)	n.d.	n.d.	n.d.	n.d.	n.d.	n.d.	13,575	25, 594	26,214
Total	272,845	280,167	991,445	1,225,676	1,475,699	1,153,651	1,409,660	2,301,191	2,420,892

Source: Civil Service Commission as cited by Mangahas and Tiu Sonco II 2011 for years 1964 to 2004. CSC at www.csc.gov.ph for more recent entries, for example, 2004–2017.

212 Maria Fe Villamejor-Mendoza and Minerva Sanvictores Baylon

TABLE 10.3 Number of government personnel, by classification of position, 2004–2017

Year	Career*	Non-career	JO/COS**	Total Employed Personnel
2004	1,316,166	159,533		1,475,699
2008	1,153,651	159,887	281,586	1,595,124
2010	1,261,285	148,375		1,409,660
2012	796,687	117,384	206,120	1,120,191
2016	1,526,450	179,579	595,162	2,301,191
2017	1,569,585	190,917	660,390	2,420,892

*Does not include third level officials, that is, those belonging to the Career Executive Service
** Job Orders/Contract of Service
Source: Civil Service Commission website.

TABLE 10.4 Levels of career appointments

Level	Coverage
First	Clerical, trades, crafts, and custodial service positions, which involve nonprofessional or sub-professional work in a nonsupervisory or supervisory capacity requiring less than four years of collegiate studies
Second	Professional, scientific, and technical positions involving professional, technical, or scientific work in nonsupervisory or supervisory capacity requiring at least four years of college work up to Division Chief level
Third	Positions in the Career Executive Service

Source: PD 807 Sec. 7.

Almost 35% (27% of which belong to the Jos/COS classification) of the total manpower of the government occupies non-career positions. LGUs employed the most number of Jos/COS employees, representing 70% of the total number of government employees under this category in 2017.

All years are more or less complete record of all personnel in government agencies, except for 2012 when only 64% of government agencies were covered (www.csc.gov.ph).

It may be noted from Table 10.3 that the size of contractuals (column of JO/COS) is increasing, a possible indicator of the possible politicization of appointments and abuse of appointing authority in the civil service. The increase and number of contractual employees is highest in the local governments.

There are safeguards put in place by the CSC to prevent abuse in the use of this appointment. For example, contractual employees must meet the education, training, and experience requirements of the position proposed by the agency heads and approved by the CSC. But eligibility is not required for this type of appointment.

Recruitment and Openness of Posts/Positions

The 1987 Philippine Constitution provides that appointments in the Civil Service shall be made only according to merit and fitness. Merit and fitness shall be determined as far as practicable by competitive examinations except for positions that are policy determining, primarily confidential, or highly technical in nature (Civil Service Commission 2017, Rule I, General Policies on Recruitment, Omnibus Rules on Appointments and Other Human Resource Actions (ORAOHRA), Revised 2018).

Recruitment and selection of employees in the civil service are guided by the principles outlined in Section 21, Chapter 5 of EO 292, namely: (1) opening of the opportunity for government employment to all qualified citizens, (2) selection on the basis of fitness to perform the duties and assume the responsibilities of the positions, (3) promotion to vacant position of employee occupying next lower position who are competent, qualified, and have appropriate civil service eligibility, and (4) formulation of a screening process by each department or agency in accordance with standards and guidelines set by the Commission.

During the martial law regime of President Marcos, he issued P.D. 1184 allowing lateral entry in government service particularly for the Philippine National Police. No longer will the applicant be required to start at the lowest position, especially if the person possesses special educational qualification as college graduates in certain technical fields needed by the services such as, but not limited to, engineers, doctors, nurses, lawyers, penologists, and forensic scientists for the crime laboratory (Sec. 13 PD 1184). Those who have met the qualifications both from inside the agency or outside of it can be appointed to higher positions. Hence, the "next in rank" concept is no longer the determining factor in promotions but competence or merit or fitness. However, this also opened up opportunities for those with the backing of government officials to be placed in higher positions, resulting in the demoralization of the insiders (*Manila Times* 2016).

One of the ways to ensure the openness of recruitment to both internal and external applicants is the posting of vacant positions. In order to ensure that all qualified applicants will have equal opportunity to work in government, NGAs, SUCs, and GOCCs with vacant positions that have been authorized to be filled are required to publish and post vacancies in at least 3 conspicuous places in the agency or online for a period of at least 10 calendar days and not less than 15 calendar days for LGUs (RA 7140, s 1991, 2017ORAOHRA, as revised).

On the part of the CSC, it is required to publish once every quarter a complete list of all the existing vacant positions in government and, thereafter, certify under oath to the completion of publication. Copies of such publication are distributed free of charge to the various personnel offices of the government where they shall be available for inspection by the public. In the case of local government units, the said publication shall be posted in at least three public and conspicuous places in their respective municipalities and provinces, or online if able. Any vacant position published shall be open to any qualified person and may not necessarily belong to the same office or who occupies a position next-in rank to the vacancy. The CSC cannot act on any appointment to fill up a vacant position unless the same has been reported to and published by the Commission.

In line with the national policy to facilitate the integration of the members of the cultural communities and accelerate the development of the areas occupied

214 Maria Fe Villamejor-Mendoza and Minerva Sanvictores Baylon

by them, the CSC gives special civil service examination for them to qualify for appointment in the civil service (EO 292, Sec 25, Chapter 5).

Recruitment Process

The current recruitment system in the Philippine civil service is based on Qualification Standards (QS), a minimum set of requirements for each position, which is comprised of education, eligibility, training, and experience. The CSC formulates and issues the minimum Qualification Standards (QS) for each position with the corresponding salary grade in government. There are 33 Salary Grades in the position classification and compensation system of the government. However, additional standards that will impose higher or stricter qualifications to positions may be done as deemed necessary by the agency.

Below is an example of a QS.

Under the 2017 CSC ORAOHR, the role of agencies to formulate their own qualification standards to be submitted to the Commission for approval was reiterated. However, special laws, which prescribe QS for specialized sectors of the civil service, for example, the Foreign Service Act (RA No. 7157), Philippine National Police (PNP) Act (RA No. 8551), Bureau of Fire Protection/Bureau of Jail Management and Penology (BFP/BJMP) Act (RA No. 9263, as amended by RA No. 9592), Local Government Code of 1991 (RA No. 7160), shall prevail (Section 34 of the Omnibus Rules).

Applicants who would like to become a civil servant must take and pass the civil service examination in order to possess the civil service eligibility. The license of professionals for their respective professions (e.g., doctor, lawyer, engineers) may be considered as an eligibility as long as the position they will occupy and the work that they will do correspond to their profession or expertise. The applicant must also possess the qualifications required under the Qualification Standards (QS) for the position being applied for.

TABLE 10.5 QS for division chiefs and executive/managerial positions in the second level

Requirements	Division Chief	Executive/Managerial
Education	Master's degree OR Certificate in Leadership and Management from the CSC	Master's degree OR Certificate of Leadership and Management from the CSC
Experience	4 years of supervisory/ management experience	5 years of supervisory/ management experience
Training	40 hours of supervisory/ management learning and development undertaken within the last five years	120 hours of supervisory/ management learning and development undertaken within the last five years
Eligibility	Career Service Professional/ Second Level	Career Service Professional/ Second Level

Source: CSC MC 05, 24 February 2016.

The Philippines **215**

A temporary appointment may be issued to a person who meets the qualifications but has no appropriate eligibility. It may be issued to this person but only in the absence of an applicant who meets all the qualification requirements. The temporary appointment shall not exceed 12 months. If issued to a person not meeting the qualifications, it shall be disapproved or invalidated by the CSC.

Each government agency is allowed to develop its own screening process, which may include tests of fitness such as examination and interview, but always in accordance with the standards and guidelines set by the CSC.

Original appointees in the career service with permanent status of appointment undergo probationary period for a thorough assessment of his/her performance and character. The duration of the probationary period is generally six months or depending on the duration of the probationary period as required by the position.

Probationary period refers to the period of actual service following the issuance of a permanent appointment. The appointee undergoes a thorough character investigation and assessment of capability to perform the duties of the position being occupied. Exempted from undergoing the probationary period are teachers who prior to the issuance of permanent appointments have acquired adequate training and professional preparation and possess appropriate civil service eligibility; first time appointees to closed career positions in State Universities and Colleges (SUCs), and scientific and research institutions if so provided under their Agency Charters; and appointees to positions exempted from it as may be provided by law.

The services of the appointee can be terminated for unsatisfactory conduct or want of capacity before the end of the second performance review on the sixth month or depending on the duration of the probationary period as required by the position.

All appointees are screened and evaluated by the Human Resource Merit Promotion and Selection Board (HRMPSB), of the agency. If applicable, a Certification from this Board will be among the appointment documents required to be submitted to the CSC.

In order to safeguard the civil servants, the law provides that no officer or employee in the Civil Service can be suspended or dismissed except for cause as provided by law and after due process. There are at least 30 grounds for disciplinary action that can be taken against a civil servant. Among these are dishonesty; neglect of duty; disgraceful and immoral conduct; and inefficiency and incompetence in the performance of official duties (AO 292, Book V, Title I, Chapter 7, Sec 34).

Competency-Based Recruitment and Qualification Standards (CBRQS)

The CSC has implemented a more integrated personnel management system to further enhance merit and fitness among civil servants. It has recently put in place the Competency-Based Recruitment and Qualification Standards (CBRQS), an upgrade from the existing qualification standards based on a minimum set of requirements comprised of education, eligibility, training, and experience. The

CBRQS is aligned with the goal of the Commission to integrate competencies in human resource systems of government agencies, starting with recruitment. The CSC defines competency, as "a set of observable, measurable, and vital skills, knowledge, and attitudes that are translations of capabilities deemed essential for organizational success" (www.csc.gov.ph).

The following serve as bases for competency-based recruitment:

- Competencies serve as objective guide in the assessment of candidates; hence it improves accuracy in assessing candidate's fitness to a particular job.
- Competency-based recruitment minimizes hiring errors as it helps prevent interviewers and selectors from assessing interviewees on the basis of characteristics that are not relevant to the job or from making hasty decisions.
- Competency-based recruitment leads to a standardized or structured selection process since the same metrics are used to assess all applicants to the same position.
- Competency-based recruitment provides clarity for the recruiters and candidates as well about the requirements for the vacant position to be filled (CSC ORAOHR 2017).
- Another major initiative of the CSC toward this direction is the Program to Institutionalize Meritocracy and Excellence in Human Resource Management (PRIME-HRM) that integrates and enhances the Personnel Management Assessment and Assistance Program (PMAAP) and the CSC Agency Accreditation Program (CSCAAP). It is a mechanism that empowers government agencies by developing their human resource management competencies, systems, and practices toward HR excellence (CSC ORAOHR 2017).

PRIME-HRM entails greater engagement not just of the human resource management officer (HRMO) but also of the officials and the rank-and-file employees of the agency. In this Program, the CSC assesses the maturity level of an agency's competencies, systems, and practices in four HR systems: (1) recruitment, selection, and placement; (2) learning and development; (3) performance management; and (4) rewards and recognition. Based on the assessment, a government agency may be classified according to four maturity levels:

1. *Transactional HRM* – HR assumes personnel function that is mostly separate from agency/business and talent needs.
2. *Process-Defined HRM* – There is a set of defined and documented SOPs established, though it needs improvement. It is characterized by goal-oriented decision making. There is some automated system but little integration of data.
3. *Integrated HRM* – Uses process metrics for continuous improvement, an HR management toolkit, and data-driven decision making. HR function supports agency business needs.
4. Strategic HRM – HR processes are focused on continually improving process performance. It is also systematically managed by a combination of process

The Philippines **217**

optimization and continuous improvement. At this level, HR helps to drive agency business decision on people, data, and insight. HR strategy is already part of the agency strategy (CSC ORAOHR 2017).

Based on the results on the maturity level, the CSC provides customized technical assistance and developmental interventions according to the determined needs of the agency (CSC ORAOHR 2017).

The Scoping Mission of the World Bank in 2018 found that the level of HRM capacity appears to be relatively low throughout the civil service. The Philippines-Australia Human Resource Development Facility (PAHRDF) and the Philippines-Australia Human Resource and Organizational Development Facility (PAHRODF) programs, which ran from 2004 until 2015,[2] supported the CSC to improve human resource capacity including the development of PRIME-HRM. This program sought to establish consistent processes and practices for a number of major human resource systems – recruitment, selection and placement, human resource development planning (learning and development), performance management systems and rewards and recognition. The system established four levels of maturity: Level 1 – Transactional HRM; Level 2 – Process-defined HRM; Level 3 – Integrated HRM; and Level 4 – Strategic HRM. (See Box 2 above and Table 10.6 for more information on PRIME-HRM and its progress.)

Under this program, the CSC was both a service provider and a beneficiary, that is, it assisted agencies with capacity development as well as participated in the program itself. As part of PRIME-HRM, a self-assessment was performed by over 1,200 government agencies to identify the level of maturity achieved (see Table 10.6). The results showed that a significant majority of agencies fell below

TABLE 10.6 PRIME HRM maturity level rating, percentage of agencies

	Maturity Level 1 Transactional HRM	Maturity Level 2 Process-defined HRM	Maturity Level 3 Integrated HRM	Maturity Level 4 Strategic HRM	Below Transactional	For Validation
Recruitment, selection, and placement	25.52	7.87	1.61	3.37	53.37	8.27
Performance management	2.89	2.49	0.56	2.49	79.61	11.96
HRD learning and development	2.09	1.61	2.33	0.0	88.92	5.06
Rewards and recognition	7.49	6.34	0.88	5.06	68.86	11.4
TOTAL RATING	9.49	4.58	1.35	2.73	72.65	9.20

Source: CSC (www.csc.gov.ph).

maturity Level 1 (i.e., below transactional level), with only 9.5% of agencies achieving an overall maturity Level 1. Encouragingly, 25% of agencies achieved maturity Level 1 for recruitment, selection, and placement; however, over half of the agencies did not meet Level 1 standards for this same system. The CSC was assessed as meeting maturity Level 1 (transactional HRM).

Employment status

The status of employment in the civil service is determined by the appointment issued, which can be any of the following:

a. Permanent
b. Temporary
c. Substitute
d. Coterminous
e. Fixed Term
f. Contractual
g. Casual (www.csc.gov.ph).

The meanings and requirements of these employment statuses can be found in Annex B.

Nature of Appointment

In terms of the nature of appointment, these are:

a. Original
b. Promotion
c. Transfer
d. Reemployment
e. Reappointment
f. Reinstatement
g. Demotion
h. Reclassification
i. Reassignment
j. Detail
k. Designation (www.csc.gov.ph).

The meanings of these appointments can be found in Annex C.

Openness of Posts/Positions

Section 21 (Recruitment and Selection of Employees), Chapter V (Personnel Policies and Standards) of EO 292 prescribes that

> opportunity for government employment shall be open to all qualified citizens and positive efforts shall be exerted to attract the best qualified to enter

The career service covers positions, which are open, closed, and appointed by the President.

the service. Employees shall be selected on the basis of fitness to perform the duties and assume the responsibilities of the positions.

The career service covers positions, which are open, closed, and appointed by the President.

- Open career positions for appointment to which prior qualification in an appropriate examination is required; (pertains to the first and second levels of career service)
- Closed Career positions which are scientific, or highly technical in nature; these include the faculty and academic staff of state colleges and universities, and scientific and technical positions in scientific or research institutions which shall establish and maintain their own merit systems;
- Positions in the Career Executive Service; namely, Undersecretary, Assistant Secretary, Bureau Director, Assistant Bureau Director, Regional Director, Assistant Regional Director, Chief of Department Service, and other officers of equivalent rank as may be identified by the Career Executive Service Board, all of whom are appointed by the President;
- Career officers, other than those in the Career Executive Service, who are appointed by the President, such as the Foreign Service Officers in the Department of Foreign Affairs;
- Commissioned officers and enlisted men of the Armed Forces which shall maintain a separate merit system;
- Personnel of government-owned or -controlled corporations, whether performing governmental or proprietary functions, who do not fall under the non-career service; and
- Permanent laborers, whether skilled or semi-skilled (EO 292).

Performance Assessments and Promotion

The Civil Service Commission developed the Strategic Performance Management System (SPMS), described as "a mechanism that links employee performance with organizational performance to enhance the performance orientation of the compensation system. It ensures that the employee achieves the objectives set by the organization and the organization, on the other hand, achieves the objectives that it has set as its strategic plan" (www.csc.gov.ph).

According to the CSC, the objectives of SPMS are: (1) to concretize the linkage of organizational performance with the Philippine Development Plan, Agency Strategic Plan, Agency Strategic Plan, and Organizational Performance Indicator Framework; (2) to ensure organizational and individual effectiveness by cascading institutional capabilities to the various levels of the organization; and (3) and to link performance management with other HR systems.

The elements of the SPMS are:

1. Goals that are aligned to agency mandate and organizational priorities

220 Maria Fe Villamejor-Mendoza and Minerva Sanvictores Baylon

2. System that is outputs/outcomes-oriented
3. A team approach to performance management
4. Forms that are user-friendly and shows alignment of individual and organizational goals
5. Information systems that support monitoring and evaluation
6. A communication plan.

The SPMS uses a five-point rating scale as shown in Table 10.7.

Performance evaluation of civil servants is conducted twice a year or by semester. The result of this performance evaluation serves as a basis for granting bonuses or incentives and for promotion purposes.

During the administration of President Benigno Aquino III (2010–2016), the Performance-Based Incentive System (PBIS), a new system of incentives

TABLE 10.7 Rating scale of the SPMS

Rating Numerical	Adjectival Rating	Description
5	OUTSTANDING	Performance represents an extraordinary level of achievement and commitment in terms of quality and time, technical skills and knowledge, ingenuity, creativity, and initiative. Employees at this performance level should have demonstrated exceptional job mastery in all major areas of responsibility. Employee achievement and contributions to the organization are of marked excellence.
4	VERY SATISFACTORY	Performance exceeded expectations. All goals, objectives, and targets were achieved above the established standards.
3	SATISFACTORY	Performance met expectations in terms of quality of work, efficiency, and timeliness. The most critical annual goals were met.
2	UNSATISFACTORY	Performance failed to meet expectations, and/or one or more of the most critical goals were not met.
1	POOR	Performance was consistently below expectations, and/or reasonable progress toward critical goals was not made. Significant improvement is needed in one or more important areas.

Source: CSC (www.csc.gov.ph).

for government employees was introduced in 20 July 2012 per EO No. 80. Under this new system, employees may receive two incentives: the Performance-Based Bonus (PBB) and the Productivity Enhancement Incentive (PEI).

Under the PBB, the employees can earn additional incentive of P5,000 (US$100) to P35,000 (US$750) a year. The grant of the performance-based bonuses aims to motivate government employees and their offices to perform better, have greater accountability, and ensure their commitment targets are met. The PBB is a top-up bonus given to employees based on their contribution to the achievement of their Department or Agency's targets and commitments. Thus, it is linked with and depends on the achievements and performance of departments under their Major Final Outputs (MFOs); the Priority Program/Project commitments; and the good governance conditions set by the Inter-Agency Task Force (IATF).

As mandated under EO 201, s. 2016, the (PEI) amounting to P5,000 (US$100) given to government employees not earlier than December 15, provided that they are still in the service as of November 30 and that they have rendered at least a total of four months of at least satisfactory service as of November 30. It covers the whole civil service as well as the military and uniformed police personnel. The PEI aims to improve the productivity of government workers. The PEI is granted to government workers, alongside the upward adjustment of the salary schedule in the bureaucracy, and new benefits such as mid-year bonus equivalent to one-month basic salary.

Those who received unsatisfactory and poor ratings are not entitled to these incentives. Moreover, these ratings can even be a ground for dismissal from office. However, due process should still be observed before a government employee can be dropped from the rolls.

In 2017, then Budget Secretary Diokno said the PBB contributed to the increase in compliance to good governance standards, instilling financial discipline and improving performance management. However, he also acknowledged the need to "tighten the system of granting the PBB, simplify the validation, and address the unintended consequences, such as the tendency of agencies to under target" (www. rappler.com accessed December 18, 2019).

Training

EO 292 upholds the career and personnel development of the workforce and the formulation and implementation of plans for such purpose. The said act establishes that "the development and retention of a competent and efficient workforce in the public service is a primary concern of government." Career and personnel development includes provisions on in-service training, overseas and local scholarships, and training grants.

Training is defined by the CSC (2017) as referring to formal or nonformal training courses and HRD interventions such as coaching, mentoring, job rotation, seminars, workshops, and others that are part of the employee's Individual Development Plan/Career Development Plan.

222   Maria Fe Villamejor-Mendoza and Minerva Sanvictores Baylon

Continuous learning and development is encouraged by the CSC. In pursuit of this, the CSC has developed the Competency-Based Learning and Development Program (CBLDP), which aims to integrate competencies in human resource systems of government agencies, not only in recruitment but also in training and employee development.

The CBLDP directly addresses the problem of competency gaps. It operates under the competency-based learning and development framework, an approach that uses competencies as the standards against which employee development needs are assessed and priorities are set against the need of the organization. CBLDP utilizes competencies as the foundation for designing targeted programs with learning outcomes that directly link to the competency requirements.

Under the CBLDP, trainings that are given to employees are focused on their needs. Opportunities for learning and development include formal classroom training, on-the-job training, self-development, and development activities and interventions. CBLDP does not only refer to training but also corresponds to upgrading the human resource maturity levels of government agencies by upgrading the competency of the individual. Learning and development interventions mold high-performing individuals who, in turn, make up high-performing organizations. At present, the CSC has begun applying competencies to its own learning and employee development processes, as it hopes to be a model in competency-based HRM for other government agencies (CSC 2017).

Another program of the CSC is the Leadership and Coaching Program. It aims to maximize employees' potential through a culture of coaching in the workplace. Coaching is a process that allows an individual to discover his or her own "best fit" and own "best self." The coach does not provide solutions but assists the individuals to find the solutions themselves in order to perform better, improve their craft, meet, or even yet exceed their targets toward the delivery of efficient and effective public service.

The CSC also conducts direct trainings and human resource development to government officials and employees through its Civil Service Institute (CSI) and its regional offices.

Guided by its vision of "Shaping the Servant-Hero towards Public Service Excellence," the CSI offers the following HR programs and services:

- competency-based training and development as well as best practices consulting services to all civil servants and government agencies – specifically focusing on HR/OD and Leadership Capacity Development, and Foundation Programs – to support them in their functions and in recognition of their ability to extend the work and mandate of CSI and ultimately influence the capabilities and capacities of civil servants
- brokers competency development solutions by creating strategic partnerships and continuing engagement with thought leaders, learning process experts and talent managers across the bureaucracy, the academe and private organizations

that help promote influx of new ideas and perspectives relevant to public service

- unifies public servant development by creating, managing and coordinating, as well as providing all these through deliberate approaches on research, knowledge management, and learning technologies, and through key partnerships throughout the bureaucracy and external stakeholders (CSC 2017).

In addition, the CSC, through Memorandum Circular 21, s 2013, adopted the following guidelines pertaining to the Qualification Standards on Training:

1. Training may be acquired from any of the following institutions:

    a. Any CSC accredited private training institutions
    b. Government training institutions
    c. Non-accredited private training institutions offering training of highly technical/specialized nature
    d. Local training institutions that are internationally acclaimed for meeting the global standards of excellence in training
    e. Institutions recognized by the Commission on Higher Education (CHED) as Center of Excellence (COE) or Development (COD)
    f. Foreign institutions that offer training for scholarship purposes or for personal advancement of participants, or
    g. Other institutions that partner with the CSC in building capabilities of civil servants.

2. Training acquired from any of the aforementioned institutions must be relevant to the position to be filled and aligned with the strategy map or development goal of the institution or organization.

As of February 2019, the total number of CSC-recognized or accredited learning and development institutions is 264. The categories and number of these institutions are shown in Table 10.8.

There is an observation that the current training and development landscape is crowded with multiple government and nongovernment actors. There is some overlapping of institutions, products, and services. Although this is not due to deliberate decisions to create intersecting institutions, the impact has created inefficiencies and restricted the rationalization of training and development products. The establishment of the Civil Service Academy, which will provide leadership and direction in all training activities and pursue a more systematic and integrated approach, provides an opportunity to develop a more consistent and strategic approach to learning and development. There are many modern approaches to training and development, which will often include a range of learning approaches, not only formal training, in recognition that knowledge is not sufficient to fully develop competencies, particularly in leadership and managerial areas (World Bank 2018).

TABLE 10.8 Category and number of CSC-recognized learning and development institutions

Category	Number
CSC Accredited Private Learning and Development Institutions	26
Government Learning and Development Institutions	44
Non-accredited Learning and Development Institutions Offering Training of Highly Technical/Specialized Nature	54
Local Learning and Development Institutions that are Internationally Acclaimed for Meeting the Excellence in Training	9
Institutions Recognized by the Commission on Higher Education as Center of Excellence or Development	99
Foreign Institutions that Offer Learning and Development for Scholarship Purposes or for Personal Advancement of Participants	7
Other Learning and Development Institutions that Partner with the CSC in Building Capabilities of Public Servants	25
TOTAL	264

Source: CSI, February 2019.

Senior Civil Service (Senior Management)

As discussed earlier, the senior officials belong to the Third Level or management class in the group of career positions in the civil service. They are appointed by the President of the Republic of the Philippines, with the consent of the Commission on Appointments.

The Career Executive Service was created by Presidential Decree No. [1] s. 1972, as amended, to "form a continuing pool of well-selected and development-oriented career administrators who shall provide competent and faithful service." This is in pursuit of and consistent with the merit-based system of appointment even of third level officials or Presidential appointees.

These positions include the Secretaries of the Department, Undersecretaries, Assistant Secretaries, Bureau Directors, Assistant Bureau Directors, Regional Directors, Assistant Regional Directors, Chiefs of Department Service, and other officers of equivalent rank as may be identified by the Career Executive Service Board (CESB) as third level positions in the Career Executive Service (CES) [Sections 7(3) and 8, paragraph 1(c), Chapter 2, Book V, EO No. 292). Entrance to said positions is prescribed by the Career Executive Service Board (an agency attached to the CSC), to serve as the governing body of the Career Executive Service and to promulgate rules, standards, and procedures on selection, classification, compensation, and career development of the CES members (PD 1 1972).

A person who meets such managerial experience and other requirements and passes such examinations, as may be prescribed by the Board, shall be included in the register of career executive eligibles.

The CES operates on the "rank concept." Career Executive Service Officers (CESOs) are "appointed" to ranks and "assigned" to CES positions. As such, they

The Philippines **225**

can be re-assigned or transferred from one CES position to another and from one office to another but not oftener than once every two years. The CES is like the Armed Forces and the Foreign Service where the officers are also appointed to ranks and assigned to positions. The Rank defines the status and compensation of the CESOs as found in Table 10.9.

CES Eligibility is conferred to a candidate who is able to successfully complete the CES Eligibility Examination Process and meet other requirements as may be prescribed by the CESB. Upon assessment of the CESB, the applicant's CES eligibility is conferred and the candidate is included in the Roster of CES Eligibles. Upon recommendation by the CESB, she/he is given a CES position and appointed by the President to a CES rank. She/He thus becomes a member of the CES (www.cesb.gov.ph).

As of June 29, 2018, there are 2,678 CES positions – a small number for a civil service of 1.7 million (1.5 CES positions for every 1,000 civil servants). Of these 2,678 positions, 1,907 were filled, indicating a total of 771 vacant positions (a rate of 29%) (www.cesb.gov.ph). This is a surprisingly high number of vacancies given the already small size of the CES relative to the rest of the civil service and the important role played by the CESOs in leading the civil service to deliver the government's policy and program priorities. Further, of the 1,907 CES positions that were filled as of June 29, 2018, as many as 859 (45%) are occupied by non-CESOs and non-eligibles (i.e., political appointees). Apart from having a relatively small leadership cadre for a civil service of 1.7 million, therefore, there is a high vacancy rate and almost half of the total number of CES positions with incumbents were filled by political appointees.[3]

The Civil Service Commission vets each and every government employee – hundreds of thousands of them every year – but it has no say when it comes to presidential appointees. Article VII, Section 16 of the 1987 Philippine Constitution gives the President the power to nominate and, with the consent of the Commission on Appointments, appoint the heads of the executive departments, ambassadors, other public ministers and consuls, officers of the armed forces from the rank of colonel or naval captain, and other officers whose appointments are vested in him in this Constitution. "She/he shall also appoint all other officers of the government whose appointments are not otherwise provided for by law, and

TABLE 10.9 Career executive service officer rank, salary grade, and equivalent CES positions

CESO Rank	Salary Grade	Equivalent CES Position
CESO I	30	Undersecretary
CESO II	29	Assistant Secretary
CESO III	28	Regional/Bureau Director
CESO IV	27	Assistant Regional/Bureau Director
CESO V	26	Director II
CESO VI	25	Director I

Source: CESB website (www.cesb.gov.ph) and EO 201 s 2016.

226 Maria Fe Villamejor-Mendoza and Minerva Sanvictores Baylon

those whom s/he may be authorized by law to appoint." Thus, although civil service appointments are based on merit, the 1987 Constitution also provides wide latitude and discretion to the President in making high-level appointments with the consent of the Commission on Appointments.

Political appointments by the President of the Republic are usually reserved to the third tier of the Civil Service, for example, the career executive service (CES), which includes the Secretaries of the Department, and all other CESOs listed in the table above (Sections 7(3) and 8, paragraph 1(c), Chapter 2, Book V, EO No. 292). These are usually for positions that are policy determining, primarily confidential, or highly technical in nature (Civil Service Commission 2017 Rule I, General Policies on Recruitment; Omnibus Rules on Appointments and Other Human Resource Actions (ORAOHRA), Revised 2018).

Political appointments short-circuit the rules on qualifications and bypass qualified civil servants who have put in years of training, service, and dedication for public service. Demoralization and fear are among the consequences. Faced with a patronage system where who you know matters more than what you know, David says, "people in government learn to be quiet, to be timid, to be politic." She says the prevailing attitude in the civil service is: "Never mind if you're wrong as long as you don't step on anybody's toes, not the mayor's, not the congressman's, not even the barangay (village) councillor's" (www.dandc.eu/en/article/civil-service-nightmares-philippines).

This political appointment is perceived to be abused (Constantino-David 2007) Moreover, recent reports (World Bank 2018) point to the growing politicization of this appointment process, with no meaningful means for vetting presidential appointees to ensure they meet the criteria and have the required qualifications for the positions to which they are appointed. Where the quality of political appointees is dubious, at best, this can adversely affect the behavior and attitudes of civil servants in several ways, including the difficulty in building and retaining capacity, lowering motivation and performance by career civil servants.

Most obviously, where political criteria carry weight in personnel decisions, competence and merit are no longer (fully) prioritized, with potentially negative implications for performance. Politicization also changes career incentives of civil servants: responsiveness to political demands becomes the key driver of success rather than impartial policy advice, unbiased implementation, and service delivery to the public (World Bank 2018).

Politicization may also shift the focus of the civil servants from serving the public to serving the politicians (Meyer-Sahling et al. 2018; Monsod 2017).

Notes

1 Professors of the Public Policy and Public Administration of the National College of Public Administration and Governance, University of the Philippines. We acknowledge the assistance of Ms. Nelin Dulpina, University Researcher of the same College.
2 PAHRDF ran from 2004 to 2010, and the PAHRODF ran from 2010 to 2015.

3 CESB data from December 31, 2017, indicated a total of 2,682 CES positions (four more than at June 29, 2018), with 1,916 being filled (nine less than in December) and 766 vacancies (compared with 771, which is five more – a rate of 28.5 percent). There were also fewer (845 or 45 percent) non-CESOs/non-eligibles in December compared with June. The question then arises as to what is the exact number of established or *plantilla* CES positions.

References

Articles

Alfiler, M. C. P. (2008) 'The Philippine administrative system as enabling institution', *Philippine Journal of Public Administration*, 52(2–4): 224–44.

Brillantes, Alex Jr. B. and Fernandez, Maricel T. (2011) 'Restoring trust and building integrity in government: Issues and concerns in the Philippines and areas for reform', *International Public Management Review*, 12(1): 55–80.

Cariño, B. V. (1987) 'The Philippines and Southeast Asia: Historical roots and contemporary linkages', in J. T. Fawceet and B. V. Cariño (eds) *Pacific Bridges: The New Immigration from Asia and the Pacific Islands* (pp. 305–25), New York: Center for Migration Studies.

Civil Service Commission (2017) *Omnibus Rules on Appointments and Other Human Resource Actions* (ORAOHRA) (Revised 2018).

Constantino-David, K. (2007) 'Politics, perils and pains of building institutions', Keynote address to the Human Development Network General Assembly, Manila.

Corpuz, O. D. (1957) *The Bureaucracy in the Philippines* (No. 4), Institute of Public Administration, University of the Philippines.

De Guzman, R. P. et al. (1988) '*The Bureaucracy*', in R. P. De Guzman and M. A. Reforma (eds) *Government and Politics of the Philippines* (pp. 180–206), New York: Oxford University Press.

Endriga, J. (1985) 'Stability and Change: Civil Service in the Philippines', *Philippine Journal of Public Administration*, 29(2): 141–74.

Legaspi, Amita (2009, September 30) 'Saludo appointment as CSC chair nixed by CA', *GMA News*, available at: https://www.gmanetwork.com/news/topstories/nation/174671/ca-rejects-saludo-one-last-time-bypasses-atienza-and-reyes/story/.

Manila Times (2016) 'Firemen demoralized over promotions scam', available at: www.manilatimes.net/2016/06/05/news/top-stories/firemen-demoralized-over-promotions-scam/266158.

Mendoza, M. F. and Baylon, M. S. (2018) 'The state of the Philippine public bureaucracy: Challenges and prospects', Paper presented at the International Conference on "The State of Public Bureaucracy in East Asia," held on 6–7 July 2018 at the Korea University, Seoul, South Korea.

Meyer-Sahling, J. H., Mikkelsen, K. S., and Schuster, C. (2018) 'Civil service management and corruption: What we know and what we don't', *Public Administration*, 96(2): 276–85.

Monsod, T. (2017) 'Political appointees in the Philippines bureaucracy: Do increasing numbers help or harm?' *Philippine Political Science Journal*, 38(1): 1–27.

Peñalosa, C. (2014) *Hanapbuhay: The Filipino bureaucrat's quest for "Ginhawa" in the workplace: Its implications for understanding bureaucratic corruption*, Doctoral dissertation, University of the Philippines.

Reyes, D. R. (2011) 'History and context of the development of public administration in the Philippines', in E. M. Berman (ed) *Public Administration in Southeast Asia* (pp. 333–54), Boca Raton, FL: CRC Press.

Tjiptoherijanto, P. (2008) 'Civil service reforms in the Philippines: The role of civil society', A Report Submitted to The Nippon Foundation Dilliman, Quezon City, Philippines.

Veneracion, J. B. (1988) *Merit or Patronage: A History of the Philippine Civil Service*, Quezon City: Great Books Trading.

World Bank (2018) 'Strengthening human resources in the Philippine bureaucracy: Developing a modern, fit for purpose civil service to support a "middle class" society', Scoping Mission Report.

Laws and other Issuances

1973 Philippine Constitution

1987 Philippine Constitution

CSC Resolution 2017 OMNIBUS RULES ON APPOINTMENTS AND OTHER HUMAN RESOURCE ACTIONS, REVISED IN 2018, "Amendments and Additional Provisions to CSC Resolution Number 1701009" issued on June 16, 2017

Executive Order No. 80 (20 July 2012) Directing the Adoption of a Performance-Based Incentive System for Government Employees

Executive Order No. 201 (19 February 2016), Modifying the Salary Schedule for Civilian Government Personnel and Authorizing the Grant of Additional Benefits for Both Civilian and Military and Uniformed Personnel

Executive Order No. 292 "Revised Administrative Code of 1987"

Presidential Decree (P.D.) No. 1, s 1972, "Reorganizing the Executive Branch of the National Government" signed on 24 September 1972

Presidential Decree (P.D.) No. 1184 s. 1977, "Integrated National Police Personnel Professionalization Act of 1977", signed on 26 August 1977.

Republic Act 7140 (05 June 1991) "An Act Requiring Regular Publication of Existing Vacant Positions in Government Offices, Appropriating Funds Therefore, and for Other Purposes"

Internet sources

www.cesb.gov.ph

www.csc.gov.ph

www.csi.gov.ph

comappt.gov.ph

rappler.com

www.dandc.eu/en/article/civil-service-nightmares-philippines

ANNEX A

Functions of the CSC Under EO 292 Entitled "Revised Administrative Code of 1987"

- Administer and enforce the constitutional and statutory provisions on the merit system for all levels and ranks in the Civil Service;
- Prescribe, amend and enforce rules and regulations for carrying into effect the provisions of the Civil Service Laws and other pertinent laws;
- Promulgate policies, standards and guidelines for the Civil Service and adopt plans and programs to promote economical, efficient and effective personnel administration in the government;
- Formulate policies and regulations for the administration, maintenance and implementation of position classification and compensation and set standards for the establishment, allocation and reallocation of pay scales, classes and positions;
- Render opinion and rulings on all personnel and other Civil Service matters which shall be binding on all head of departments, offices and agencies and which may be brought to the Supreme Court on *certiorari*;
- Appoint and discipline its officials and employees in accordance with law and exercise control and supervision over the activities of the Commission;
- Control, supervise and coordinate Civil Service examinations. Any entity or official in government may be called upon by the Commission to assist in the preparation and conduct of said examinations including security, use of buildings and facilities as well as personnel and transportation of examination materials which shall be exempt from inspection regulations;
- Prescribe all forms for Civil Service examinations, appointment, reports and such other forms as may be required by law, rules and regulations;
- Declare positions in the Civil Service as may properly be primarily confidential, highly technical or policy determining;
- Formulate, administer and evaluate programs relative to the development and retention of qualified and competent work force in the public service;

230 Maria Fe Villamejor-Mendoza and Minerva Sanvictores Baylon

- Hear and decide administrative cases instituted by or brought before it directly or on appeal, including contested appointments, and review decisions and action of its offices and of the agencies attached to it. Officials and employees who fail to comply with such decisions, orders, or rulings shall be liable for contempt of the Commission. Its decisions, orders or rulings shall be final and executory. Such decisions, orders, or rulings may be brought to Supreme Court on certiorari by the aggrieved party within 30 days from receipt of the copy thereof;
- Issues *subpoena* and *subpoena duces tecum* for the production of documents and records pertinent to investigations and inquiries conducted by it in accordance with its authority conferred by the Constitution and pertinent laws;
- Advise the President on all matters involving personnel management in the government service and submit to the President an annual report on the personnel programs;
- Take appropriate actions on all appointments and other personnel matters in the Civil Service including extension of service beyond retirement age;
- Inspect and audit the personnel actions and programs of the departments, agencies, bureaus, offices, local government including government-owned or controlled corporations; conduct periodic review of the decisions and actions of offices or officials to whom authority has been delegated by the Commission as well as the conduct of the officials and the employees in these offices and apply appropriate sanctions whenever necessary;
- Delegate authority for the performance of any functions to departments, agencies and offices where such functions may be effectively performed;
- Administer the retirement program of government officials and employees, and accredit government services and evaluate qualification for retirement;
- Keep and maintain personnel records of all officials and employees in the Civil Service; and
- Perform all functions properly belonging to a central personnel agency such as other functions as may be provided by law

Source: EO 292, s. 1991

ANNEX B

Employment Status in the Civil Service

Permanent – an appointment issued to a person who meets all the qualification requirements of the position to which he/she is being appointed to, including the appropriate eligibility, in accordance with the provisions of law, rules and standards promulgated.

Temporary – issued to a person who meets the education, experience and training requirements for the position to which he/she is being appointed to except for the appropriate eligibility. A temporary appointment may only be issued in the absence of an applicant who meets all the qualification requirements of the position as certified by the appointing authority. The appointment shall not exceed 12 months from the date the appointment was issued. The appointee may be replaced sooner if a qualified eligible who is willing to accept the appointment becomes actually available.

Substitute – issued when the regular incumbent of a position is temporarily unable to perform the duties of the position, i.e., on approved leave of absence, under suspension, on a scholarship grant or is on secondment. A substitute appointment is allowed only if the leave of absence of the incumbent is at least 3 months except in the case of teachers.

Coterminous – issued to a person whose tenure is limited to a period specified by law or whose continuity in the service is based on the trust and confidence of the appointing authority or head of the organizational unit where assigned. There are 4 categories under it – coterminous with the appointing authority, with the head of the organizational unit where assigned, primarily confidential in nature, and with the lifespan of the agency.

Fixed term – issued to a person with a specified term of office, subject to reappointment as provided by law such as Chairperson and members of commissions and boards, SUC President, and Head of Agency appointed by the Board

Contractual – issued to a person whose employment in the government is in accordance with a special contract to undertake local or foreign-assisted projects or a specific work or job requiring special or technical skills not available in the employing agency, to be accomplished within a specific period. Appointment is limited to one year but may be renewed every year, based on performance, until the completion of the project or specific work. They must meet the education, training and experience requirements of the positions as proposed by the respective agency heads and approved by the CSC

Casual – issued only for essential and necessary services where there are not enough regular staff to meet the demands of the service and for emergency cases and intermittent period not to exceed one year

Source: Source: Rule IV, 2017ORAOHRA, CSC Resolution N0.1800692

ANNEX C

Nature of Appointment

Original – the initial entry into the career or non-career service

Promotion – advancement of a career employee from one position to another with an increase in duties and responsibilities as authorized by law, and usually accompanied by an increase in salary

The movement may be from one department or agency to another or from one organizational unit to another in the same department of agency.

Transfer – a movement of an employee from one position to another which is of equivalent rank, level or salary without gap in the service involving the issuance of an appointment

Reemployment – appointment of a person who has been previously appointed to a position in the government service but was separated therefrom as a result of reduction in force, reorganization, retirement, voluntary resignation, or other non-disciplinary action

Reappointment – issuance of an appointment as a result of reorganization, devolution, salary standardization, recategorization, rationalization, or similar events

Reinstatement – any person who has been permanently appointed to a position in the career service and who has, through no delinquency or misconduct, have been separated may be reinstated to a position in the same level for which he/she is qualified

Demotion – movement of an employee from a higher position to a lower position where he/she qualifies, if a lower position is available. It entails reduction in duties, responsibilities, status or rank, which may or may not involve reduction in salary

Reclassification – a form of staffing modification and/or position classification which is applied only when there is a substantial change in the regular duties and responsibilities of the position

Human Resource Actions not requiring the issuance of an appointment but an Office Order issued by the appointing authority

Reassignment – movement of an employee across the organizational structure within the same department or agency which does not involve a reduction in rank, status or salary

Detail – temporary movement of an employee from one department or agency to another which does not involved a reduction in rank, status or salary

Designation – movement that involves an imposition of additional and/or higher duties to be performed by a public official/employee which is temporary and can be terminated any time at the pleasure of the appointing authority

Source: Rule IV, 2017ORAOHRA, CSC Resolution No. 180069

CONCLUSION

Chong-Min Park, Yongjin Chang, and Yousueng Han

Comparing civil service systems turns out to be a big methodological challenge (Demmke and Moilanen 2010). Yet, accounting for their national differences is an even bigger theoretical challenge (Pollitt and Bouckaert 2011; Peters 2021). In this study we propose four modes of public employment to compare contemporary civil service systems at the operational level: bureaucratization, professionalization, politicization, and marketization. We presume that there are no pure or clear-cut models and that contemporary civil service systems are likely mixed or hybrid systems that combine, at varying degree, these modes of public employment. Yet, we find some patterns of public employment across East and Southeast Asia.

At the risk of simplification, we may summarize notable features of civil service systems across the region: Japan, South Korea, and Taiwan develop civil service systems with high levels of bureaucratization and low levels of politicization; Singapore and Hong Kong, civil service systems with high levels of professionalization or marketization and low levels of politicization; Indonesia and the Philippines, civil service systems with high levels of bureaucratization and moderate levels of politicization; Malaysia, a civil service system with high levels of bureaucratization and politicization; Thailand, a civil service system with high levels of bureaucratization and low levels of politicization; and Vietnam, a civil service system with high levels of politicization and bureaucratization.

The question now would be why they differ in combining elements of each mode of public employment. Painter and Peter (2010) emphasize the legacy of the past as a basis of understanding contemporary administrative systems. Considering that initial choices made at the critical juncture in the past shape subsequent choices, they argue that local administrative traditions and imported models of modern administration under colonial rule may shape contemporary administrative systems (Peters 2021). Pollitt and Bouckaert (2011) suggest that state traditions and political institutions may affect responses to administrative reform pressures,

DOI: 10.4324/9781003326496-14

resulting in different public administrative systems. Following these lines of inquiry, we focus on local traditions, foreign transplants, and types of political regime.

Painter and Peter (2010) classify East and Southeast Asian countries into four groups in terms of local traditions and European transplants. First, Japan, South Korea, Taiwan, China, Vietnam, Hong Kong, and Singapore have the Confucian administrative tradition while Indonesia, Thailand, Malaysia, and the Philippines, non-Confucian administrative traditions. Second, Japan, South Korea, Taiwan, China, Vietnam, Indonesia, and Thailand have administrative transplants of Continental European origin while Hong Kong, Singapore, Malaysia, and the Philippines,[1] those of Anglo-American origin.[2]

The Confucian administrative tradition is a combination of Confucianism and the traditional administrative practices of Imperial China (Painter and Peters 2010). One of the core characteristics of the Confucian administrative tradition includes a meritocracy based on an examination system to recruit scholar-officials (Woodside 2006). The examination system in the Confucian tradition emphasizes general competence, largely through testing of knowledge about Confucian classics. Hence, we may expect that where the Confucian administrative heritage remains strong, meritocratic recruitment, especially exam-based, for civil servants is likely to prevail. As the name suggests, however, the cases with the non-Confucian tradition constitute a catch-all category. They differ widely in cultural traditions: Indonesia and Malaysia, Islamicist tradition; Thailand, Buddhist tradition; and the Philippines, Catholic tradition. It remains unclear what administrative traditions they share. But the Confucian administrative tradition may be distinguishable from the non-Confucian traditions in support for meritocracy as an ideal.

Imported models of modern administration at the critical juncture have more direct influence on contemporary civil service systems. Two Western administrative traditions are relevant for East and Southeast Asia: one is the Anglo-American tradition and the other, the Continental European one. In the Anglo-American tradition, the state is a byproduct of interests in society and the state bureaucracy is subject to the influence of political institutions. In this anti-statist tradition, the law is a tool to constrain the power of the state. Although politics is separated from administration, political accountability is emphasized as a primary mechanism of controlling the state bureaucracy. The blurring of the boundaries between the public and private sectors weakens the legal status of civil servants. No public law status is given to the civil servant and public sector employment is not much different from private sector employment. The Anglo-American pragmatic tradition is closely linked to the "public interest" model of administrative system (Painter and Peters 2010; Pierre 1995; Pollitt and Bouckaert 2011).

In the Continental European tradition, whether French or German, the state is autonomous from interests in society and the state bureaucracy is assumed to be above politics. In this statist tradition, any administrative reform to weaken the power of the state is likely resisted. The law is an instrument of the state in expanding its power. Legal or specialized training is a necessary qualification of civil servants. The civil servant is given a public law status to bind them to the

Conclusion **237**

state and the civil service tends to be kept distinct from private sector employment. Legal accountability is emphasized as a primacy mechanism of controlling the state bureaucracy. The Continental European legalistic tradition is closely linked to the *Rechtsstaat* model of administrative system (Painter and Peters 2010; Pierre 1995; Pollitt and Bouckaert 2011).

Overall, the civil servants in the Continental European tradition are trustees or representatives of the state while their counterparts in the Anglo-American tradition, servants of political masters (Hood and Lodge 2006). Hence, countries with a legacy of the Anglo-American model are more open to the politicization of public employment than those with a legacy of the Continental European model. Since the Anglo-American tradition is less likely to emphasize the distinction between public and private sectors than the Continental European tradition, countries with a legacy of the Anglo-American model are more open to the professionalization or marketization of public employment than those with a legacy of the Continental European model. By contrast, countries with a legacy of the Continental European model are more readily open to the bureaucratization of public employment than those with a legacy of the Anglo-American model.

The patterns of public employment found in East and Southeast Asia seem largely consistent with these expectations. Of our six cases with the Confucian tradition, Japan, South Korea, Taiwan, and Vietnam transplanted the Continental European model. It should be added that after the Communist revolution Vietnam adopts the Soviet model on top of the Continental European model.[3] By contrast, Singapore and Hong Kong imported the Anglo-American model. Since the Confucian tradition emphasizes meritocratic recruitment based on formal examination and the Continental European model is more linked to Weberian bureaucracy than the Anglo-American model, South Korea, Taiwan, and Japan maintain civil service systems which are more bureaucratized than professionalized. Singapore and Hong Kong, where the Anglo-American model was imported under direct colonial rule, maintain civil service systems which are more professionalized than bureaucratized. Singapore and Hong Kong, where pragmatic administrative tradition remains strong, are more open to market-based reform of public employment than Japan, South Korea, and Taiwan, where the legalistic tradition remains prevalent. In general, the civil service systems of non-Confucian cases tend to be less bureaucratized than those of Confucian cases. Yet, due to the differences in imported models of modern administration, they differ in the extent of bureaucratization of public employment. The civil service systems in Indonesia and Thailand where the Continental European model was transplanted are more bureaucratized than those in Malaysia and the Philippines where the Anglo-American model was transplanted.

Local traditions and foreign transplants are not the only factor shaping contemporary civil service systems. The types of political regime may shape the behavior of government leaders in interpreting and responding to administrative reform pressures, resulting in different civil service systems (Pollitt and Bouckaert 2011). Similarly, Lodge (2012) notes the relationship between civil service systems and the wider political systems. Another institutional factor includes the relationship between political parties and public bureaucracies, which are crucially shaped by the relative timing of democratization and bureaucratization (Shefter 1994).

In competitive electoral regimes, the separation of politics from administration is well established although political accountability of the public bureaucracy is emphasized. Hence, the politicization of public employment tends to be moderated. In noncompetitive electoral regimes, political responsiveness, if not democratic accountability, is emphasized such that the public bureaucracy remains a key source of political leadership. In one-party regimes, the public bureaucracy officially exists as a party organization and public employment is primarily based on loyalty to the party rather than technical competence. We may expect that competitive electoral regimes are more likely to develop modern civil service notions such as neutral competence and protection of civil servants from political interference than noncompetitive electoral regimes or single-party dictatorships.

As expected, in Japan, South Korea, and Taiwan, stable competitive electoral regimes, the civil service systems display low levels of politicization. In Indonesia and the Philippines, unstable competitive electoral regimes, the civil service systems exhibit moderate levels of politicization. Singapore, Malaysia, and Hong Kong may be regarded as noncompetitive electoral regimes. Yet, the level of politicization of public employment varies: the civil service system in Malaysia displays high levels of politicization while those in Singapore and Hong Kong, low levels. It should be added, though, that the civil service system in Hong Kong becomes more politicized than before since its transfer to China. In Thailand, a noncompetitive electoral regime under a coalition of military and civilian bureaucratic elites, the civil service system is not much politicized. In Vietnam, where the ruling Communist party commands the public bureaucracy, the civil service system is highly politicized. Overall, the civil service systems in Japan, South Korea, and Taiwan appear to be distinguishable from those in Southeast Asia.

As Shefter (1994) emphasizes, the relative timing of democratization and bureaucratization may shape the character of political parties as a major source of public employment. When political democratization proceeds bureaucratic development, political parties tend to serve as an important source of public employment, especially in partisan politics. By contrast, when bureaucratic development proceeds political democratization, political parties face difficulties with expanding the extent of political appointment. If the public bureaucracy is established before democratization, the politicization of public employment would be moderated or restrained. By contrast, when the public bureaucracy was established after or along with democratization, the politicization of public employment could be intensified. Democratization seeks political accountability by extending political appointments and strengthening the role of political parties. Consistent with these expectations, in Japan, South Korea, and Taiwan, where bureaucratic development proceeded long before democratization, the civil service systems display low levels of politicization (Evans and Rauch 1999). Even in Singapore and Hong Kong, where bureaucratic development proceeded before limited democratization, the civil service systems display low levels of politicization. By contrast, in Indonesia

Conclusion **239**

and the Philippines, where democratization occurs along with or before bureaucratic development, the civil service systems display moderate levels of politization.

The ten East and Southeast Asian cases examined here differ in local administrative traditions, imported Western models of modern administration, types of political regime, and the relative timing of democratization. The region's contemporary civil service systems appear to reflect, to some extent, these differences. Japan, South Korea, and Taiwan inherited the Confucian tradition and transplanted the Continental European system of modern administration. They establish liberal democracies long after bureaucratic development. Hence, their civil service systems tend to display high levels of bureaucratization and low levels of politicization, featuring exam-based recruitment, neutral testing of general competencies, and lifelong tenure. Singapore and Hong Kong inherited the Confucian tradition and transplanted the Anglo-American system of modern administration and maintain noncompetitive electoral regimes after bureaucratic development. Hence, their civil service systems tend to display high levels of professionalization or marketization and low levels of politicization, featuring skills-based recruitment, wide-open search for candidates, and high pay competitiveness. Vietnam inherited the Confucian tradition and established a Soviet-style political-administrative system on top of the Continental European model of modern administration. Hence, its civil service system tends to display high levels of politicization and bureaucratization.

The civil service systems found in non-Confucian cases are more complicated and varied than those found in the Confucian cases. Indonesia imported the Continental European model of modern administration and establishes an electoral regime before or along with bureaucratic development. Hence, its civil service system tends to display high levels of bureaucratization and moderate levels of politicization. Malaysia imported the Anglo-American model of modern administration and establishes a noncompetitive electoral regime before or along with bureaucratic development. Hence, its civil service system tends to display high levels of politicization and bureaucratization. In this ethically heterogeneous society the bumiputra policy including affirmative action in the public sector contributes to the politicization of public employment while discourages bureaucratization or professionalization. The Philippines, with a legacy of Spanish colonial rule, imported the Anglo-American model of modern administration and establishes an electoral regime before bureaucratic development. Hence, its civil service system tends to display high levels of bureaucratization and professionalization and moderate levels of politicization. Lastly, Thailand imported the Continental European model of modern administration and maintains a military-bureaucratic regime. Hence, its civil service system tends to display high levels of bureaucratization and low levels of politicization.

Since the end of World War II, newly independent countries in East and Southeast Asia have faced administrative reform pressures associated with modernization, democratization, and globalization at the societal level (Wong and Chan 1999). In the context of socioeconomic modernization, they have been under pressure to modernize the civil service system by weakening cronyism and nepotism and

240 Chong-Min Park, Yongjin Chang, and Yousueng Han

developing legal-rational institutions of administration. Reform measures emphasized the establishment of a merit-based public bureaucracy through either bureaucratization or professionalization of public employment. In the context of political democratization, they have been under pressure to strengthen institutions of democratic accountability and responsiveness including political parties. Reform measures emphasize the increasing role of representative institutions through politicization of public employment. In the context of globalization, they have been under pressure to improve the efficiency and effectiveness of the public sector through marketization of public employment. Given administrative traditions and political institutions, they distinctively responded to these reform pressures, resulting in civil service systems with different modes of public employment. National strategies and responses to these challenges are clearly of time and context-contingent nature. Contemporary civil service systems in East and Southeast Asia appear to have several layers each of which is associated with context-specific responses to modernization, democratization, and globalization at the societal level. The landscape of civil service systems in the region consists of a variety of hybrid systems, failing to converge into a clear-cut model.

Notes

1 Although the Philippines was earlier colonized by Spain, which shares the Napoleonic administrative tradition, research indicates the influence of American colonialism on its contemporary civil service system (Reyes 2011; Endriga 2001)
2 The legacy of British colonial rule in East Asia can be found in Singapore, Malaysia, and Hong Kong. It is argued that through British colonization, a modern bureaucracy that emphasizes meritocracy, legalism, political neutrality, and general administrators was introduced in these countries (Berman 2011)
3 In the Soviet model one party rule is combined with a centralized state. Party rule imposes political control over all institutions of the state. Loyalty to the party ideology is essential for entry and promotion in the cadre bureaucracy. Meritocracy or professionalism is just a secondary consideration.

References

Berman, E. M. (2011) 'Public administration in Southeast Asia: An overview', in E. M. Berman (ed) *Public Administration in Southeast Asia: Thailand, Philippines, Malaysia, Hong Kong, and Macao* (pp. 1–26), Boca Raton, FL: CRC Press.
Demmke, C. and Moilanen, T. (2010) *Civil Services in the EU of 27: Reform Outcomes and the Future of the Civil Service*, Frankfurt am Main: Peter Lang.
Endriga, J. N. (2001) 'The national civil service system of the Philippines', in J. P. Burns and B. Bowornwathana (eds) *Civil Service Systems in Asia*, Cheltenham, UK: Edward Elgar.
Evans, P. and Rauch, J. E. (1999) 'Bureaucracy and growth: A cross-national analysis of the effects of "Weberian" state structures on economic growth', *American Sociological Review*, 64(5): 748–65.
Hood, C. and Lodge, M. (2006) *The Politics of Public Service Bargains*, Oxford: Oxford University Press.
Lodge, M. (2012) 'Administrative patterns and national politics', in B. G. Peters and J. Pierre (eds) *The SAGE Handbook of Public Administration, Concise*, 2nd. (pp. 479–94), Los Angeles: SAGE.

Painter, M. and Peters, B. G. (2010) 'Administrative traditions in comparative perspective: Families, groups, and hybrids', in M. Painter and B. G. Peters (eds) *Tradition and Public Administration* (pp. 19–30), London: Palgrave Macmillan.

Peters, B. G. (2021) *Administrative Traditions: Understanding the Roots of Contemporary Administrative Behavior*, Oxford: Oxford University Press.

Pierre, J. (1995) 'Conclusion: A framework of comparative public administration', in J. Pierre (ed) *Bureaucracy in the Modern State: An Introduction to Comparative Public Administration* (pp. 205–18), Aldershot: Edward Elgar.

Pollitt, C. and Bouckaert, G. (2011) *Public Management Reform: A Comparative Analysis*, 3rd edn., Oxford: Oxford University Press.

Reyes, D. R. (2011) 'History and context of the development of public administration in the Philippines', in E. Berman (ed) *Public Administration in Southeast Asia* (pp. 333–54), Boca Raton, FL: CRC Press.

Shefter, M. (1994) *Political Parties and the State: The American Historical Experience*, Princeton: Princeton University Press.

Wong, H. and Chan, H. S. (eds) (1999) *Handbook of Comparative Public Administration in the Asia-Pacific Basin*, New York: Marcel Dekker.

Woodside, A. (2006) *Lost Modernities: China, Vietnam, Korea, and the Hazards of World History*, Cambridge: Harvard University Press.

INDEX

Act on Officials with Fixed Term of Office (Japan) 35

Act on Personal Exchange between the Government and Private Enterprises (Japan) 35–36

administrative systems: grand general theory, formulation 2; "public interest" model 236

Administratorial Position (Jabatan Administrasi) (Indonesia) 129, 141

Anglo-American model: import 17, 19, 20, 239; legacy 237; transplantation 18; usage 21

Anti-Extradition Bill (Hong Kong) 80

Anugerah Perkhidmatan Cemerlang (APC) (Malaysia) 190

Aparatur Sipil Negara (ASN) (Indonesia) 120–121; composition *131*; training 139

appointments 233–234

Aquino, Corazon 204

Badan Kepegawaian Negara (BKN) 121, 122–123, 125; functions 122–123; public, social media communication *132*

Badan Siber dan Sandi Negara (BSSN) (Indonesia) 127

Badawi, Abdullah Ahmad 173

Bakar, Azwar Abu 121

best-suited candidate (selection), professionalization (emphasis) 14

bureaucracy: meritocracy, increase 124; reform, meritocracy (impact) 124

bureaucratic agencies, political neutrality 43

bureaucratization 1, 3, 235; approach (Vietnam) 20; display 16; level, ascertaining 13; levels, comparison 235; modernization, impact 12; prevalence 18; private-public distinction 10–11; professionalization, contrast 4, 5, 7–8; public employment mode 5–6; usage 18

Cabinet Bureau of Personnel Affairs, establishment (Japan) 41

career advancement, predictability 4

career civil servants, CSEE recruitment (Taiwan) 63–64

career incentives (change), politicization (impact) 226

central administration, civil service rank system (South Korea) *49*

central government agencies, training institutes (Taiwan) **68**

central human resource management (HRM) unit: Hong Kong 83–84; Indonesia 120–125; Philippines 205–209; Singapore 72–73; South Korea 46; Taiwan 62–63; Vietnam 100–103

Central Officials' Training Institute (COTI), creation (South Korea) 52

Central Personnel Administrative Agency (Japan) 29–30

Chan-ocha, Prayuth 152

civil service: employment status 231–232; inside/outside, mobility 11; mobility 109; neutrality act, enactment 61;

Index

political neutrality 82; reforms, promotion (Malaysia) 21
Civil Service Bureau (CSB) (Hong Kong) 83–85, 87–88
civil service classification/status 31–33; Singapore 74; South Korea 45, 48–50; Taiwan 64–65
Civil Service College (CSC) programs (Singapore) 76
Civil Service Commission (Indonesia) 121
Civil Service Commission (South Korea) 46
Civil Service Commission (CSC), functions (EO 292) 229–230
Civil Service Protection and Training Commission (CSPTC) (Taiwan) 62
Civil Service Reform, flexibility (Hong Kong) 87
Civil Service Regulation (CSR), increment grant (Hong Kong) 92
civil service systems: comparison 1; comparison, methodological challenge 235; definition 2; historical evolution 3; Indonesia 120; Japan 27; non-Confucian cases 239; professionalization 8; public employment institution 2–5; Singapore 72–77; South Korea 46–55; Taiwan 62–69; Thailand 152
Civil Service Training and Development Institute (CSTDI), responsibility (Hong Kong) 93–94
Civil Service Training Institute and Programs (Hong Kong) 93–94
closed career system 18; Japan 30, 41
Common Recruitment Examination (Hong Kong) 19–20
"Common Recruitment Examination" (CRE) (Hong Kong) 85
Communist Party, function 20
Competency-Based Learning and Development Program (CBLDP) (Philippines) 222
Competency-Based Recruitment and Qualification Standards (CBRQS) (Philippines) 215–218
Computer Assisted Test (CAT): Indonesia 125, 126; introduction 20
computer-assisted testing system (CAT) (Indonesia) 127
Confucian administrative tradition, characteristics 236
Confucian tradition: cases 18, 21; examination system 236; inheritance 17

Continental European model: import 17, 18, 20; legacy 237; Soviet-style political-administrative system, impact 239; transplantation 18; usage 21
Contract-Based Government Employees (Indonesia) 129
contractual employment, statutory employment (contrast) 107–108
contrast-based employment, flexibility 11
country-specific responses, cumulative outcomes 5
Court Organization Act (South Korea) 48
COVID-19 pandemic 45
"Cross Assignment/Cross Fertilisation" programme (Malaysia) 189–190
"Cyber Learning Centre Plus" (CLCP), CSTDI maintenance (Hong Kong) 94
Cyber National Official Examination Center, South Korean government operation 47

democratization, timing (impact) 238–239
Directorate-General of Personnel Administration (DGPA), setup (Taiwan) 62–63
double piece model (Japan) 39, *40*

East Asia, public employment 12–17; modes **13**
economic incentives, usage 4
Employee Work Objectives (Sasaran Kerja Pegawai: SKP) 134–135
employment, flexibility 11
employment status 218, 231; career civil servant enjoyment 65; civil servant usage 107–108; Hong Kong 87–88; Indonesia 125; Thailand 159; types 181–182
exam-based neutral testing 123
external mobility 65, 88–90, 109, 187–190
external recruitment 88; availability 19–20; positions, opening 65, 67; usage 14

Famli, Ridzuan Kushairi Mohd 196
financial incentives, providing 51
fixed-term administrative grade employees, hiring (Japan) 35
fixed-term temporary employment, permanent/lifelong employment (contrast) 107–108
Foreign Service Officials Act (South Korea) 48
foreign transplants, impact 237–238
Functional Position (Jabatan Fungsional) (Indonesia) 141

244 Index

General Intelligence Test (Indonesia) 127
globalization, impact 12
Golongan Karya (Golkar) civil servant
    brackets (Indonesia) 119–120
Good Governance: concepts 158–159;
    principles 155
Governmental Regulation of Performance
    Appraisal for Civil Servant 30/2019
    (Indonesia) 136
Government Commission on Organization
    and Personnel (Vietnam) 107
Government-Linked Companies (GLCs)
    exchange program (Malaysia) 190
government office terms, Yuan office terms
    (contrast) (Taiwan) **61**
Government Regulation of Performance
    Appraisal for Civil Servant Apparatus
    30/2019 (Indonesia) 136, 138

Handover (Hong Kong) 82
Harun, Azhar 181
Ho Chi Minh National Academy of
    Politics, management (Vietnam)
    112–113
Hong Kong, civil service: administrative
    grade, policy cabinet source 95–96;
    "Administrative Officer" 86;
    administrative officers, generalist
    grade 95; Anti-Extradition Bill 80;
    Basic Law 80, 84–85; British basis 86;
    central human resource management
    (HRM) unit 83–84; central human
    resource management (HRM) unit,
    name/location/organizational type 83;
    central human resource management
    (HRM) unit, tasks/functions 83–84;
    citizen expectations 81–82; Civil
    Service Bureau (CSB) 83–85, 87–88;
    Civil Service Reform, flexibility 87;
    Civil Service Regulation (CSR),
    increment grant 92; Civil Service
    Training and Development Institute
    (CSTDI), responsibility 93–94; Civil
    Service Training Institute and Programs
    93–94; classification status 86–88;
    classification status, employment
    status/conditions 87–88; classification
    status, functional level/grade 86–87;
    classification status, job security 87–88;
    Commendation Award Scheme 91;
    Commendation Letter Scheme 91;
    Common Recruitment Examination
    (CRE) 19, 85; Confucian tradition,
    inheritance 17; context/overview

80–83; "Cyber Learning Centre Plus"
(CLCP), CSTDI maintenance 94;
democratization 81–82; "Developmental
Grades" 86; "Directorate Pay Scale D1
to D8" 94; ex-civil servants, selection/
appointment 90; executive-led system
81; "Executive Officer" 86; former civil
servants, principal officials (numbers)
90; General Disciplined Services 88;
"Generalist Grades" 86; Handover
82; Hospital Authority, management
81; Independent Commission Against
Corruptions (ICAC), recommendations
93; internal/external mobility 88–90;
internal/external recruitment 88; Joint
Recruitment Examination (JRE),
occurrence 85; Long and Meritorious
Service Travel Award Scheme 91; Master
Pay Scale 86; merit-based promotion
91; "National studies programmes" 94;
Non-Civil Service Contracts (NCSC),
adoption 83, 87; Notional Annual
Midpoint Salary (NAMS) System 84;
"One Country, Two Systems" (OCTS)
framework 80; "Pay for Performance"
(Civil Service Bureau scheme) 92;
performance assessment 90–93;
performance assessment, sanctions
92–93; performance assessment,
types/tools/criteria/frequency 90–91;
performance management, ongoing
process 90–91; "permanent secretary"
role 95; Political Appointment
System, appointments 83; political
pressures 82–83; political system,
dysfunction 81–82; politicization 80;
politicization, political appointment
system (relationship) 82–83; posts/
positions, openness 88–90; Principal
Official Accountability System (POAS)
82; promotion 90–93; promotion,
incentives 91–92; Public Accounts
Committee 84; public management,
change 83; Public Service Commission,
consultation 92–93; recruitment 84–86;
recruitment, competitive examination
85; recruitment, definition/eligibility
84–85; recruitment, direct application
85; recruitment, monitoring 85–86;
SAR Government governance crisis 82;
Secrétariat on Civil Service Discipline
(SCSD) 92; senior civil service (senior
management) 94–96; "senior civil
service," official definition (absence)

94–96; "Senior executive development" focus 93–94; service, officers (exit numbers) **89**; Special Autonomous Region (SASR) 80; state, hollowing-out 83; system 83–96; training 93–94; Urban Renewal Authority, employment 81; Water Revolution 80

horizontal mobility 145–146

Hospital Authority, management (Hong Kong) 81

human resource management (HRM): centralization (Thailand) 20–21; functions 19; unit (*see* central human resource management unit)

Human Resource Merit Promotion and Section Board (HRMPSB) (Philippines) 215

human resources program (HRD) (Philippines) 205

incentives 15, 91–92; career incentives (change), politicization (impact) 226; employee receipt 221; employment security/professionalism, usage 39; factors 135; financial incentives, providing 51; grade 130; granting 220; introduction 11; market mechanism 10–11; monetary incentives 190–191; Performance-Based Incentive System (PBIS), introduction 220–221; performance incentives, problem 135–136; performance incentives, provision 135; protection 131; providing 48; social/economic incentives, usage 4; usage 135

Independent Commission Against Corruptions (ICAC), recommendations (Hong Kong) 93

Indonesia, civil service 119–120; 360-degree assessment 135; 360-degree evaluation 147; Administratorial/ Functional Positions 133; Administratorial Position (Jabatan Administrasi) 129–130, 141; Aparatur Sipil Negara (ASN) 120; Aparatur Sipil Negara (ASN), composition *131*; Aparatur Sipil Negara (ASN), developmental trainings 139; Aparatur Sipil Negara (ASN), human resource management (institutional responsibility) 120–121; Aparatur Sipil Negara (ASN), recruitment 130; Aparatur Sipil Negara (ASN), senior executive service requirements 143; Aparatur Sipil

Negara (ASN), training 139; Badan Kepegawaian Negara (BKN) 121, 122–123, 125; Badan Kepegawaian Negara (BKN), public (social media communication) *132*; Badan Siber dan Sandi Negara (BSSN) 127; Basic Competence 127; BKN Cloud Computing System 127; bureaucracy, meritocracy (increase) 124–125; bureaucracy, reform (institutionalization) 144; Bureaucratic Reform 120; capacity building program 139; central human resource management (HRM) unit 120–125; civil servants, human resources quantity 128; civil servants, number/ qualification (absence) 128; civil servants, positions **142**; civil servants, promotion 136; civil servants, promotion/rotation/ career *137*; civil servants, recruitment process *124*; civil servants, reform 124; civil servants, rules (government application) 133; Civil Service Law 5/2014 123, 125, 129, 134, 136, 138, 145; classification/status 129–131; computer-assisted test (CAT) 125, 126; computer-assisted testing system (CAT) 127; Contract-Based Government Employees 129; cross-agencies collaboration 140; Diaspora formation, government allocation 126; diklatpim, development 139–140; Echelons I/II 128; education/training centers *(pusat pendidikan dan pelatihan)* 139; Employee Work Objectives (Sasaran Kerja Pegawai: SKP) 134–135; employment status 125; executive training mode, change 140; Functional Position (Jabatan Fungsional) 129, 130, 141; General Intelligence Test 127; Golongan Karya (Golkar) civil servant brackets 119–120; Governmental Regulation of Performance Appraisal for Civil Servant 30/2019 136; Government Regulation of Performance Appraisal for Civil Servant Apparatus 30/2019 136, 138; graduation *(ikatan dinas)* 139; human resource management (HRM) process 131; inducement (prajabatan) training stage 139; information and communication technology (ICT), track record system 146; integrated human resource management (HRM) system 145–146; Kementerian BUMN 134; Kementerian Dalam Negeri 128–129; Kementerian Pendayagunaan

246 Index

Aparatur Negara dan Reformasi Birokrasi (Kemen-PANRB) 120–122, 125, 134; Kementerian Pendidikan dan Kebudayaan/Kemendikbud 127; Kementerian Sekretariat Negara 129; Komisi Aparatur Sipil Negara (KASN) 121, 123–124; Lembaga Administrasi Negara (LAN) 121, 124–125; Lembaga Non-Struktural (LNS) nonstructural state institution 123; Lembaga Pemerintah Non-Kementerian (LPNK) government agency 122; MENPAN 122; meritocracy development 120, 141–143; meritocracy, guardian 123; Merit System 120; merit-system formulation 123; National Civil Service Agency 121, 125; National Cyber and Crypto Agency 127; Nationality Concept Test 127; neutrality, embracing 119–120; New Order Regime 119–120; non-Aparatur Sipil Negara (ASN), senior executive service requirements 144; Old Order Regime 119; organizational outcomes/individual outputs, performance gaps 147; oversight/accountability 147–148; Pegawai Negeri Sipil (PNS) 129; Pegawai Pemerintah dengan Perjanjian Kerja (PPPK) 129, 143; Pejabat Pembna Kepegawaian (PPK) 123; performance assessment 134–138; performance-based compensation 145–147; performance incentives, problem 135–136; performance incentives, provision 135; performance management, importance 146; performance management, improvement *138*; Personal Characteristic Test 127; Personnel Development Officer (Pejabat Pembina Kepegawaian) (PPK) 129, 141; politics, bureaucracy (separation) 146; politics, neutrality 146; positioning, conflicts 145; posts/positions, openness 131–134; pre-recruitment training 139; Presidential Decree of Grand Design of Bureaucratic Reform 134; Presidential Instruction of Government Institution Performance Accountability 7/1999 134; promotion 134–138, *137*; Public Personnel Law 43/1999 119, 146; recruitment 125–129; recruitment, computer assisted test (CAT) 127; recruitment, conflicts 145; recruitment, document-based selection 126; recruitment, registration 126;

recruitment, result/announcement 127–129; *Reformasi Birokrasi* 122; Reform Leader Academy (RLA) program 140; reforms, institutional deficiencies 144–148; Regulation 60/2008 147; Road Map of Civil Servant Development in Indonesia 120; Seleski Kompetensi Bidang (SKB) 127; Seleski Kompetensi Dasar (SKD) 127; senior civil service 141–144; Senior Executive Service (Jabatan Pimpinan Tinggi) (JPT) 129, 130, 141; Senior Executive Service (SES) 134; senior executive service (Jabatan Pimpinan Tinggi) (JPT) positions, hierarchical level/typology **142**; senior executive service (Jabatan Pimpinan Tinggi) (JPT), professional experience/educational background requirements 143–144; State Civil Servant Apparatus 120; system 120; Technical Competence 127; tenured civil servants (pegawai negeri sipil: PNS) 122; Tes Intelegensia Umum (TIU) 127; Tes Karakteristik Pribaldi (TKP) 127; Tes Wawasan Kebansaan (TWK) 127; training 138–141; vertical/horizontal mobility, integration 145–146; World Class Government 120

Institute for Youth Research Malaysia (IYRES) 181
Institute of Integrity Malaysia (IIM), founding 173
Institute of Public Administration (INTAN) (Malaysia) 185
internal mobility 88–90, 187–190
internal promotion 4
internal recruitment 65, 88, 108

Jabatan Fungsional (Indonesia) 129
Jabatan Perkhidmatan Awam (JPA) (Malaysia) 177
Jabatan Pimpinan Tinggi (Indonesia) 129
Japan, civil service: Act on Officials with Fixed Term of Office 35; Act on Personal Exchange between the Government and Private Enterprises 35–36; administrative officials *(jimukan)*, distinction 31; *amakudari* ("descent from heaven") 36, 39–40; bureaucracy-lewd policy, increase (possibility) 43; bureaucratic agencies, political neutrality 43; bureaucratization, display 16; Cabinet Bureau of Personnel Affairs, establishment 41; career candidates,

personnel management 31; Career Track
(sōgō-shoku) Examination 30; Central
Personnel Administrative Agency
29–30; classification/status 31–33;
closed career system 30, 41; "collective
bargaining rights" 32; Constitution,
establishment (1946) 27; current
system 28–43; deputy director-general
(shingikan), promotion 36; designated
positions 41; director-general *(kyokuchō)*,
impact 36; double piece model 39,
40; eligibility screening 41; evaluation
results, utilization *38*; fixed-term
administrative grade employees, hiring
35; fixed-term recruitment, system 33;
fundamental skills test 30; General Track
(ippan-shoku) Examination 30; history
27–28; "independent kingdom" 31;
labor rights *33*; mid-career recruitment,
system 33; ministerial personnel
management 30, 41; National Personnel
Authority *29*, 29–32, 40; National
Personnel Authority, independence
27; National Personnel Authority,
Regulations 1–24 35; National
Personnel Authority, training 40–41;
National Personnel Authority, training
programs *42*; national public employees,
categorization 28; national public
employees, posts/positions (openness)
33, 35; National Public Service
Act 27–28, 32, 36; national public
service personnel system, recruitment
30–31; non-career positions, usage
31; non-career-track employees,
competition 39; non-career track
employees, defining 31; permanent
vice-minister *(jimujian)*, promotion 36;
personnel evaluation system, framework
37; political neutrality/responsiveness,
prioritization 43; "private sector
compliance" 32; public-private
partnerships 39; public-private personnel
exchange 35–43; Remuneration Act
28; "right to organize" 32; section
chief/director *(kachō)*, impact 36; senior
civil service (senior management)
41, 43; system, Confucian tradition
27; technical officials *(gikan)*. 31;
theme-based programs 41; third-year
follow-up sessions 40
job security: civil servants 108, 186–187;
Hong Kong 87–88; worsening (private
sector) 50

Joint Recruitment Examination (JRE),
occurrence (Hong Kong) 85

Kementerian BUMN (Indonesia) 134
Kementerian Dalam Negeri (Indonesia)
128–129
Kementerian Pendayagunaan Aparatur
Negara dan Reformasi Birokrasi
(Kemen-PANRB) (Indonesia)
120–122
Kementerian Pendidikan dan Kebudayaan/
Kemendikbud (Indonesia) 127
Kementerian Sekretariat Negara
(Indonesia) 129
Ketua Setiausaha Negara (KSN)
(Malaysia) 196
key performance indicators (KPIs)
162–163, 190, 196
Komisi Aparatur Sipil Negara (KASN) 121,
123–124
Koya, Latheefa 181

labor: rights (Japan) *33*; vertical/horizontal
specialization 7
Laporan Nilaian Prestasi Tahunan (LNPT)
(Malaysia) 190
Lembaga Administrasi Negara (LAN) 121,
124–125
Lembaga Non-Struktural (LNS)
nonstructural state institution
(Indonesia) 123
Lembaga Pemerintah Non-Kementerian
(LPNK) government agency
(Indonesia) 122
local administrative traditions,
difference 239
local traditions, impact 237–238

Malaysia, civil service: administrative
authority (punca kuasa), sources
175–176; advanced training 194;
Anglo-American mode, import 239;
Annual Performance Assessment
Report (Laporan Nilaian Prestasi
Tahunan) (LNPT) 190; Anugerah
Perkhidmatan Cemerlang (APC)
190; assessors, impact 196; Barisan
Nasional, defeat 174; basic training 194;
career advancement 191–192; central
agency 177–180; central agency, tasks/
functions 177–180; certifications 184;
Chartered Tax Institute of Malaysia
(CTIM) 194; civil servants, job security
186–187; civil servants, promotion

248 Index

considerations/criteria 192; civil servants, recruitment process 184–185; civil servants, secondment/temporary transfer/permanent exchange *187*; civil servants, training 193–196; civil service classification/status 186–187; civil service reform, promotion 21; closed service **188**; common (open) service **188**; Corporate Communication Unit 179; "Cross Assignment/Cross Fertilisation" programme 189–190; Development and Management of Strategic Information Division 179; Diplomatic Administrative Officers (Pegawai Tadbir Diplomatik) (PTD) 185; Economic Planning Unit (EPU) 181; employment status, types 181–182; Establishment Office of Malaysia (EOM) 175; examinations, objectives 185–186; Exit Policy 21, 191; external mobility 187–190; fast-track promotions 193; Federal Establishment Office (FEO) 175; First Malaysian Development Plan 171; Government-Linked Companies (GLCs) exchange program 190; government structure *174*; Head of Service (Ketua Perkhidmatan) 180; High Potential Leadership program 191; Human Capital Development Division 177–178; human resource training policy, objectives 194; Institute for Youth Research Malaysia (IYRES) 181; Institute of Diplomacy and Foreign Relations (IDFR) 194; Institute of Integrity Malaysia (IIM), founding 173; Institute of Public Administration (INTAN) 185; Integrity Unit 179; intermediate training 194; Internal Audit Unit 179; internal mobility 187, 188–189; interviews/personal communication 201–202; Jabatan Perkhidmatan Awam (JPA) 177; Ketua Setiausaha Negara (KSN) 196; key performance indicators (KPIs) 190, 196; Legal Adviser, task 179; Mahathir rule 172–173; Malaysian Administrative Modernisation and Management Planning Unit (MAMPU) 172; Malaysian Anti-Corruption Commission (MACC) 181; Malaysian Civil Service, job security 186–187; Malaysian Education Certificate (Sijil Pelajaran Malaysia) (SPM) 184; Malaysian Establishment Office (MEO), founding 175; Malaysian Qualifications

Agency (MQA) 184; Management and Professional group (Pengurusan dan Profesional) (P&P) 188; Ministry of Foreign Affairs (MOFA) 189, 194; monetary incentives 190–191; National Institute of Public Administration (INTAN) 179; New Economic Model (NEM) 173–174; New Economic Policy (NEP), formulation/implementation 172; Organizational Development Division 178; overview 171–175; Pakatan Harapan (PH), victory/rule 174–175, 177, 181; Pakatan Keadilan Rakyat (PKR) 181; Panduan Pelaksanaan Sistem Penilaian Prestasi Pegawai Perkhidmatan Awan Malaysia 190; PEMUDAH (Pasukan Petugas Khas Pemudahcara Perniagaan) 173; Perbadanan Golf Subang 181; Perbadanan Stadium Malaysia 181; performance assessment 190–191, 193; Perikatan Nasional (PN), rule 175; Pingat Perkhidmatan Cemerlang (PPC) 190; Post-Service Division 178; posts/positions, openness 187–190; pre-placement training 194; promotion 190; promotion, civil servant criteria 193; promotion, criteria 192–193; Psychology Management Division 178; public officers, political alignment 181; public servants, number (breakdown) **176**; Public Service Commission (Suruhanjaya Perkhidmatan Awam) (SPA) 182, 185; Public Service Department (PSD), administrative authority sources 175–176; Public Service Department (PSD), career advancement 191–192; Public Service Department (PSD), divisions 177–180; Public Service Department (PSD), human resources management 177; Public Service Department (PSD), organizational chart *178*; Public Service New Remuneration 174; public service system 175; recruitment 180–186; Remuneration Division 178; Research Planning and Policy Division 179; rural areas *(kampung)*, PTD cadet placement 185; Saraan Baru Perkhidmatan Awam (SBPA) 174; secondment *187*; secondment, concept 189; senior civil service 196; Service Division 178; Service Management Division 179; Special Task Force to Facilitate Business

173; Special Unit for High Potential and Subject Matter Expert (SUPREME) 191; staff assessment, characteristics 190; standard operating procedure (SOP) documents, usage 172; Subject Matter Expert (SME) 191, 192; support staff, importance 187–188; tests 186; Think, Lead, Speak, and Act (TLSA) 192; training 193–196; training institutes/providers **195**; training structures, schemes/classifications (phases) 194; transition training 194; underperforming staff, Exit Policy 191

marketization 1, 3, 235; measures 18–19; professionalization, compatibility 11; public employment mode 10–12

Master Pay Scale (Hong Kong) 86

Merican, Johan Mahmood 180–181

merit-based promotion (Hong Kong) 91

merit-based recruitment 14; civil service system, equivalence 2; entry level 185; guarantee 64, 84–85

merit criteria 9–10

meritocracy 9; basis 236; bureaucracy reform 124; development 120, 141–143; emphasis 20; guardian 123; increase 124; manifestations 146–147; personnel management principle, importance 72; professionalism, embracing 120; Program to Institutionalize Meritocracy and Excellence in Human Resource Management (PRIME HRM) maturity level rating 216, **217**

ministerial personnel management 18, 30, 41

Ministry of Foreign Affairs (MOFA) (Malaysia) 189, 194

Ministry of Home Affairs (MOHA) (Vietnam): organization chart 101–102, *102*; tasks/functions 102–103

Ministry of Personnel Management (MPM), impact (South Korea) 46, 48

Ministry of Public Administration and Security (MOPAS), impact (South Korea) 46

mobility: civil service, inside/outside (mobility) 11; civil service, mobility 109; external mobility 65, 88–90, 109, 187–190; horizontal mobility 145–146; internal mobility 88–90, 187–190; opportunity 159; upward mobility, problem 91; vertical/horizontal mobility, integration 145

Mohamad, Mahathir 175, 177

monetary incentives 190–191

National Academy of Civil Service (NACS) (Taiwan) 67

National Academy of Public Administration (NAPA) training center (Vietnam) 113

National Civil Service Agency (Indonesia) 121

National Cyber and Crypto Agency (Indonesia) 127

National Human Resources Development Institute (NHI), impact (South Korea) 46, 52

National Institute of Public Administration (Indonesia) 1212

National Institute of Public Administration (INTAN) (Malaysia) 179

Nationality Concept Test (Indonesia) 127

National Officials' Training Institute (NOTI), founding (South Korea) 52

National Personnel Authority (Japan) *29*; training 40–41; training programs *42*

national public employees, posts/positions (openness) (Japan) 33, 35; remuneration recommendation, process *34*

National Public Service Act 27–28

national public service personnel system, recruitment (Japan) 30–31

neoliberal managerial reform, impact 3

neutrality: civil service political neutrality 82; embracing 119–120; merit system 156–157; political neutrality, protection 208; political neutrality/responsiveness, prioritization 43; politics, neutrality 145, 146; public bureaucracy, political neutrality (emphasis) 18

New Public Management (NPM) 83; administrative reform 45; concept 158–159; global trend 72; government adoption 196; transition 100

New Public Management (NPM) reform: aim 15; measures 19–20; movement 10

Non-Civil Service Contracts (NCSC), adoption (Hong Kong) 83, 87

noncompetitive electoral regime, establishment 239

non-Confucian traditions 236

Notional Annual Midpoint Salary (NAMS) System (Hong Kong) 84

Office of Civil Servant Commission (OCSC) (Thailand) 152–154; responsibilities 154; structure 152–154;

250 Index

sub-commissions, appointment duties/
responsibilities 153–154
officials, status (bureaucratization/
professionalization protection) 11
"One Country, Two Systems" (OCTS)
framework (Hong Kong) 80
Onn, Tun Hussein 172
open competition, market mechanism
10–11
openness of positions. *see* posts/positions
organizational model, professional model
(contrast) 4–5
organization-centered meritocratic control,
emphasis 5

Pakatan Keadilan Rakyat (PKR)
(Malaysia) 181
Panduan Pelaksanaan Sistem Penilaian
Prestasi Pegawai Perkhidmatan Awan
Malaysia 190
party-based political appointment 10
patronage-based political appointment 10
"Pay for Performance" (Civil Service
Bureau scheme) (Hong Kong) 92
pay-for-performance system 20
Pegawai Negeri Sipil (PNS)
(Indonesia) 129
Pegawai Pemerintah dengan Perjanjian
Kerja (PPPK) (Indonesia) 129, 143
Pegawai Tadbir Diplomatik (PTD)
(Malaysia) 185
Pejabat Pembina Kepegawaian
(Indonesia) 129
Pejabat Pembna Kepegawaian (PPK)
(Indonesia) 123
Pengurusan dan Profesional (P&P)
(Malaysia) 188
performance assessment: Hong Kong
90–93; Singapore 74–75; South Korea
51–52; Taiwan 65–67; Thailand
160–161; Vietnam 109–111
Performance-Based Incentive System
(PBIS) (Philippines) 220–221;
introduction 220–221
performance-related pay, assessment 15–16
Personal Characteristic Test (Indonesia) 127
personnel authorities, focus (Taiwan) *59*
Personnel Development Officer (Pejabat
Pembina Kepegawaian) (PPK)
(Indonesia) 129, 141
personnel evaluation system, framework
(Japan) *37*
Philippines, civil service: Act No. 5
(Civil Service Act) 204; Americans,

arrival 204; appointment, nature 218;
Attrition Law 209; barangays 203;
bonuses/incentives, granting 220;
Bureau of Civil Service (BCS) 204;
Bureau of Fire Protection/Bureau of
Jail Management and Penology (BFP/
BJMP) Act (RA No. 9263) 214; career
appointments, levels 210, **212**; Career
Executive Service Board (CESB) 224;
Career Executive Service (CES), creation
224; Career Executive Service (CES)
Eligibility Examination Process 225;
Career Executive Service (CES) office
rank/salary grade positions **225**; Career
Executive Service Officers (CESOs),
appointment 224–226; career incentives
(change), politicization (impact) 226;
career officers, appointment 219;
career service, positions 219; Center
of Development (COD) 223; Center
of Excellence (COE) 223; central
human resource management (HRM)
unit 205–209; Civil Service Academy,
establishment 223; Civil Service
appointments 213; Civil Service
Commission (CSC), features/functions/
relationships 205, 207; Civil Service
Commission (CSC) HR programs/
services 222–223; Civil Service
Commission (CSC), importance 21;
Civil Service Commission (CSC),
organizational chart *206*; Civil Service
Commission (CSC), personnel (number)
208; Civil Service Commission (CSC),
recognized learning/development
institutions (category/number) **224**; Civil
Service Decree 204; Civil Service Law
of 1959 204; classification/status 209,
210–212; closed career positions 219;
Commission on Appointments (CA)
207; Commission on Higher Education
(CHED) 223; Competency-Based
Learning and Development Program
(CBLDP) 222; Competency-Based
Recruitment and Qualification Standards
(CBRQS) 215–218; competency-based
recruitment, bases 216; CSC Agency
Accreditation Program (CSCAAP)
216; definition 209; division chiefs,
Qualification Standards (QS) **214**;
employment status 218; executive/
managerial positions, Qualification
Standards (QS) **214**; Executive Order
292 204–205, 208, 219; Foreign Service

Act (RA No. 7157) 214; government agency, maturity level classification 216–217; government-owned/government-controlled corporations (GOCCs) 209, 210, 213; government-owned/government-controlled corporations (GOCCs), personnel (career service position) 219; government personnel, number **211**, **212**; historical background 203–205; human resource management (HRM), control 208; human resource management officer (HRMO), role 216; Human Resource Merit Promotion and Section Board (HRMPSB) 215; human resources development (HRD) programs 205; integrated HRM 216–217; Inter-Agency Task Force (IATF) 221; laws/issuances 228; Local Government Code 210; Local Government Code of 1991 (RA No. 7160) 214; Local Government Units 209; Major Final Outputs (MFOs) 221; martial law regime 213; Memorandum Circular 21 223; non-career service 210; Omnibus Rules on Appointments and Other Human Resource Actions (ORAOHRA) 213, 214, 216, 217, 226; open career positions 219; PD 1 (1972) 204; PD 807 204; performance assessments 219–221; Performance-Based Bonus (PBB) 221; Performance-Based Incentive System (PBIS) 220–221; permanent laborers, career service position 219; Personnel Management Assessment and Assistance Program (PMAAP) 216; Philippine Civil Service, establishment 204; Philippine National Police (PNP) Act (RA No. 8551) 214; political appointment, perception 226; political neutrality, protection 208; posts/positions, openness 212, 218–219; process-defined HRM 216–217; Productivity Enhancement Incentive (PEI) 221; Program to Institutionalize Meritocracy and Excellence in Human Resource Management (PRIME HRM) maturity level rating 216–217, **217**; promotion 219–220; Qualification Standards (QS) 214; Qualification Standards on Training, CSC guidelines 223; R.A. 2260 (Civil Service Law of 1959) 204; RA 6040 (1969) 204; RA 7041 (Attrition Law) 209; recruitment 212–219; recruitment process 214–215; senior civil service (senior management) 224–226; size 209–210; Spanish colonial regime, impact 203–204; State Universities and Colleges (SUCs), career positions 215; strategic HRM 216–217; Strategic Performance Management System (SPMS), elements 219–220; Strategic Performance Management System (SPMS), rating scale **220**; system 205; training 221–223; training, acquisition 223; transactional HRM 216, 218

Pingat Perkhidmatan Cemerlang (PPC) (Malaysia) 190

Police Officers Act (South Korea) 48

political neutrality, protection 208

politicization 1, 3, 235; levels 17; low levels 238; political appointment system, relationship (Hong Kong) 82–83; private-public distinction 10–11; public employment mode 8–10

politics, neutrality 145, 146

position-focused open civil service systems, professional model (relationship) 4

post-entry specialization 4, 7

posts/positions, openness: Hong Kong 88–90; Indonesia 131–134; Japan 33, 35; Malaysia 187–190; Philippines 212–219; Singapore 73; South Korea 50–51; Vietnam 108–109

Presidential Decree of Grand Design of Bureaucratic Reform (Indonesia) 134

Presidential Instruction of Government Institution Performance Accountability 7/1999 (Indonesia) 134

Principal Official Accountability System (POAS) (Hong Kong) 82

private sector compliance (Japan) 32

professionalization 1, 3, 235; bureaucratization, contrast 4, 5, 8; display 18; emphasis 8; levels 14, 16–17; marketization, compatibility 11; measures 18–19; public employment mode 7–8; specialization, contrast 6; usage 18

professional model: open system basis 4; organizational model, contrast 4; position-focused open civil service systems, relationship 4; profession-centered meritocratic control 5; profession-related education/training 4

professionals, operational autonomy 8

252 Index

promotion: Hong Kong 90–93; Indonesia 134–138, *137*; internal promotion 4; Malaysia 190, 192–193; Philippines 219–220; Singapore 74–75; South Korea 51–52; Taiwan 65–67; Thailand 160–161; Vietnam 109
Prosecutor's Office Act (South Korea) 48
public administration reform (PAR) (Vietnam) 99–100
public bureaucracy, political neutrality (emphasis) 18
Public Educational Officials Act (South Korea) 48
public employment: bureaucratization 6–7, 12–14; East Asia/Southeast Asia 12–17; marketization 11; marketization, globalization (impact) 12; modes 3, 5–12, **13**, 16; patterns 237; political control 10; politicization, misunderstandings 9; professionalization 7, 14; professionalization (facilitation), modernization (usage) 12
public officials, training (South Korea) 52–54
public-private distinction, making 2
public-private personnel exchange (Japan) 35–43
Public Sector Leadership Programme (PSLP) (Singapore) 77
public servants, categories (South Korea) 48
Public Service Commission (PSC), authority (Singapore) 72
Public Service Commission, consultation (Hong Kong) 92–93
Public Service Division (PSD), impact (Singapore) 72–73

Quality of Governance Institute (QoG), Expert Survey 12

Rahman, Tunku Abdul 171
Razak, Tun Abdul 171, 172
Rechtsstaat model, Continental European legalistic tradition (link) 237
recruitment: Hong Kong 84–86; Indonesia 125–129; Malaysia 180–186; South Korea 47–48; Vietnam 103–106
Reformasi Birokrasi (Indonesia) 122
Reform Leader Academy (RLA) program (Indonesia) 140
Remuneration Act (Japan) 28
remuneration recommendation, process (Japan) *34*
results-based control, usage 11

Road Map of Civil Servant Development in Indonesia 120
rules-based control, replacement 11

Saraan Baru Perkhidmatan Awam (SBPA) (Malaysia) 174
Sasaran Kerja Pegawai (SKP) (Indonesia) 134–135
Secrétariat on Civil Service Discipline (SCSD) (Hong Kong) 92
selection procedure 105–106; favoritism 19; subjective judgment/bias, minimization 64
Seleski Kompetensi Bidang (SKB) (Indonesia) 127
Seleski Kompetensi Dasar (SKD) (Indonesia) 127
senior civil service 18, 45; Indonesia 141–144; Malaysia 196; NACS training programs 67
Senior Civil Service (SCS) (senior management) (South Korea) 47–48, 51, 54–55
senior civil service (senior management): Hong Kong 94–96; Japan 41, 43; Philippines 224–226; Singapore 77; Taiwan 68–69; Vietnam 114
Senior Executive Service (Jabatan Pimpinan Tinggi) (Indonesia) 129, 141
Senior Executive Service (SES) (Indonesia) 134
seniority-based advancement 4
Sijil Pelajaran Malaysia (SPM) (Malaysia) 184
Singapore, civil service: AIM framework 75; background 71–72; central human resource management (HRM) unit 72–73; centralized training 75–76; civil service classification/status 74; Civil Service College (CSC) centralized training 76; Civil Service College (CSC) programs 76; Confucian tradition, inheritance 17; Currently Estimated Potential (CEP), public officer assessment 75; Directors' Developmental Experience 76; Empowered to Lead Programme 76; Executive Leadership Programme 76; human resource management (HRM) functions 73; in-house training 75–76; job vacancies, advertisement 73; leaders, diversity 77; LEARN mobile app (CSC) 76; Learn to Lead Programme 76; officers, performance appraisals 75; on-the-job training 76; performance

Index **253**

assessment 74–75; performance-related pay, assessment 15–16; posts/positions, recruitment/openness 73; promotion 74–75; Public Sector Leadership Programme (PSLP) 77; Public Service Commission (PSC), authority 72; Public Service Division (PSD), impact 72–73; Public Service officers, appointment 74; senior civil service (senior management) 77; Senior Management Programme 76; Singapore Public Service, origin 71–72; Singapore Public Service, training categories 75–76; Singapore-Thailand Leadership Development Program 166; Singapore-Thailand Senior Officials Development Programme (SG-TH SODP) 166; Smart Nation drive 76; system 72–77; talent identification 77; training 75–77; transformation 71; VITAL 73
social incentives, usage 4
Southeast Asia, public employment 12–17; modes **13**
South Korea, civil service: Administrative Bureau of the State, personnel functions (movement) 46; Appeals Commission 46; central administration, civil service rank system *49*; central human resource management (HRM) unit 45, 46; Central Officials' Training Institute (COTI), creation 52; "Central Selection Committee," MPM establishment 50–51; Civil Service Commission (CSC), establishment 46; classification/status 48–50; composition *49*; context/overview 45; Court Organization Act 48; Cyber National Official Examination Center, government operation 47; financial incentives/promotion points, providing 51; Foreign Service Officials Act 48; general service (career service) 48; Government Administration, public personnel functions 46; ministries, transfer 51; Ministry of Personnel Management (MPM), impact 46, 48, 50; Ministry of Public Administration and Security (MOPAS), impact 46; Ministry of the Interior and Safety 46; National Human Resources Development Institute (NHI), impact 46, 52; National Officials' Training Institute (NOTI), founding 52; New Public Management (NPM) administrative reform 45; performance assessment 51–52; Police Officers Act 48; political service (non-career service) 48; posts/positions, openness 50–51; private sector job security, worsening 50; professional tools, usage 54–55; promotions 51–52; Prosecutor's Office Act 48; Public Educational Officials Act 48; public officials, training 52–54; public servants categories 48; recruitment 47–48; recruitment examinations, types 47; Senior Civil Service (SCS) (senior management) 47–48, 51, 54–55; special administrative service (non-career service) 48; special service (career service) 48; State Public Officials Act 52, 54; system 46–55; training program *53*
Spanish-American War 204
specialization, professionalization (contrast) 6
Special Unit for High Potential and Subject Matter Expert (SUPREME) (Malaysia) 191
State Administration Act of 2002 (Thailand) 158–159
State Civil Servant Apparatus (Indonesia) 120
State Public Officials Act (South Korea) 52
Strategic Performance Management System (SPMS) (Philippines) 219–220
Subject Matter Expert (SME) (Malaysia) 191, 192
Sun Yat-sen 59, 60
Suruhanjaya Perkhidmatan Awam (SPA) (Malaysia) 182, 185

Taiwan, civil service 58; assessment result 66; background 59–61; career-based system 59; career civil servants, CSEE recruitment 63–64; career civil servants, lifelong employment status 65; central government agencies, training institutes **68**; central government, structure *59*; central human resource management (HRM) unit 62–63; Civil Service Development Institute (CSDS) 67; civil service entrance examinations (CSEEs) 59–60, 63–65; Civil Service Protection and Training Commission (CSPTC) 62, 67; classification/status 64–65; democracy, defect 59–60; Democratic Progressive Party (DPP), power 61; democratic transition 61; development, trend 59–61; Directorate-General of Personnel Administration (DGPA),

254 Index

setup 62–63; double merit/double demerit 66; Examination Yuan, jurisdiction 58, 60–64, 69; Executive Yuan 69; experimental reform, failure 64; government office terms, Yuan office terms (contrast) **61**; Institute of Diplomacy and International Affairs 67; internal promotion 67; internal recruitment 65; *Kuomintang* (KMT) power, reassumption 61; *Kuomintang* (KMT) retreat 64; *Kuomintang* (KMT) rule 58, 60; Legislative Yuan 61; line management, application 63; Ministry of Civil Service (MCS) 62; Ministry of Examination (ME) 62; National Academy of Civil Service (NACS) 67; neutrality act, enactment 61; performance assessment 65–67; personnel authorities, focus *59*; position classification system 64; positions, openness 65; profile 58–59; promotion 65–67; rank-in-person system, adoption 64; senior civil service (senior management) 68–69; system 62–69; Taiwan Police College 67; training 67; yearly appraisal, criteria 66

Technical Competence (Indonesia) 127

tenured civil servants (pegawai negeri sipil: PNS) (Indonesia) 122

Tes Intelegensia Umum (TIU) (Indonesia) 127

Tes Karakteristik Pribaldi (TKP) (Indonesia) 127

Tes Wawasan Kebansaan (TWK) (Indonesia) 127

Thailand, civil service: background 151–152; civil servant positions, categories 155–156; Civil Servants 4.0 167; Civil Service Act (1928) 151; Civil Service Act (2008) 151, 154–159, 162, 164, 166; Civil Service Commission (CSC), duties/responsibilities **155**; Civil Service Commission (CSC), members **153**; Civil Service Commission (CSC), supervisory role 152–153; Civil Service Executive Development Program (CSED1) 168; classification/status 158–161; competency assessment 163–164; competency-based assessment, hybrid scale (usage) **164**; competency-based performance assessment 164; competitive examination 157; deduction points criteria **164**; development programs, examples 166–167; Digital Literacy Project 167; employment status 159; executives (civil servant position) 155; Extra Training Courses for Senior Executives 168; Forms I/II/III 162–163; general positions (civil servant position) 156; Good Governance concepts 158–159; Good Governance principles 155; High Performance and Potential System (HiPPS) 167; hybrid scale model, usage 163–164; Information Act of 1997 155; key performance indicators (KPIs) 162–163; King Rama VII, bureaucracy reformation 151; King's Scholarship 158; knowledge worker positions (civil servant position) 156; Leadership for Change 167; managerial positions (civil servant position) 156; mobility opportunity 158; National Economic and Social Development Board (NESD) role 152–153; national strategic plan, proposal 152; neutrality, merit system 156–157; New Public Management (NPM) 158–159; Office of Civil Servant Commission (OCSC) 152–154; Office of Civil Servant Commission (OCSC), establishment 151; Office of Civil Servant Commission (OCSC), responsibilities 154; Office of Civil Servant Commission (OCSC), structure 152–154; Office of Civil Servant Commission (OCSC), subcommission duties/responsibilities 153–154; performance appraisal system 161–165; performance appraisal tools 162–163; performance assessment 160–161; performance criteria 161–162; performance management process 160–161; performance measurement levels **162**; personnel, qualifications 156; personnel, recruitment 154, 156–158; personnel, selection process 156–158; position classification (PC) 158; Prime Minister's Delivery Unit (PMDU), establishment 152; probation 164–165; promotion 160–161; public sector, performance management process *160*; retirement 159; Royal Thai Government Scholarship 158; self-learning study 165; senior civil service development 167–168; Senior Executive Development Program 168; Senior Executive Service (SES) 167–168; Service Executive Development Program (SED1/SED2) 166; Singapore-Thailand Leadership Development Program 166;

Singapore-Thailand Senior Officials Development Programme (SG-TH SODP) 166; State Administrative Act of 2002 154, 158–159; system 152; training 165–167; training programs, examples 166–167
Think, Lead, Speak, and Act (TLSA) (Malaysia) 192
training: Hong Kong 93–94; Indonesia 138–141; Malaysia 193–196; Philippines 221–223; Singapore 75–77; South Korea 53; Taiwan 67; Vietnam 112–114
Treaty of Paris 204
Tung Chee-hwa 82

upward mobility, problem 91
Urban Renewal Authority, employment (Hong Kong) 81

vertical/horizontal mobility, integration 145
Vietnam, civil service: bureaucratization, approach 20; cadres/civil servants, policy implementation (MOHA guidance/supervision) 102–103; career advancement 111–112; central human resource management (HRM) unit 100–103; civil servants, annual evaluations 110; civil servants, appraisal process 110; civil servants, employment status/condition 107–108; civil servants, grades 99; civil servants, job security information 108; civil servants, leading/managerial positions 109; civil servants, number **101**; civil servants, poor performance (sanction methods) 111; civil servants, recruitment process 104–105; civil servants, rewards/incentives 111; civil servants, training system 112–113; civil service classification, functional level/guide 106–107; civil service classification/status 106–108; civil service recruitment examinations, subject knowledge 104; commune civil servants, movement 109; Commune Civil Servants, unit heads 107; Confucian tradition, inheritance 17; Constitution (2013) 99; context/overview 98–100; Continental European model, import 17; Decision No. 414/TCCP-VC 107; employment status 107–108; executive bodies, levels 98; external mobility 109; foreign language test 104; Government Commission on Organization and Personnel 107; Government Decree No. 56/ND-CP 111; Government Decree No. 114/2020/ND-CP 103; Government Decree No. 1382020/ND-CP 103; government provisions, implementation (MOHA guidance/supervision) 103; Ho Chi Minh National Academy of Politics, management 112–113; human resource management (HRM) unit, information 100–101; human resources planning, MOHA building 103; internal/external candidates, post openings 108; internal mobility 109; internal recruitment 108; job security information 10; judicial bodies, levels 98; Law of Anti-corruption 99; Law of Cadres and Civil Servants 99, 104, 106, 108, 111; Law on Legal Documents Issue 99; Law on Local Government 99; Law on Public Servants 106; leaders/managers appraisal process 110; legal provisions, implementation (MOHA guidance/supervision) 103; legislative bodies, levels 98; local administrative organizational levels *106*; local levels 99; Ministry of Home Affairs (MOHA), central ministry 100; Ministry of Home Affairs (MOHA), organization chart 101–102, *102*; Ministry of Home Affairs (MOHA), tasks/functions 102–103; National Academy of Public Administration (NAPA) training center 113; national government, structure **101**; new employees, training 114; performance assessment 109–111; performance-related pay, assessment 15–16; permanent/lifelong employment, fixed-term/temporary employment, contrast 107–108; posts/positions, openness 108–109; posts, recruitment openness 108; promotion 109; promotion, criteria 112; promotion, rewards/commendations/disciplines 111; provinces 99; public administration institutional 99; public administration machinery 98; public administration reform (PAR) 99–100; public officials, basic salary 106; public servants **101**; Public Servants, official role 107; rank promotion competitions, MOHA organization 103; recruitment 103–106; recruitment criteria 105–106; recruitment exams, probation condition 105; selection procedures 105–106; senior civil service (senior management) 114; State, branches

256 Index

98; state management, principles 99; statutory employment, contractual employment (contrast) 107–108; system 100–114; training 112–114; training institute system *113*; training programs, institutional offerings 113–114; training programs/plans, implementation (MOHA guidance/supervision) 103

Water Revolution (Hong Kong) 80

Weberian bureaucracy: Continental European model, link 237; features/characteristics 5, 7, 12; legal-rational basis 8; technical competence 6

World Bank on Global Report: Public Sector Performance 127

Yuan office terms, government office terms (contrast) (Taiwan) **61**

Printed in the United States
by Baker & Taylor Publisher Services